David Morgan
RETHINKING FAMILY PRACTICES

Eriikka Oinonen
FAMILIES IN CONVERGING EUROPE
A Comparison of Forms, Structures and Ideals

Róisín Ryan-Flood
LESBIAN MOTHERHOOD
Gender, Families and Sexual Citizenship

Sally Sales
ADOPTION, FAMILY AND THE PARADOX OF ORIGINS
A Foucauldian History

Tam Sanger
TRANS PEOPLE'S PARTNERSHIPS
Towards an Ethics of Intimacy

Tam Sanger and Yvette Taylor (editors)
MAPPING INTIMACIES
Relations, Exchanges, Affects

Elizabeth B. Silva
TECHNOLOGY, CULTURE, FAMILY
Influences on Home Life

Lisa Smyth
THE DEMANDS OF MOTHERHOOD
Agents, Roles and Recognitions

Yvette Taylor
EDUCATIONAL DIVERSITY
The Subject of Difference and Different Subjects

Palgrave Macmillan Studies in Family and Intimate Life
Series Standing Order ISBN 978–0–230–51748–6 hardback
978–0–230–24924–0 paperback
(*outside North America only*)

You can receive future titles in this series as they are published by placing a standing order. Please contact your bookseller or, in case of difficulty, write to us at the address below with your name and address, the title of the series and the ISBN quoted above.

Customer Services Department, Macmillan Distribution Ltd, Houndmills, Basingstoke, Hampshire RG21 6XS, England

Living Alone

Globalization, Identity and Belonging

Lynn Jamieson
University of Edinburgh, UK

Roona Simpson
University of Glasgow, UK

palgrave
macmillan

First published 2013 by
PALGRAVE MACMILLAN

Palgrave Macmillan in the UK is an imprint of Macmillan Publishers Limited, registered in England, company number 785998, of Houndmills, Basingstoke, Hampshire RG21 6XS.

Palgrave Macmillan in the US is a division of St Martin's Press LLC, 175 Fifth Avenue, New York, NY 10010.

Palgrave Macmillan is the global academic imprint of the above companies and has companies and representatives throughout the world.

Palgrave® and Macmillan® are registered trademarks in the United States, the United Kingdom, Europe and other countries.

ISBN 978–0–230–27192–0

This book is printed on paper suitable for recycling and made from fully managed and sustained forest sources. Logging, pulping and manufacturing processes are expected to conform to the environmental regulations of the country of origin.

A catalogue record for this book is available from the British Library.

A catalog record for this book is available from the Library of Congress.

To the memory of generous friends who created hospitable homes alone, sometimes with others, and were always a positive force in the lives of those around them: Helen Corr 1955–2013, Christine Redmill 1961–2003 and Anne Witz 1952–2006

Contents

Tables

Series Editors' Preface

The remit of the *Palgrave Macmillan Studies in Family and Intimate Life* series is to publish major texts, monographs and edited collections focusing broadly on the sociological exploration of intimate relationships and family organization. As editors, we think such a series is timely. Expectations, commitments and practices have changed significantly in intimate relationship and family life in recent decades. This is very apparent in patterns of family formation and dissolution, demonstrated by trends in cohabitation, marriage and divorce. Changes in household living patterns over the last 20 years have also been marked, with more people living alone, adult children living longer in the parental home and more 'non-family' households being formed. Furthermore, there have been important shifts in the ways people construct intimate relationships. There are few comfortable certainties about the best ways of being a family man or woman, with once conventional gender roles no longer being widely accepted. The normative connection between sexual relationships and marriage or marriage-like relationships is also less powerful than it once was. Not only is greater sexual experimentation accepted, but it is now accepted at an earlier age. Moreover, heterosexuality is no longer the only mode of sexual relationship given legitimacy. In Britain as elsewhere, gay male and lesbian partnerships are now socially and legally endorsed to a degree hardly imaginable in the mid-twentieth century. Increases in lone-parent families, the rapid growth of different types of stepfamily, the de-stigmatization of births outside marriage and the rise in couples 'living-apart-together' (LAT) all provide further examples of the ways that 'being a couple', 'being a parent' and 'being a family' have diversified in recent years.

The fact that change in family life and intimate relationships has been so pervasive has resulted in renewed research interest from sociologists and other scholars. Increasing amounts of public funding have been directed to family research in recent years, in terms of both individual projects and the creation of family research centres of different hues. This research activity has been accompanied by the publication of some very important and influential books exploring different aspects of shifting family experience, in Britain and elsewhere. The *Palgrave Macmillan Studies in Family and Intimate Life* series hopes to add to this list of influential research-based texts, thereby contributing to existing knowledge and informing current debates. Our main audience consists of academics and advanced students, though we intend that the books in the series will be accessible to a more general readership who wish to understand better the changing nature of contemporary family life and personal relationships.

We see the remit of the series as wide. The concept of 'family and intimate life' will be interpreted in a broad fashion. While the focus of the series will clearly be sociological, we take family and intimacy as being inclusive rather than exclusive. The series will cover a range of topics concerned with family practices and experiences, including, for example, partnership, marriage, parenting, domestic arrangements, kinship, demographic change, intergenerational ties, life course transitions, stepfamilies, gay and lesbian relationships, lone-parent households, and also non-familial intimate relationships such as friendships. We also wish to foster comparative research, as well as research on understudied populations. The series will include different forms of books. Most will be theoretical or empirical monographs on particular substantive topics, though some may also have a strong methodological focus. In addition, we see edited collections as also falling within the series' remit, as well as translations of significant publications in other languages. Finally, we intend that the series has an international appeal, in terms of both topics covered and authorship. Our goal is for the series to provide a forum for family sociologists conducting research in various societies, and not solely in Britain.

Graham Allan, Lynn Jamieson and David Morgan

Acknowledgements

This book could not have been produced without the contributions of several people involved in the *Rural and Urban Solo Living: Social Integration, Quality of Life and Future Orientations* study. Particular thanks to Fran Wasoff, a co-investigator in that study. We are also appreciative of the insights of Sue Kelly and Helen Willmot who also contributed to this study. Our gratitude, too, to the Economic and Social Research Council for funding this research (award reference RES-062-23-0172). We are indebted, most of all, to the 140 men and women who took part in this study and generously shared their experiences and views of living alone. Thanks to the staff at the Centre for Research on Families and Relationships for various forms of occasional help and particularly Dawn Cattanach, Kathryn Dunne and Vivien Smith. We would also like to thank David Morgan for his perceptive comments on an earlier draft of the book. Roona would like to express her appreciation to friends and family for their encouragement and succour over the past few years, with particular thanks to Alison Young for her copy-editing skills and support.

1
Introduction

This introduction begins by briefly summarizing why people who live alone are of interest to us all and an appropriate subject of research. The reasons given also explain how the book is structured. Next, we explore definitions of 'living alone', followed by further explanation of the scope, focus and sources of evidence of the book.

Three sets of reasons for studying and knowing more about people living alone

Popular stereotypes

The need for evidence to counterbalance the confusion of popular stereotypes and messages about this growing trend provides the first set of reasons for studying living alone. Living alone is increasingly common across the globe, thereby becoming an object of popular interest. In Asia, Europe and North America, for some commentators the trend is symptomatic of current problems and spells further threats for the future, but for others it is a harbinger of new freedoms and opportunities. Differences in viewpoint sometimes reflect perspectives of different generations and genders. Two negative stereotypes recur among a jumble of others: the carefree self-absorbed person who is oblivious to the responsibilities of family, kin or community and the sad, lonely, neglected and excluded person. The former is often depicted as a young person and the latter as an older person, albeit without any consideration of if or how these biographies might join up across an individual life course. Sometimes the former is also imagined as a young migrant to an urban area, and the latter as an older person left behind by the loss of a partner and migration of children without support in depopulating rural areas. Although negative stereotypes of people living alone can

1

refer to both men and women in the popular culture of many parts of the world, particular disdain is reserved for a woman who lives outside of conventional family arrangements (Allerton, 2007).

This book draws together the existing evidence that comes mainly from Asia, Europe and North America and contributes our own research on people living alone in the United Kingdom at ages more conventionally associated with living with a partner and children. The first set of evidence to counterbalance stereotypes is provided in the introduction to Part I and in Chapter 2. International differences in reactions to men and women living alone are contextualized in Chapter 2 by discussion of variation across global regions.

Debate about identity and personal life

The second set of reasons for studying living alone comes from its significance to discussions within social science, particularly sociology, about the nature of personal relationships and the dynamics of personal life. While the text is written with the intention of being readable for any audience, it is structured by engagement with a number of academic discussions.

Those who live alone exemplify the separation of living arrangements and personal relationships and present an extreme case of considerable theoretical interest. The separation of living arrangements and personal relationships enables focused consideration of factors shaping identity, social integration and social isolation. People living alone may see themselves as 'loners' or in terms of the parts they play in the lives of others. In popular psychology, solitary reflection can be an aid to 'knowing oneself' and a means thereby to self-development and creativity, as well as laying the basis for reaching out to others. On the other hand, being alone too much and loneliness are routinely regarded as unhealthy for a person's state of mind and sense of self. How people living alone experience this balance is a theme that runs through subsequent chapters. In cultures where there has traditionally been no respectable way of living alone, to do so without being an 'outcast' indicates fundamental social change. Do people who live alone tend to start with or develop a narrative of the self that incorporates living alone as part of 'who I am', for example, as 'a loner', 'outcast', a person who is more creative or productive because of time alone, or as 'sad and lonely'?

People living alone have varying degrees of personal ties to kin, family and friends. Some maintain relationships across households with partners, children, parents and siblings who, for other people or at other stages of life, are within their home. For some, new technologies play an important part in sustaining connections. Understanding how connected people living alone are to others can be informative about the resilience of 'family', demonstrating whether and how such relationships are sustained across households. How they maintain 'being connected' contributes to discussion of the relative significance of face-to-face versus mediated communication and the impact of digital technologies on everyday life. The meaning of 'home' to a person living alone, and how they go about the business of transforming a dwelling into a home, is also very revealing. In many cultural contexts, the idea of home conventionally centres on family or kin, intimacy and belonging to a wider kindred or community. Are those constructing a home alone creating an individualized subjectivity and personal identity in preference to affinity with others? Is this symptomatic of the home becoming 'a conduit of atomization' as Richard Ronald and Yosuke Hirayama provocatively suggest is the case for younger generations in Japan (2009)? How people reflect on and manage eating in the context of living alone is another more specific focus that is theoretically interesting and sheds light on processes of social integration, given that eating with others is a universal means of sustaining and celebrating relationships. Similarly, there are lessons to learn from whether and how those who live alone participate in holidays and festivals that conventionally express family and community relationships.

Such issues are of direct relevance to the theorization of the interplay between personal life, identity and the wider social fabric. These issues are taken up in Chapters 3–5. Chapter 3 focuses on the orientation to partnering and parenting of men and women living alone at ages more conventionally associated with living with a partner and children. Chapter 4 focuses on the meaning and construction of home by people living alone, and Chapter 5 focuses on their experiences of meals and eating, holidays and festivals.

'Globalization' and individualized consumers

The vision conjured up in academic discussion of the intersections between 'globalization' and individualization of self-absorbed consumers with no ties to any particular place or strong affiliations provides the third set of reasons for studying living alone. In this discussion, there is some suggestion of an 'elective affinity' between the residential arrangement of living alone and the mindset and self-image of a growing number of people. They do not see themselves as sad and lonely people living alone because they have been left behind, but as persons who are exercising choice. This sense of choice, nevertheless, coincides with being swept along by trends that are often seen as facets of 'globalization': late twentieth and twenty-first century patterns of development, mobility, communication and consumption enabled by interconnected systems of globalized capitalist mass production, petroleum-based rapid transport and instantaneous digitized communication. Commentators focused on the environmental consequences of globalization fear a trend towards living alone will escalate 'carbon footprints' in developing countries as well as in the richer parts of the world.

For some theorists, the trend of living alone is an outcome of an era that facilitates individual mobility and dislocation from moorings to place and people of origin without automatically severing connections to loved ones; however, for other theorists, disconnection is always a likely outcome, given 24/7 media encouragement of self-absorption in personalized consumption. Pessimistic accounts focus on social processes that separate individuals from each other, individualization, and individualism, an ideology that celebrates the individual above all else. Our own evidence of the social networks, connectedness and community integration of people living alone is the focus of Chapter 6. This discussion is extended through a more specific focus on place, mobility and migration in Chapter 7. Clearly, debates about the nature of contemporary personal life and relationships overlap with the more general discussions of 'globalization', dislocation, consumption and identity. So the contents of Chapters 6 and 7 are interconnected and build on the discussion in Chapter 3, which includes relationships with family and use of Internet dating, and to Chapters 4 and 5 focusing on the uses of home and patterns of consumption and their environmental consequences.

Definitions: A one-person household, dwelling and conducting domestic life alone

Our focus is on one-person households meaning not only a person who is the sole occupant of a dwelling but also a person who lives a domestic life alone. The term 'household' is used to describe a unit of people who live together, sharing resources as well as their living space, for example, food acquired from pooled effort or income. Occupants of a cluster of one-person dwellings who eat together in a shared dining hall or in the open air around a communal fire are not living alone as one-person households. In some cultures, everyday use of 'living alone' has a less restricted meaning than 'one-person household'. For example,

Yunxiang Yan (2003, p. 163) describes how in the Chinese rural village the term *danguo*, meaning living independently and living alone, was used to describe both an elderly couple living by themselves and a solo elderly person living alone because both are equally outside the traditional and once expected arrangement of living with a married son. However, only the solo elderly person is considered as living alone in the sense in which it is used here. The essence of the definition of living alone is simple: nobody else lives in the same living space or routinely shares everyday domestic life.

Fuzziness of 'one-person household'

While it is possible to provide a clear definition of a 'one-person household',[1] like many categories of human arrangement, in practice the boundaries of the category are not so clear-cut but rather become fuzzy at the edges. Regular visitors create one form of fuzzy edge. Many people living alone, as the sole occupant of a dwelling most of the time, have others staying with them some of the time. Obviously occasional visitors and guests do not threaten the classification, but how do we classify routine arrangements that involve the presence of others for more than half of the time? For example, if children or a partner with another residence elsewhere regularly and routinely stay overnight, say up to three or four times a week, are they then part of the household rather than simply frequent guests? If seeking to resolve this sociologically, the perception of those involved might be given particular weight, rather than applying formal classificatory rules such as those used by governmental agencies when extracting taxation or delivering benefits.

However, there are also difficulties with taking vernacular definitions as a starting point rather than an objective definition of 'one-person household'. In parts of Asia with long traditions of multi-generational and extended family households, even couples alone together are sometimes described using language signifying 'living alone' (Yan, 2003), but their experience obviously differs from one-person households. Cultural taboos against the idea of choosing to live alone are sufficiently strong for some people doing so temporarily to deny a categorization of 'living alone'. Among interviewees living in one-person households discussed as living alone in Chapter 3, Kapoor (a young professional migrant from India) claims 'it's not living alone' because he knew his marriage would be arranged and that he would be living with his spouse by the age of 30.

Sharing some aspect of space or household facility creates another form of blurred boundary. People living in one roomed apartments, including the form of cheap rented accommodation that the British call 'bedsits', with a bed, sitting area, sink and cooking facilities, would generally be classified as living alone, even if they share a bathroom. Similarly, residents of 'single room occupancy dwellings' such as those in low-budget hotel residences accommodating poor people in some parts of the United States are so classified even if they have a shared bathroom or laundry facilities. More ambiguous cases include some types of hostel, and rented space within a household or multiply sub-divided dwelling in which all cooking and washing facilities are shared. Residents might be regarded or regard themselves as living alone if each has the exclusive use of their own room and their access to shared space does not lead to a sense of forming a household, connection or common cause with others. However, for lodgers within family households, some incorporation into the landlord/landlady's household is common and undermines the categorization of living alone. In lodgings and hostels, people are often subject to additional rules and regulations limiting their control over even their private space, making them institutional settings rather than collections of one-person households.

The fact that people move in and out of living alone across time (Chandler et al., 2004; Glanville et al., 2005; Smith et al., 2005; Wasoff et al., 2005; Williams et al., 2008) creates another sense of fuzziness around the category of living alone. For example, when re-contacting a sample of 140 men and women aged 25–44 who were identified as one-person households in a household survey, by the time of our interviews, about a year after this initial survey, 9 per cent were no longer living alone because they were now living with a partner, one was now living with her mother, and one had an unofficial lodger.

Solo-living versus going solo, choice versus constraint

Finally, note that living alone should not be confused with 'being single'. Although solo-living is often used to mean living alone, sometimes being so used in this text, this can be confusing since 'going solo' sometimes means living without a partner or leaving a partner. Solo-living, living alone, need not mean being solo in this sense of without a partner. Partnership status and living arrangements are analytically separate dimensions of human arrangements and in some circumstances they are physically separate. It is perfectly possible to live alone and be partnered, just as it is possible to be single and living in shared arrangements. 'Single' itself, as a term for partnership status, can have several meanings, two using legal classificatory systems, 'never married' or 'not currently married' (never married, widowed, divorced) and it is also used in the more experiential sense of 'currently without a partner'. As Chapter 3 discusses at length, some people who live alone are in couple relationships with partners, whether seen as potential life partners or short-term sexual relationships who live elsewhere, and some who live alone have no partner. Some who have no partner and live alone have a legal partnership status of single but others are divorced or widowed; some have never experienced living with a partner and others have exited from cohabiting relationships.

It has been suggested that people living alone can be usefully classified as two groups, those who elected to live alone and those forced to do so (Bennett and Dixon, 2006). Understanding the routes people take into living alone and the factors driving their move to this living situation is very important as these routes and drivers clearly impact on the experience of living alone. Living alone because of bereavement in a space that was previously shared with a long-loved partner is clearly a different experience from setting up home alone prior to any partner relationship. These circumstances are also likely to be encountered at different ages and stages of the life course, compounding experiential difference. It is not necessarily easy or helpful to reduce differences among people living alone into those who choose versus those arriving by accident or constraint. Something of the difficulties and dubious helpfulness is illustrated in discussion of whether to classify those who are single or childless by whether or not it was 'chosen'. 'Choice' is in itself a notoriously misleading concept often signalling individualized decision-making as if the wider social context could be safely bracketed off even though individual choices are typically socially shaped. As is discussed in Chapters 2 and 3, even those who use the language of choice in describing setting-up home alone prior to partnering in younger adulthood can also feel that this is something that they have to do. This is not generally because they are being forced out of their family home by violence or adverse circumstances, although that can also happen, but because of normative understandings of being too old to continue to live with parents that are part of the cultural context of much of northern and western Europe.

Scope and sources of evidence

Some notable previous American studies have been published with titles designed to challenged negative views of living alone such as:

Going Solo: The Extraordinary Rise and Surprising Appeal of Living Alone (Klinenberg, 2012) and *Singled Out: How Singles Are Stereotyped, Stigmatized, and Ignored, and Still Live Happily Ever After* (de Paulo, 2006). While we share the intention of counteracting inappropriate stereotypes, it will become clear throughout the subsequent chapters that there is never only one story to be told about living alone. Experience varies with resources and by age and stage in the life course. This in turn is connected to the intersecting demographic and biographical circumstances that precipitate living alone. It makes a difference whether living alone is caused by the loss of a partner through death or divorce or whether by running away from, forced exit from, or planned and scheduled departure from a family household or transitional lodgings entered in lieu of living with a family. In most cultures, these different routes into living alone will also be reacted to and experienced differently according to the gender of the person living alone and will be navigated differently by the economically advantaged and disadvantaged. Different regions of the globe, and different rural and urban contexts within the same region, offer specific combinations of locally and globally generated social, economic and cultural conditions. These in turn modify the potential quality of life of a person living alone. In many Asian cultures, women suffer social death as well as bereavement with the death of a husband, and a poor woman with no independent means of support has to rely on and is vulnerable to abuse from kin. In European and North American contexts, when older people have economic independence and women have traditionally been the 'kin keepers', connecting kin and bringing families together, men losing their wives in older age can be more at risk of isolation than widows. Social scientists have become increasingly attuned to the intersection of different dimension of social differentiation and inequality in individual biographies, such as age, social class, ethnicity, gender, health, region and sexuality. We avoid the rather awkward phrase 'intersectionality' that is now sometimes used as shorthand for analysis that focuses on the consequences of such intersections but, nevertheless, remain mindful of this approach in our use of evidence.

Age, generation and gender

This book focuses more on men and women of working age but also discusses those living alone at older ages. Our reasons for more strongly focusing on younger ages and on both men and women address some particular concerns. Popular worry and excitement about the trend of living alone focus on possible shifts in power between generations and gender, particularly in cultures that afford significant respect to the authority of the old over the young and of men over women. Surprisingly, there are continuities of concern in cultures which formally celebrate equality. Here the trend is sometimes associated with the fear held by some that women are matching men in pursuing their own interests rather than devoting energies to family life, amplifying the fragility of personal life and making everyone a casualty. However, there is a mismatch between the idea that women are now pioneering this social change and the statistical reality that a larger number of men of working age live on their own than women across countries leading the trend. In order to address these issues strategically, we have focused our own research on both men and women choosing the age span 25–44, conventionally associated with being partnered, giving birth to and nurturing the next generation. Our discussion also turns back to the evidence of researchers studying other age groups. It is important to contextualize our focus by also looking across age: experience at younger ages may influence what happens in later life, while experiences at older ages may portend what is ahead for those who are younger.

Locality, regions and globalization

Chapter 2 shows that there are very significant differences across the globe in the proportions of people living alone. We draw on Göran Therborn's (2004, 2011) division of the world into a small number of regions with distinctive ways of organizing personal life. This categorization by historical and geographical divisions in thinking about, organizing and ordering life courses, as ways of partnering, parenting and developing households, is suggestive of why some regions have high and some low rates of living alone. However, although rates are varied, a trend of increase is discernible even in regions where rates are very low. Therborn is one of a number of authors who discuss global processes impacting on all regions that have sometimes been labelled with the shorthand 'globalization', albeit that he dislikes the label in his earlier work (2004). Subsequent chapters draw on our own research which has been conducted within north-western Europe, the region with the highest rate of living alone. Our own qualitative research, which is drawn on in Chapters 3–7, is conducted specifically in Scotland, the northern country within the United Kingdom. As in all parts of the world, some of the factors impacting on those living alone in Scotland have a global reach, such as the state of the 'global economy'. Some of those who live alone there are migrants from other parts of the globe; our own study included migrants from near neighbours including other parts of the United Kingdom, Ireland and other European countries, as well as Africa and Asia. Throughout our use of Scottish evidence, we cross-refer to available research from other countries and regions and maintain mindfulness of both commonality and difference in the circumstances that precipitate, enable and inhibit living alone and in the circumstances that enhance or detract from consequent quality of life. Everywhere, just as global trends can be seen in the local, the local can be seen as contributing to the global, and this is a perspective we seek to maintain.

Rural and urban contexts

Subsequent chapters touch on rural and urban differences within regions. In South Asia and in parts of many regions of the 'global south', the majority of the population lives in small settlements and rural areas. Such areas in many 'developing' and 'developed' regions of the global north suffer from depopulation and, particularly, the loss of young people. Rural areas with small populations in village localities where potentially 'everybody knows everybody' are often assumed to have much more sense of community that exercises more collective social control over individuals than cities with the anonymity of large-scale and mobile populations. Evidence from many parts of the world shows that living alone among older people is rising in rural and urban areas. In societies which are dramatically urbanizing, rates of increase are often higher in rural areas, as is the case in China (Yan, 2010). While in north-western Europe there are higher concentrations of working-age men and women living alone in urban areas, their increase also in rural areas raises interesting questions. Do those living alone in rural localities indicate the demise of localized community or are they withdrawing from or participating in such communities? In our own research, we considered it important to include the experiences of men and women from both urban and rural areas. People living alone in rural areas may be a particular barometer of social change of 'community'. Understanding living alone among working-age rural populations is particularly important to fragile rural communities concerned with attracting or retaining people of working age as workers, as helpers to older generations and as potential parents of new generations. An urban–rural comparison addresses both theoretical and policy-related reasons for getting underneath the trend towards solo-living, recognizing how solo living can impact on future demand for housing and for care and income support in older age, both of which present rather different challenges in urban and rural areas.

Sources

We draw on collations of census data across countries over time to identify trends in living alone. This is complemented by attending to the growing body of research in English on the topic from across the globe, and we pay particular attention to work that has involved listening directly to people who live alone. There are qualitative studies of elderly people living alone in almost all regions of the world although fewer studies encompassing people of working age. Nevertheless, there are notable studies with a direct focus on working-age people living alone in Asia, Europe and North America, as well as bodies of research on overlapping topics, which include people living alone, such as studies of single people, parenting relationships and couple relationships conducted without co-residence, over distance or 'living apart together'.

Much of the text is informed by our own research, which records the voices of 140 men and women aged between 25 and 44 years in one-person households living in Scotland. They were identified as one-person households through a large household survey, the Scottish Household Survey.[2] Using a household survey as a sampling frame has the advantage of it being constructed by statistical techniques designed to ensure a representative sample of the population. We cannot claim our subsequent subsample is statistically representative of people living alone as the numbers are relatively small and our procedures disproportionately sampled women and people living alone in rural areas in order to produce equal numbers of men and women and people living alone in urban and rural localities. Nevertheless, it is reasonable to assume that, within those categories, the achieved sample is likely to be fairly typical of that particular population and certainly more so than if we had started with a convenience sample. Appendix 1 provides additional information on the characteristics of our sample.

Scotland has somewhat higher rates of solo-living, lower fertility and more extreme ageing of its population than its neighbour, England.[3] Scotland's landmass is disproportionately rural and sparsely populated with the majority of the population of five million people concentrated in urban areas. The Scottish context contains remote rural areas with ongoing concerns about the shrinking and extreme ageing of their populations and cities, which are major hubs of employment, attracting professional in-migrants and high rates of young solo-living. This makes Scotland a very appropriate place to explore the trend to living alone in different types of urban and rural localities. Analysis of any locality requires mindfulness of the interaction of global and local processes but Scotland's particular mix of high solo-living, urban density and rural areas provides a small-scale example of concerns that are repeated in much larger populations and in many parts of the world. The research employs comparison of people living alone in 'large urban areas' with settlements of over 125,000 with those living in either remote small towns, settlements of 3–10,000 that are more than 30 minutes by car from larger settlements, or rural areas, settlements less than 3000.

We have also conducted secondary analyses of European and UK household surveys. Some tables derived from the European surveys are reported in Chapter 2, and analyses of the most recent available data from the Scottish Household Survey are used to contextualize our qualitative research in Scotland. A series of tables presented in Appendix 2 shows how people living alone at working ages compare with those living with others across a number of economic and social domains. Where sample sizes permit, additional tables show how people living alone at ages 25–44 compare with people living alone across the wider working age.

Theoretical debate

This section provides some elaboration and referencing of the debates about personal life, 'globalization', dislocation, consumption and individualization alluded to above. The person living alone stands in a position of particular theoretical importance within these debates.

Selves, subjectivity and globalization

Within social science, debates about how to theorize human subjectivity, agency and identity run alongside discussion of social change in personal life. Two terms recur in summaries of how societies and social worlds are changing in the present: 'modernity', sometimes qualified by adjectives indicating it is past or in a new phase, and 'globalization'. Both terms are fuzzy with multiple uses. 'Modernity' is often used loosely to refer to a pervasive sense of a break with the past rather than a period that is more clearly delimited by a span of years. 'Globalization' is taken to mean processes with a near global reach including forms of economic exchange, political governance or systems of ideas

(Therborn, 2011). In this sense, globalization is not new, but the term is more commonly a shorthand for very recent social processes, sometimes also presented as a new modernity or postmodernity. This use of globalization focuses on step changes in capitalist production, capitalist markets, mass media and consumption, often particularly highlighting global socio-technical systems emergent from the digital revolution. This globalization is widely seen as fostering a new modernity, an era of unprecedented possibilities that reduce distance, speed up travel and generate various forms of social good alongside unprecedented threats to the sustainability of the planet and human life itself. Stereotypes and images of people living alone feed on the contested claims concerning the overall effect of 'globalization' and its new 'modernity' on people's sense of themselves and their place in the world.

In sociology, social psychology and philosophy, theories of how we come to develop a sense of our self as an agent in the world often emphasize the connection between inner dialogue, embodied feelings and our relationships with others. There is an ongoing debate about how this is modified if relationships are increasingly mediated by use of consumer goods, commercial services and digital communications. While some of this discussion refers to the development of a secure sense of self in early childhood (sometimes referred to as 'ontological security'), the quality, intensity and resilience of relationships with others across adulthood are consequential, according to many commentators. A classic account that remains influential is that of the theorist George Herbert Mead (1927). He described how an infant's interactions with his or her first carers prompts not only the learning of symbols and language but the development of internal dialogue between an active enquiring 'I', and a reactive 'me' incorporating a 'generalized other', a sense of the voice of the relevant wider social world, enabling anticipation of normative reactions. Mead's theoretical perspective developed in a 'Western' context. Non-Western studies show that some cultures strongly emphasize interconnection and immersion in a web of relationships in their understandings of personhood and lack the emphasis on the separation and autonomy of the individual attributed to 'Western' understandings of the self (Allerton, 2007; Bell and Coleman, 1999; Strathearn, 1988; Trawick, 2003). However, although Mead's vocabulary includes an individualized 'I' and a 'me', his understanding profoundly emphasizes the dependence of the self on relationships.

Twenty-first century theorists, working across a range of social science disciplines and traditions of thought, seek to theorize the impact of mediated discourse, fluid and fleeting relationships on 'the self'. It is accepted that a sense of self can be modified by belonging to communities that exist more in imagination than interaction (Calhoun, 2003), by membership of transient and multiple categories and temporary performance of diverse roles (Butler, 1999; Hewitt, 2007). It is widely accepted that the dislocating changes fostered by globalization, including unprecedented exposure to images of alternative lifestyles, competing claims of knowledge and loss of certainties such as life-long marriage, enhance questioning self-reflexivity (Beck, 1992; Beck and Beck-Gernsheim, 2001; Giddens, 1990, 1991, 1992; Lasch, 1994). In seeking to theorize this modern subjectivity, some contemporary theorists see the self as shaped more by ephemeral and pervasive 'discourse', the disembodied knowledge of experts, government and the like (Rose, 1996). The emphasis on discourse can go too far towards disregarding embodied personal relationships. Mead's 'generalized other' can be re-conceptualized as part of an inner dialogue that is one of the many forms of self-reflexivity (Archer, 2007; Brownlie, 2011), a constantly updated synthesis that typifies and normalizes 'what people think' and 'what people do' based on both face-to-face interactions and the global flows of popular culture or expert discourse (Holdsworth and Morgan, 2007). The pervasive part played by mass-produced goods and socio-technical systems in personal life has also led theorists to refurbish understandings of the interdependence of the self and things (Latour, 2005), including the use of goods and services, for performance, self-presentation and sense of distinction from others (Goffman, 1959; Slater, 1997; Southerton, 2009). The work of Pierre Bourdieu is the most cited in this latter respect (Bourdieu, 1984) and provokes much debate about the fit between practices of self-formation and the reproduction of power relationships, hierarchies and inequalities. For Bourdieu, preferences and dispositions are acquired by processes of interaction in childhood, like those described by Mead, but then become unconsciously embodied and only amenable to conscious thought in particular conditions (Adkins, 2004).

In the early 1970s, reflecting on their own social world, the American sociologist Peter Berger and his co-authors place particular emphasis on the couple relationship (Berger and Kellner, 1964; Berger and Luckman, 1971) as the key 'significant other' interlocutor, sustaining a person's sense of self across adult life. By the end of the twentieth century, some theorists of personal life in Europe and North America question the continued primacy of the couple relationship as the ideal sought by the majority of adults, and many observe that more varied constellations of personal relationships are the 'significant others' in people's lives, particularly those who do not identify themselves as heterosexual (Weeks et al., 1996, 2001; Weston, 1991, 1998). Some twenty-first-century scholars suggests that a more fluid pattern is becoming more common (Budgeon and Roseneil, 2004; Raine and Wellman, 2012). This is consistent with the understanding that 'globalization' has extended freedoms to create increasingly diverse and differentiated biographies and identities, albeit without erasing long-standing social inequalities such as those of gender.

Individualization, individualism and living alone

Many commentators hint at an association between living alone, and changes in individualization or individualism as a result of 'globalization', often in ways that reinforce negative stereotypes about living alone. This section reviews the history of some of these arguments, in the hope of moving on from themes that might obscure rather than clarify subsequent discussion.

The term 'individualization' usually refers to social processes separating out, delimiting, focusing on or giving place to the individual, allowing some differentiation from rather than being subsumed within social categories and collectivities, and enabling room for manoeuvre rather than constraining through anchorage to traditional moorings. Individualism refers to ideas about personhood, an ideology, philosophy or set of beliefs that celebrate or place particular significance on the individual. The distinction can be illustrated by current discussion of social change in China. The anthropologist Yunxiang Yan argues that the Chinese socialist state sponsored individualization but not individualism when it embraced market capitalism. The break-up of the previously collectivized farms and industries, encouragement of private business and promotion of self-development through education, mobility, enterprise and consumption are aspects of modern China encouraging individualization. However, scholars note that they did not end traditional respect for collective values nor signal state adoption of an ideology of individualism (Yan, 2003, 2009, 2010). Yan describes how members of the rural village he studied from 1949 to 1999 pursued more privacy and 'increasingly have been demanding the rights of self-development, happiness and security against the backdrop of age-old teachings of collective well-being' (Yan, 2009, p. xviii). Similar arguments about individualization without abandonment of collectivism or embracing an ideology of individualism are made with respect to South Korea (Chang, 2010).

The discussion of individualization, individualism and modernity in China and South Korea adds a new chapter to discussion initiated by the founding figures of sociology. Emile Durkheim (1984 [1893]) identified moral individualism, acknowledging and respecting the rights of others, as a new form of solidarity that emerged with complex divisions of labour of modern societies. Max Weber (1976 [1904/1905]) identified an elective affinity between the activities of capital accumulation in capitalism and a set of beliefs about the individual's responsibility for his or her destiny. In both these classic accounts, social processes of differentiation between individuals and belief systems of individualism develop in tandem. Yan (2003, 2009, 2010) describes how in China, individualization (but not, he argues, individualism) has resulted in young newly-weds preferring to form separate family households rather than continuing in traditional three-generational families. The consequent growth of 'empty nest' family households, in turn, increases numbers of older people living alone on the death of a spouse. It remains to be seen whether individualization in China will also continue in ways that result in growing numbers of young adults who have not yet married establishing households in which they live alone and whether individualization will continue without growing commitment to individualism. A Weberian understanding of the relationship between systems of human activity and ideas might suggest an elective affinity between processes of individualization and ideologies of individualism that will develop in the longer term, but such a view is speculative and contentious. It is clear, however, that social processes fostering individualization are as centrally implicated as ideas about individualism in the trend towards living alone in Europe and North America, although it is individualism that has been more routinely cited and draws notoriety.

The history of individualization as an aspect of personal life in Europe and North America has sometimes been overstated and remains contested. In the twentieth-century decades of 1950–1980, American functionalist sociologists advanced a view of history suggesting Americans had turned away from their wider kin relationships to focus on nuclear family households because this family form fitted the demands of industrial capitalism (Goode, 1970; Parsons and Bales, 1956). These accounts blossomed despite the more or less simultaneous emergence of compelling historical evidence that nuclear families had been a key feature of western European societies long before industrial capitalism (Laslett, 1965; see also Anderson, 1980; Coontz, 1992; Hartmann, 1979; Jamieson, 1987; Thornton, 2005). Another critique of the argument came through a burgeoning of empirical research documenting the contemporaneous significance of kin relationships across households as the primary sources of help in times of trouble and the main providers of care. Kin remain significant across the globe; even in the ideological heartland of the nuclear family, the United States, people routinely draw on wider networks of kin and friendship to sustain family life (Hansen, 2005). The myth that people are now choosing to live alone in order to look after no one but themselves is more persuasive when a fictitious history of how Europeans and Americans recently turned away from extended kin continues to circulate.

European and North American academics of the late twentieth century began to comment on diversification of the life course and family life consistent with intensification of individualization, a theme that recurs into the first decades of the twenty-first century. As is discussed in Chapter 2, deviation from previously normative ages and sequencing of leaving home, marrying, establishing a co-resident household, and becoming a parent become common. While some young people become parents at an early age prior to partnering or establishing an independent home, many have an extended period of transition to adulthood sometimes missing or reordering once conventional milestones. The emergent diversity in family life includes partnerships without marriage, parenting without co-residence and various forms of 'blended', 'reconstituted' and 'chosen' family. The life course is relabelled a 'choice biography', a personalized project involving strategic life planning, adaption to changing circumstances and reflexivity (Giddens, 1991, p. 58; Beck, 2000, p. 53).

> With the extension of the dynamic of individualization into the family, forms of living together begin to change *radically*... The lifelong standard family... becomes a limiting case, and the rule becomes a movement back and forth amongst various familial and *non*familial forms of living together, specific to the particular phase of life in question... Each person lives through several family lives as well as nonfamilial forms of life, depending on the life phase, and *for that very reason* lives more and more his/her *own biography*... marriage can be subtracted from sexuality, and that in turn from parenthood; parenthood can be multiplied by divorce; and the whole thing can be divided by living together or apart, and raised to a higher power by the possibility of multiple residences and the ever-present potentiality of taking back decisions.
>
> (Beck, 1992, p. 114–116, emphasis in original)

At the same time, European and North American research demonstrated that the most disadvantaged groups in societies typically gain least by 'choice biographies' and that so-called choice biographies continued to reproduce long-standing patterns of difference and inequality by regions, by gender and in terms of socio-economic circumstances (Crompton, 2006; Dykstra and Poortman, 2010; Furlong and Cartmel, 2007; Furstenberg, 2010; Goldscheider and Goldscheider, 1999; Holdsworth and Morgan, 2005; Iacovóu, 2010; Iacovou and Skew, 2010; Irwin, 1995; Pfau-Effinger, 1998).

While in the 1970s European and North American academics saw families as accommodating increasing demands for individual autonomy, privacy and self-expression (Goode 1970; Stone, 1979) as the 'realm of individual freedom' (Zaretsky, 1976), by the millennium these very demands for personal satisfaction are seen by some as threatening the viability of family life (Bellah, et al., 1985; Hochschild, 2003; Cherlin, 2009). Again, the writings of Ulrich Beck and Elisabeth Beck-Gernsheim are particularly iconoclastic, suggesting that a person living alone, childless and outside of relationships is the apex of market-driven individualization and individualism (Beck, 1992; Beck and Beck-Gernsheim, 1995).

> Everyone must be independent, free for the demands of the market...the market subject is ultimately the single individual.... The ultimate market society is a *childless* society.
>
> (Beck and Beck-Gernsheim, 1995, p. 116)

The pessimism of these particular authors dissipates with a later shift in focus, but, in this strand of their writing, the direction of change is towards being doomed to be alone, desperate for love and coupledom but, simultaneously, unwilling to make the sacrifices necessary to sustain relationships. Much of feminist-informed research places the emphasis rather differently on women's desires for more equal relationships rather than a self-interested turning away from familial concerns. In this version of change, it is men's unwillingness to meet women halfway which contributes to strains in marriage and the increase in 'solos' and 'singles' (for example, Crompton, 2006; Gerson, 2010; Hochschild, 1990; Lewis, 2001; Skolnick, 1991).

In contrast, the British author Anthony Giddens (Giddens, 1990, 1991, 1992) was much more optimistic. Yet Giddens shared Beck's and Bauman's view of a new modernity in which people are more radically individualized and disembedded from traditional ties. Rather than gloom about the fragility of equal relationships that lack the entrapment of financial dependency or constraining institutional structures, this body of work emphasizes positive opportunity; new intensities of intimacy and democracy are constructed through a dialogue of mutual self-disclosure in the process of jointly creating 'narratives of the self' and 'pure relationships' sustained by the dynamic of mutual satisfaction without reliance on institutional structures. Rather than seeing women as displaying the same selfishness as men, women, as the more skilled practitioners of self-disclosing intimacy, play the leading role in this process, which simultaneously democratizes personal relationships. Living-apart-together, an arrangement in which couples maintain long-term relationships without pooling resources or jointly conducting domestic affairs in co-residence, is perfectly consistent with Giddens' vision of 'pure relationship' and conducting democratic personal lives.

While Giddens adopted a positive view of individualism (Santore, 2008), many varieties are named in the academic literature along with critiques and denials. Feminist work critiques the hidden gendered assumptions of individual autonomy in the historical account of the emergence of 'rational man' as patriarchy-serving illusion that denies and distorts his historical dependence on division of labour between men and women (Pateman, 1988; Smith, 1987). Individualism is more often used negatively, as in selfish-individualism, emphasizing a tendency to deny connection to and responsibility for others. Anthony Elliott and Charles Lemert (2009) suggest the modern consumer's sense of freedom to choose expresses 'manipulated individualism', and Zygmunt Bauman (2001, 2003, 2005) suggests that capitalism's promotion of self-expression through hyper-consumption (see also Bellah et al., 1985; Illouz, 2007) has created an emphasis on fluidity, mobility and disposability, which undermine the human capacity to sustain durable and meaningful relationships. Earlier twentieth-century American scholars of family life offer positive accounts of the alliance between individualization, individualism and capitalism in a period when American modernity was still more unequivocally admired (Goode, 1970; Parsons, 1959; Shorter, 1975; Zaretsky, 1976). By the 1990s, American visions of their post-industrial modernity had become grim and the same trope had a pessimistic cant. Richard Sennett (1998), for example, argues that working practices exemplified by the portfolio-career of late capitalism virulently undermine all forms of loyal relationships; loyalty at home is lost along with loyalty to the firm (Sennett, 1998). While some of the assumptions about capitalist labour processes in such accounts are found wanting (Wajcman and Martin, 2002), the genre of caricaturing selfish man (or woman) remains powerful. These multiple forms of the idea that an ideology of 'individualism' is inimical to ties to kin and community help to set up the negative stereotype of the young person living alone.

Networked individuals and relationship to place

The fear that people who live alone are particularly disengaged from social ties makes assumptions about engagement in civic life, community and locality; it suggests inhabitants living as-if-blinkered-and-passing-through, with no need for meaningful connection to people living locally or to the place itself. Writing about a 'Western' context, Giddens was optimistic that he was witnessing a move to a more democratic personal life, which would help reinvigorate other forms of democratic civic engagement. This was again a contrasting tack to the more pessimistic North American accounts claiming to document deterioration in forms of sociability and social solidarity over time, such as that of Robert Putnam's (2000) text, *Bowling Alone*, which became one of the most cited books of its decade. Meanwhile, other North American authors focusing on the new opportunities for making relationships created by the communication technologies of the digital age were claiming a change in the type of ties people have rather than a deterioration of ties as such (Castells, 1996). Barry Wellman and his co-authors suggested a historical shift towards a type of social solidarity that they describe as 'networked individuals'. Their claim is that 'networked individualism' is increasingly taking over from prior forms of social solidarity – being embedded in close-knit groups or neighbourhood-based local ties with well-known others. Perhaps understating the continued significance of kin and friendship relationships (Jamieson, 2013), Wellman and his co-authors argue the reduced relevance of residential arrangements to social connections and solidarity. For networked individuals, 'the individual – and not the household, kinship group, or work group – is the primary unit of connectivity... people must actively network to thrive or even to survive comfortably. More passive or unskilled people may lose out, as the group (village, neighbourhood, household) is no longer taking care of things for them' (Wellman et al., 2006, p. 164–165). Wellman's more recent writing (Raine and Wellman, 2012) stresses continuity as well as change since social networks that include some weaker ties to lesser known others beyond the neighbourhood, and 'glocalized' ties that combine some weak and strong ties in constellations of global and local relationships, can be documented for many societies and historical periods. However, an emphasis on networks as the key social unit of an individual's life is particularly appropriate in the period following the Internet and mobile phone revolutions (Raine and Wellman, 2012). In his discussion of living alone, Klinenberg (2012) suggests that attractions and pleasures are opened up by new mobile telephone and Internet possibilities facilitating living alone as a networked individual.

Research has also qualified claims about disengagement from communities of place by exploration of urban–rural and social class differences. Since Simmel (1950 [1903]), a disengaged relationship to locality and co-residents has been regarded as an urban phenomenon. Research has documented different patterns of networks in urban and rural areas showing how they emerge from their different opportunities and constraints. The former provide much greater choice and possibilities for diversity in personal relationships, and the latter offer fewer more multiplex relationships and a need for circumspection given the durability and unavoidability of one's neighbours (see, for example, Fischer, 1982). There is also a growing body of research on class differences in local and dispersed networks and their modification by mobility. Michael Savage and his co-authors (2005) concluded on the basis of a study in the north of England that an attitude of the mobile consumer pervades how some people approach their locality of residence, as if they inhabit a blank canvas with no clutter of previous history or other noteworthy prior social contexts that need to be negotiated. Research on localities in the United Kingdom often argues that those most rooted by local ties are working-class people without the resources to be geographically or socially mobile. Locally based social networks facilitate more frequent informal contact, and UK studies comment on class differences in parents' expectations of frequent contact with grown-up children such as 'popping in' and speaking on the telephone (Charles et al., 2008). Exploration of the relationship between residence arrangements, mobility histories and orientations to locality and community is sharpened by comparison across rural and urban localities. However, in an era of networked individualism, new interaction opportunities are extended to the rural community and the difference between the urban and rural diminishes. As noted above, comparison of those living alone in rural and urban contexts will help clarify the relationship between residence alone and social and local engagement. Are urbanites living alone or their rural equivalents any less likely to conform to the stereotype of disengagement and social distance?

These interlinked theoretical debates on subjectivity and the self, on individualization and individualism and on relationship to place in the context of globalization, form the background to our investigation of the trend of increase in living alone across the globe. We begin with detailed analysis of international patterns in living alone and possible explanations for differences across regions and between countries. More in-depth analysis follows, drawing on our UK study, before returning to reconsider these discussions.

Part I

Living Alone, Life Course and Life Transitions

Part I looks first at the international and geographical pattern of living alone. Living a domestic life alone would be practically impossible or extremely difficult in some parts of the world. There are regions where such a way of being is almost unthinkable, where to live alone steps outside of normal life and defies moral order. Those who do so are likely to feel outcasts, unless they can claim to be pioneers of social change. However, Chapter 2 shows that even in regions with very low rates of living alone, a trend of increase is typical. Discussants of 'globalization' and large-scale demographic trends suggest changes that make living alone both more possible and thinkable.

After a focus on demographic trends and geographical diversity of cultures in Chapter 2, Chapter 3 refocuses on the biographical experiences of people who are living alone at ages more conventionally associated with partnering and parenting. Their perspectives on alternative domestic and familial arrangements are explored. How intentionally and happily are they living alone? Do they think of themselves as in any way pioneers or victims of social change?

Living alone and restructuring of the life course

The trend to living alone is part of a package of demographic changes, the restructuring of life events – partnering, parenting, household formation, death – that constitute populations, the individual life course and the institutional arrangements that structure it, such as marriage. Demographic trends such as age of marriage, rates of living alone and the duration of life are not randomly and independently fluctuating, but complexly interconnected. Göran Therborn (2004, 2011) has tried to capture such interconnections by use of the compound noun 'family–sex–gender system'. For living alone to be possible for young adults, women as well as men require the demise of traditional family–sex–gender systems that lock young people quickly into life-long arrangements in which women are subordinate to and economically dependent on male kin.

The elements of interconnected systems of demographic change that require particular attention are different for living alone in older age and at working age. The former is most obviously linked to increased longevity and the decrease in three-generational households as a standard arrangement. Longevity is now, in almost every nation, typically greater for women than men, but it also varies markedly within countries by levels of economic advantage. In India, for example, poor widows, who have no economic independence and lower social worth than widowers, have very high mortality if they are not supported by a son (Chen, 2000). On a global scale, the residence arrangements of the population who reach old age are changing; the number living as a couple by themselves is notably increasing, including in some parts of the world where this is not conventionally the desirable or appropriate form of household. Thus, in much of Asia, a parenting couple should not experience the 'empty nest' stage, since the desired arrangement does not involve all children leaving home to set up their own households elsewhere. In parts of the world where couples routinely live by themselves, old people typically face living alone and doing so for long periods if a partner's death is premature and remarriage does not follow.

Where the trend to living alone among adults of working age is already very visible, it has emerged as part of a package of demographic changes that typically include fertility below population replacement levels, linked to postponement of starting a family, delayed marriage and acceptability of cohabiting before marriage, often referred to as 'the second demographic transition' (Goldscheider, 2000; Kaufmann, 1994; Lesthaeghe, 2010; Lesthaeghe and van de Kaa, 1986).[1] Delayed marriage can mean young adults spending an extended period in the parental home or cohabiting with a partner before marriage but, in many countries, it is also associated with young adults spending time living independently of parents and without a partner. The move to living alone in young adulthood has its roots in this stage of independence. Such trends are more marked in the richer or 'developed' countries that mainly cluster in the 'global north' (Table 2.1). In the European settler societies of North America, Australia and New Zealand, and in north-western Europe, the pattern of demographic change also includes high rates of couple dissolution and significant numbers of one-parent families and 'non-resident fathers' living without their children. They too contribute to the trend of living alone.

What makes living alone possible? Levels of 'development' and material cultures

Living a domestic life alone requires the minimal resources of a dwelling that provides shelter from inclement weather and sufficient means to maintain a domestic life and the essentials of living. In many contexts of poverty and earning modest livings, including subsistence farming that remains the means of support for large proportions of the population in much of the 'global south', survival is labour intensive and relies on family labour. In such contexts, solo exit from a family home without the blessing of kin is to have nowhere to go and no means of support. Such a move invites the dangers and hardships of sustained itinerant homelessness and risks of never finding sufficient income or resources to set up home alone. Even the occupation of land without payment, building a home from found materials collected by scavenging, as is characteristic of the creation of barrios and shanty towns, necessarily involves many hands working together, drawing on community and kinship ties (Kellett, 2000).

Regions and nations vary in the extent to which material infrastructures and means of economic support facilitate living alone. In countries of the 'global north' with long-established and relatively generous welfare regimes, welfare systems may provide financial support when other means of making a living fail and may offer routes into government-funded 'social housing'. However, the possibility of access to tenancy of a dwelling and an economic means of support can never be simply read from the level of a country's 'development', housing infrastructure or the existence of welfare regimes. The United Kingdom is a society with long-standing welfare provisions and social housing, but charities campaign on behalf of the 'single homeless' because housing policies have long regarded them as a low priority, while laws exclude some categories of migrants from access to such benefits.

How thinkable is living alone? Family–sex–gender systems

In some cultures, living alone is unthinkable as a desirable arrangement. For example, the anthropologist Catherine Allerton (2007) describes how the Manggarai people in Eastern Indonesia consider that sleeping in a room alone is spiritually and emotionally dangerous and not desirable for men or women. Allerton's ethnography identifies economically active never married women beyond the conventional age of marriage living in their parents' or brothers' households and enjoying a degree of independence and status, albeit not sexual freedom; it is possible for Manggarai women to remain unmarried but not to live alone, even although women have possibilities of independent income from weaving and sometimes have their own plots of land.

Therborn's (2004, 2011) analysis of historical change in family systems provides a broad-brush account of why living alone is more thinkable in some parts of the world than others. He uses 'family–sex–gender system' to capture durability and interconnectedness of arrangements for organizing family life, sexuality, the life course and relationships between men and women. He depicts seven geographically anchored family–sex–gender systems persisting over long historical periods. These have emerged as the legacy of the world's five 'main civilizations' – the Sinic, the Indic, the West African, the European and the sub-Saharan African – producing, respectively, the Confucian East Asian family, the South Asian Hindu family, the Islamic West Asian/North African family, the Christian-European family and the sub-Saharan African set of family systems, as well as two hybrid systems – the Southeast Asian systems and an American Creole pattern. Some family–sex–gender systems made living alone unthinkable in the past and this legacy continues, more or less intact, in the present. This is the case where patriarchy, the rule of the father or male kin, is at its most virulent, marriage is at an early age, leaving no room for youth independence, and frail old people expect to be looked after in three-generational families or households of extended kin.

Patriarchy, and its expression in 'the relative rights and duties of parents and children, of men and women' (Therborn, 2004, p. 8), and the institution of marriage, are particularly relevant to living alone in early adult life. Living alone is only possible as a socially acceptable option for both men and women when moral respectability is not dependant on being married or remaining within a domain of patriarchal supervision. In many parts of Africa, Asia, and for some ethnic and religious minorities in Europe and America, conventions continue to subject women to constant supervision. Remaining unmarried and living beyond the supervision of kin remains difficult, particularly for women in the Confucian East Asian family system, with its traditional emphasis on filial piety, and the sub-Saharan African family system, characterized by polygyny, and even more so in the South Asian Hindu and the Islamic African family systems. In these systems, marriage is not an individualized personal choice but a responsibility to a collectivity, a community and kindred. In such cultures, an arranged marriage that consolidates collective ties is much preferable to a dangerous loss of self, kin and community in individualised dyadic romantic love. Women who do not marry face significant social disapproval and sometimes physical threats. Living alone and remaining unmarried is also at complete odds with the Islamic West Asian/North African family in which female chastity is fundamental to family honour.

The family systems which create the most room for living alone to be thinkable in the earlier part of adult life are those that exercise lighter parental control over marriage and have a history of tolerance of those who never marry. In these terms, Therborn identifies the Western European variant of the Christian-European family as providing favourable conditions for living alone. The nuclear household form of the Christian-European family has also been more hospitable to the idea of living alone in older age, since there is no expectation of an older age lived in three-generational or extended-family arrangements. The preference for separate residential arrangements once children reach adulthood is not typically reversed when a parent becomes a widow or widower, is bereaved and living alone. From the perspective of other family systems, living alone in older age has conventionally been viewed as a sign of neglect, albeit that this is changing in many countries and rapidly in some within the Confucian system. The care of older people living alone is discussed in Chapter 6, but we note here that sharing a household does not guarantee intergenerational care and living in separate households does not necessarily signify its absence. The cultural expectation across systems is that children should provide care to those who parented them. In the Western-European tradition, the ideal living arrangement involves older people living near to, but separately from, their children, facilitating flows of care across households. Research has shown, for example, that despite the different incidence of living alone, there is no profound difference between patterns of care for elderly people between Beijing in China and Liverpool in the United Kingdom, because kin are the main carers, whether within the same family household or across family households (Wenger and Liu, 2000).

Globalization as exogenous change, individualization and internal agency

The term 'globalization' is a shorthand for a range of economic, technical and cultural revolutions. Therborn's account tries to encapsulate how waves of 'globalization' change social worlds, modifying the fundamentals of life, such as the means of making a living and restructuring populations, life courses and family systems (2004, 2011). In discussing how the necessary skills for participation in available means of making a living are transformed, he draws on a range of historical resources including economic histories of shifting global divisions of labour between rich and poor sectors of the globe and of the shifting balance in local economies towards service and financial industries, from manufacturing and primary production. Globally, a higher proportion of young people are drawn into extended education, which sometimes modifies mental horizons as well as life courses. While acknowledging that the association is not a simple one, Therborn sees demographic changes, longer life and lower fertility, as basically facilitated by the level of capitalist development, increased demand for education and welfare, rising living standards and high rates of consumption; more people live longer in smaller and more diverse families, although strong regional differences persist. He believes patriarchy is losing ground everywhere although it has retained stronger cultural and social support, sometimes still underpinned by economic support, in some family–sex–gender systems. Although he does not use the term 'individualization', his description of the diminishing authority of men over women and old over young refers to processes promoting individualized rights and autonomous self-expression, which loom large in debates about 'individualization' and 'individualism' reviewed in the last section of Chapter 1.

For Therborn, change comes in spasms responding to waves of 'globalization'. The causes of change are 'exogenous' (2004, p. 297), always outside the family–sex–gender system modifying its internal balance. This theoretical emphasis is not intended to deny individual agency, but puts less weight on the momentum that families and personal lives bring to historical transitions than some theoreticians, including historians, using a 'life course approach' (Elder, 1998; Hareven, 1991). Proponents of this latter approach focus on the historical detail of the intermeshing of individual and familial conduct of personal life with opportunities and constraints in the wider environment. Personal and interpersonal management of biographical transitions brings much more than reactively adjusting. As agents of synchronization, individuals and families are drivers as well as conduits of social change. Within social science there are many theoretical attempts to acknowledge the interdependence of social structures, which have durability and reach far beyond individuals, and activities of individuals, both habitual and purposive, which build and sustain institutions (Giddens, 1984).

Researchers documenting personal life and social change frequently note misalignments between lived realities and cultural ideals; these may be exacerbated in times of rapid social change. For example, older people across many family systems experience gaps between continued rhetoric emphasizing traditional commitment to their care, and the realities of actual caring. Rapid 'modernization' and rising standards of living in Asia have been associated with three generational and joint households losing ground as young couples increasingly opt to form new households on marriage rather than brides moving to the family household of her husband's kin. This in turn may have helped to make more imaginable setting up a home alone. This is particularly so in urbanizing and developing counties where economic prospects for young adults are improving. Consequently, there are extensive concerns and research literatures discussing the demise of filial piety in Confucian East Asian family systems (Ikels, 2004; Janelli and Yim, 2004; Liu, 2008; Yan, 2009). In India, unemployment remains high among educated young people (Jeffrey, 2010, 2011) and young people living alone remains relatively rare, but here too there are complaints of reciprocal ties across generations weakening and impacting on the care of older people (Lamb, 2000). The plight of widows made unwelcome in the homes of their sons and daughters-in-law has been a particular focus of research in India (Chen, 1998, 2000).

Optional partnering and parenting: Resisting the discourse of love

Revolutions in mass media and communication loom large in accounts of globalization impacting on personal lives, and some analysts have turned their attention to how a global Hollywood/Bollywood discourse of romantic love may complicate how people live out regional and local differences in family–sex–gender systems. One major difference in such systems is the degree of parental control over partnering, and the extent to which never partnering and childlessness is permitted without consequent 'social death'. Chapter 3 shifts focus from an overview of trends to the perspective of people living alone. It discusses how men and women see partnering and parenting from particular locations within the clustering of demographic changes that constitute the European family–sex–gender systems. It considers how the perspectives of those who live alone vary with whether they have never partnered and are childless; have a past partnership and/or parenting relationship now no longer in their lives; or are a continuing partner and/or parent without co-residence.

While the European family systems do not exercise the kind of pressure to marry that still operates in many regions and particularly South Asian and Islamic Africa, being 'single' still remains a more problematic identity for women than men. Research exploration of understandings of 'single' among women in the United Kingdom concludes it remains a 'troubled category' (Reynolds and Wetherell, 2003, 2007). Tuula Gordon's (1994) earlier research in Britain, Finland and the United States finds single women feeling socially excluded from much of social life, and a more recent US study of a younger group of white college-educated women (aged 28–34) still finds women worrying about a 'missed transition' and living 'in the shadow of marriage' (Sharp and Ganong, 2007). Eric Klinenberg's more recent US study also finds women worrying that their satisfaction living alone reflects a personal failure (2012, p. 68). However, Kay Trimberger's (2006) US-based study of an ethnically diverse set of older respondents who have lived alone over years indicates the erosion of any real sense of regret over time. This finding is also confirmed by some of Klinenberg's interviewees (2012). Roona Simpson's UK research suggests that the constant circulation of negative discourse makes it difficult to claim contentment with being single (Simpson, 2006, 2009). Yet acknowledging any desire to be partnered runs the risk of being negatively stereotyped as deficient and desperate (MacVarish, 2006). A sense of being outside the mainstream and socially excluded has been sufficiently strong to inspire networking sites in the United States, such as Quirkyalone.net and SingularCity.com, and has also given rise to campaigning organizations, which aim to combat discrimination and advocate the value of being single and childless (de Paulo, 2006; Klinenberg, 2012; Trimberger, 2006).[2]

The trend towards living alone across many regions of the globe seems at odds with a pervasive discourse of love focused on couple relationships. Anthropologists document both diversity in cultural understandings of love and the universality of a genre of romantic love stories in popular culture, sometimes read as 'Western' and consistent with Giddens' account discussed in the previous chapter. The story line involves falling in love and overcoming obstacles to be with 'the one', he or she who is loved, in an intensely intimate relationship (Cole and Thomas, 2009; Hirsch and Wardlow, 2006; Jankowiak, 2008; Mody, 2008; Rebhun, 1999; Uberoi, 2006). Dominant ideas about 'love' in popular culture enter individual lives in complex ways and are often called on when people explain their story of finding a partner. In some cultural contexts, 'love' can be appealed to as justification for a diverse range of sexual relationships, and does not always preclude the creation of alternative intimacies to the sexual couple (Roseneil, 2010). Love stories have a very different resonance where the dominant way of becoming a couple is through arranged heterosexual patriarchal marriage and where marriage is the only context for legitimate sexual intercourse. The extensive historical and sociological literature on love in 'Western' contexts (see, for example, Cancian, 1987; Coontz, 2005; Evans, 2003; Goode, 1959; Langford, 1999; Swidler, 2003) includes a tradition of feminist exposé of how discourses of 'falling in love' have supported patriarchal marriage in which women became like servants to men. Swidler (2003) argues that the ideal of monogamous life-long marriage and the myth of 'true love' remain mutually supportive. Her lengthy interviews with middle class Americans in the 1980s explored how they drew on such cultural resources as popular stories and advice in their everyday uses of love. Swidler's interviewees often lurched back and forth between a film version of 'love at first sight', forever and with 'the one and only' that they recognized as 'mythic' and a 'prosaic realism', in which love is ambiguous, gradual and uncertain.

People who live alone cannot be assumed to be living without love or outside of couple relationships; rather, this has to be a matter for empirical investigation. The term 'LAT', couples 'living apart together', was coined to describe a mooted new trend of people who are socially recognized as a couple and committed to pursuing a life together, but who are nevertheless living apart. The acronym was intended to signal a new phenomenon (Levin, 2004), although, as the literature acknowledges, there have been, and are, many historical and cultural contexts in which people who share social recognition as a couple, nevertheless, spend long periods of time living apart. For example, across continents and historical periods, there are many patterns of economic activities requiring absence from a family household in seasonal and circular migration. Institutionalized marriage arrangements sometimes also include long periods in which couples live apart, such as a long and formal courtship before co-residence in marriage, or childhood marriage with co-residence delayed until adulthood. However, the term LAT suggests a distinctive late twentieth- and twenty-first-century Euro-North American form of dual residence coupledom in which people seek to combine aspects of the freedom of living alone with the intimacy of being a couple, what Levin calls the 'both/and' approach, both intimacy and autonomy.

Chapter 3 explores how people living alone deal with love and intimacy. In the following chapter, we consider trends in living alone alongside other related demographic trends, of which shifts in patterns of partnering and parenting are part.

2
Geographies and Biographies of Living Alone

This chapter draws on census and large-scale survey data[1] to explore the geography of living alone. We start by looking across countries at trends in the proportions of one-person households.[2] Attention is also given to the biographical context of living alone. This includes drawing on a range of literature considering living alone in relation to other life course transitions and using trend data on first marriage, first childbirth as well as data on fertility rates and the proportion of women who remain childless.

Solo-living and global social change

Table 2.1 lists 42 countries from five continents.[3] It shows the total of all men and women living alone, that is, all one-person households, as a percentage of all private households. Countries are listed in rank order according to the proportion of one-person households with the highest ranking country at the top of the table and the lowest at the bottom. The difference between Sweden at the top and India at the bottom of the selection is more than tenfold. Living alone has increased in all but India and has often increased dramatically. The pace of change in some countries starting from a low base has been particularly rapid; for example, quadrupling in 30 years in Japan. Projected trends in family and household structures to 2030 anticipate that one-person households will grow for all countries for which projections are available, mainly as a consequence of ageing populations (OECD, 2011a).[4] The subsequent discussion refers back to Therborn's classification of family–sex–gender systems as a starting point for consideration of why some countries are high and some low. Three systems are discussed in more detail drawing on supporting research literature: the South Asian Hindu family

Table 2.1 One-person households as per cent of all households (selected countries ranked high to low by latest year for which data available)

Rank	Country	1950[a]	1980[b]	1990[b]	2000[b,c]	2010[b,d]
1	Sweden	21	33[a]	44	47	49
2	Finland	18	27	32	37	41
3	Norway	15	28	34	38	40
4	Denmark	14	30[a]	34	37	39
5	Germany	12	30	35	36	39
6	Switzerland		29	32	36	37
7	The Netherlands	9[e]	22	30	33	36
8	Austria	18	28	28	30	36
9	Estonia				34	35
10	Belgium	16[e]	23	28	31	34
11	Japan[f]	5	20	24	28	31
12	Iceland[g]	18				31
13	France	19	25[a]	26	31	30
14	Slovakia		20	22	30	
15	The United Kingdom	11	22	27	29	29
16	Luxembourg	9[e]	21	26	29	
17	Hungary		20	24	26	29
18	Italy	10	18[a]		23	29
19	The Czech Republic		24	27	30	27
20	The United States	9[h]	23	25	26	27
21	Canada		20	23	26	27
22	Australia[i]		16	19	24	27
23	Ukraine				21	24
24	New Zealand[g]					23
25	Ireland	11[e]	17	20	23	21
26	Slovenia		17	18	22	
27	Poland		17	18	22	
28	Russian Federation				22	
29	Croatia		16	18	21	
30	Greece	9	15[a]		20	
31	Romania			17	19	
32	Israel		14	15	17	18
33	Portugal	8	13[a]	14	17	
34	Spain		8	10	12	18
35	Hong Kong[j]				16	17[d]
36	Cyprus	12[e]	10	13	16	
37	Brazil[k]				8	
38	China[l]				8[l]	10[l]
39	Argentina[k]				7	

40	Mexico[g,k]	2	8
41	Chile[k]	2	
42	India[m]	4	4

[a]Wall (1989, p. 377).

[b]Unless otherwise indicated the source is the United Nations Economic Commission for Europe (UNECE) Statistical Division Database, compiled from national and international official sources (Eurostat, UN Statistics Division Demographic Yearbook, WHO European health for all database and UNICEF TransMONEE): http://w3.unece.org/pxweb/Dialog/varval.asp?ma=08_GEFHPrivHouse_r&ti=Private+households+by+Household+Type%2C+Measurement%2C+Country+and+Year&path=../DATABASE/Stat/30-GE/02-Families_households/&lang=1 (accessed 24 May 2012).

[c]Or nearest year: Data concern 2001 for Croatia, Cyprus, the Czech Republic, Greece, Hungary, Luxembourg, Portugal, Slovakia; 2002 for Romania, Russian Federation, Slovenia.

[d]Or latest year available: Data concern 2005 for Hungary, Iceland, Mexico; 2006 for Australia, Canada, Hong Kong, New Zealand; 2008 for the Czech Republic, Germany, Ireland, Spain; 2009 for Belgium.

[e]Data from 1946.

[f]Japan: Population Census of Japan: http://www.stat.go.jp/english/data/chouki/02.htm (accessed 5 August 2012); http://www.stat.go.jp/english/data/nenkan/1431-02.htm (accessed 5 August 2012).

[g]OECD (Organisation for Economic Co-operation and Development) Family Database, compiling information from different OECD databases and databases maintained by other (international) organizations: http://www.oecd.org/els/soc/oecdfamilydatabase.htm (accessed 24 May 2012).

[h]The United States: Figure for 1950 from US Census Statistics: http://www.census.gov/hhes/www/housing/census/historic/livalone.html (accessed 20 June 2012).

[i]De Vaus and Richardson (2009, p. 4).

[j]Hong Kong: http://www.bycensus2006.gov.hk/en/data/data3/statistical_tables/index.htm#D1 (accessed 20 June 2012).

[k]Central and southern America data 2001: http://www.zonalatina.com/Zldata226.htm (accessed 20 June 2012).

[l]China: Figures for 2001 and 2009 from China Statistical Database: http://219.235.129.58/search.do?query=numberofhouseholds&collId=4,5,6&rand=0.6003325412460865, Number of family households and number of households by size and by region (accessed 5 August 2012).

[m]Census of India: http://www.censusindia.gov.in/2011census/hlo/hlo_highlights.html (accessed 27 July 2012).

system represented in Table 2.1 by India, the East Asian Confucian family systems represented by China, Hong Kong and Japan and the Christian European family system represented by the majority of the countries in the table.

South Asia

In India, only 4 per cent of households are one-person households. This is consistent with the enduring strength of patriarchal arrangements in the South Asian family and earlier remarks about what makes living alone possible and thinkable. India is a complex and diverse society, yet material culture and mindsets throughout the region work strongly against living alone for the majority of people across a range of caste, class and religious backgrounds and particularly for women. India's population remains predominantly rural; economic development and the increase in the proportions of the population accessing higher levels of education have not disrupted near universal marriage, the persistence of marriage arranged by parents and family elders or the early marriage of the majority of rural women close to and sometimes below the legal minimum age of 18. Even in urban contexts, access to education does not routinely translate into a radical change in women's economic position or social mobility for men; for example, unemployment is very high among college-educated young men (Jeffrey, 2010, 2011) and educational content is not always a progressive force for social change (Mensch et al., 2005). Popular anxieties about young people are often focused on difficulties associated with the business of marrying, anxieties that delay will result in reduced chances of a good match, inflation in the cost of dowries or difficulties in finding partners given shifting, regionally variable, imbalance in sex ratios, partly produced by continued 'daughter aversion' (Jeffery, 2013). Unlike in East Asia, the presence of independent unmarried young women is not sufficiently visible to generate vilification in the popular press, since parents successfully push most towards early marriage; rather, the subject of public scandal is those who dishonour their families by running away to make 'love marriages' (Mody, 2008).

The conditions are generally unfavourable to living alone at all ages and stages of the life course. Women who have lost their husbands, a condition more common in but by no means limited to midlife and older age, face significant social and economic barriers to living alone. Women's rates of employment remain low and the stigma of a woman without a husband remains high. Living alone is also not typically seen as desirable for men. The culturally taken-for-granted significance of kin ties and connectivity are not conducive to imagining the pleasures of living alone. Only a small proportion of Indian elderly people have a pension or other form of economic independence and most elderly people rely on support from and co-residence with their children or extended family and this is unlikely to change in the foreseeable future (Chaudhuri and Roy, 2009; Croll, 2006; Guilmoto, 2011; Jeffery, 2013; Lamb, 2000; Rajan, 2008). Capacities to care for the elderly continue to vary with economic position, and India's economic development has not resulted in the opening up of access to employment to all nor transformed economic inequalities or access to social mobility (Jeffery, 2013). Multiple changes in economic and demographic conditions have the potential to modify relationships between generations and may lead to weakening the commitment of children to care for their parents in old age and an increase in elderly people living alone. Young people's migration from villages, in some regions, disrupts traditional patterns of residence and elder care. Falling family sizes, the increasing costs of childcare and increased longevity modify burdens of care but again these changes vary markedly by region. Nuclear family households are slightly increasing at the expense of households in which married sons live with their parents but the speed of change is modest in comparison to parts of East Asia.

Divergence between practice and the dominant view that elderly people should be cared for by their extended family is not uncommon, particularly in the case of widows, but the majority of older people neglected by kin lack the resources to live alone. For example, Martha Chen's studies of widows in rural India (2000) and a study of older age people in Bengali North India (Lamb, 2000) document widows living in the house or compound of one or more sons with the daily disappointment of sparse emotional or practical support. It is extremely rare for women to own land or any property but by convention, on the death of her husband, this passes to sons, whereas a man may retain some control of property until his own death. Vera-Sanso (2012) notes the increased pressure for older women in poorer communities to contribute to the household economy of younger family members, with economic globalization necessitating the provision of domestic and caring work to free daughters and daughters-in-law to earn an income in situations of privation. Most young widows remarry but traditionally upper caste Hindu widows are prohibited from remarrying and should live a secluded chaste life of perpetual mourning, upholding the honour and purity of her husband's lineage, while receiving maintenance from his kin (Chen, 2000). Older people, and particularly widows, may spend periods of time on pilgrimages, a socially sanctioned way to step outside of kin relationships, and a practice often seem as a necessary preparation for death. Some older people live outside of a network of ties to others as wandering beggars or as old-age home dwellers (Lamb, 2000, p. 128–137). These options are sometimes more possible and thinkable than living in their own homes alone. Only a small privileged minority would have the resources to allow living alone if the inclination to do so developed.

East Asia

China is also close to the bottom of Table 2.1, ranked 38 out of the 42 countries listed, but already a clear step up from India, with 10 per cent of households being one-person households and evidence of a rising trend. Readily available statistics do not disaggregate the trend by age and gender but studies of rural and urban China are documenting an increase in older people living alone and rapid modification of expectations of co-residence with children (Lin, 1995; Xin and Chuliang, 2008; Yan, 2003, 2009; Zhang, 2004). The absence of pensions in rural areas means that living alone without some financial support from kin is not possible for all, but a growing number of older people have accumulated savings and material goods during the period of China's rapid economic development. A larger proportion of elderly people can afford to live alone in urban areas (Lin, 1995; Xin and Chuliang, 2008). Living alone as an older person is now also much more thinkable even if living with a married son and being looked after by a daughter-in-law is still regarded as the ideal. This is powerfully illustrated by Yunxiang Yan's description of the tragic case of a 64-year-old man who drank a bottle of pesticide in 1991. His suicide was in response to an unhappy life locked in conflict with his daughter-in-law. The opinion among older rural villagers was, 'since he had accumulated a large amount of cash savings and a good house, he could have had a comfortable retirement living alone' (2009, p. 58), a view that Yan notes as unthinkable 20 years earlier.

Hong Kong is also in the bottom quadrant of the table, but not the other representative of the East Asian Confucian family, Japan. Therborn describes Japan as 'the pace setter' within East and South-East Asia in matters of sexual freedom and youth autonomy because of its earlier economic success (2011, p. 162) but, nevertheless, its high ranking seems inconsistent with Therborn's depiction of the Confucian family–sex–gender systems. Japan's pattern of living alone seems much closer to a north-western European pattern, which means a combination of both elderly people living alone and a rise in living alone at working age. There is discussion in the literature of relevance to both of these trends. For example, Zeng Yi (1994) and his co-authors compared age of leaving home in China, Japan and South Korea against selected Western countries. Focusing on the 1970s, they showed the distinctiveness of Japan; young men were leaving home much earlier than in China or South Korea, albeit in smaller proportions than the comparators of Sweden and the United States. This difference within East Asia is attributed to Japan's more advanced economic development and the associated earlier expansion of higher education. The wider literature on youth transitions attributes tertiary education with a major role in fostering a stage of youth independence across countries; education potentially makes living alone more possible and thinkable by providing a route to living away from home, credentials that improve means of economic independence and shifts in mindsets, often towards more individualistic, egalitarian and liberal views (Heath and Cleaver, 2003; Lesthaeghe and Moors, 2000; Schofer and Meyer, 2005).

In Japan, men are more likely to leave home for employment or education than women, making Japan one of the very few countries in which women are older than men when they leave their parental home (Fukuda, 2009). Since the stalling of Japan's economy in the 1990s, the visibility of young people postponing partnership and parenting has increased. Both those living alone and those living longer in the parental home have attracted critical media commentary; women have been particularly vilified for apparent unwillingness to take up the role of mothers (Nemoto, 2008; Ronald and Hirayama, 2009; Yamada, 2005). Kumiko Nemoto (2008) documents ambivalence about marriage and difficulties in partnering among highly educated women who resent cultural expectations of giving up work on marriage and the association of femininity with submissiveness and subordination. Lyons-Lee (1998) notes a similar problematizing of partnering among tertiary-educated women in Singapore, and also argues such women have not rejected marriage, but rather traditional constructions of gender roles within the family.

But Japan's ranking in Table 2.1 is also influenced by the preponderance of elderly people in its population and their increased incidence of living alone. Many Japanese elderly people are living alone, although the Confucian emphasis on filial piety remains influential and, as in China, this is not regarded as the ideal arrangement for old age (Hashimoto, 1996; Jenike, 2004). Japan's departure from the traditional household composition of the East Asian Confucian family system is often attributed to the period of post-war reconstruction and is more advanced in urban than rural areas, albeit significantly advanced in both. The demise of the multi-generational family as a household arrangement is often linked to the abolition of the primogeniture system with the Family Law of 1947 passed during the American Occupation, although commentators agree that filial piety as a revered ideal remained (Hashimoto, 2004). A move to nuclear family forms in conjunction with the ageing of the Japanese population inevitably produced an increase in older people living alone, although it remains much more common for Japanese people aged over 65 to live with older and younger generations than in north-western Europe. Nevertheless, as Table 2.2 illustrates, this experience has radically shrunk, while the proportion living in couple only households, with children who are not married or living alone has increased over time. The rows in the table show how the households of over 65 year olds are distributed in any one year. Reading down the table shows the change across years in a particular category. The proportion of one-person households doubled from 11 per cent in 1980 to 22 per cent in 2005.

As Table 2.3 shows, the proportions living alone also vary in relation to locality. The trend of living alone is more marked in highly urbanized prefectures, as administrative division are called in Japan, but there are also significant increases in less urbanized prefectures (Tokyo prefecture is the most populous, Tottori prefecture is the least populous and Iwati is the most sparsely populated prefecture on the main island of Honshu).

Japan may point the way for China. The increase in living alone over 50 years in Japan has been rapid in international terms from a

Table 2.2 Japan, 1980–2005: percentage distribution of private households by household type, men and women age 65 and over

	Couple only	A couple or alone with own child(ren) only	As parent(s) or in-laws or other relatives to a couple (with or without children)	One person	Total (100%)
1980	16	13	60	11	8,124,354
1990	21	15	49	15	10,729,464
2000	26	19	35	20	15,044,608
2005	28	21	28	22	17,204,473

Source: Statistical Survey Department, Statistics Bureau, Ministry of Internal Affairs and Communications (authors' own analysis)

Table 2.3 Japan and selected prefectures, 1950–2010: One-person households (all ages) as a percentage of all private households

	1950	1960	1970	1980	1990	2000	2010
Japan	5	5	11	20	24	28	31
Tokyo prefecture	9	10	21	33	36	41	45
Tottori prefecture	5	4	8	14	17	23	26
Iwati prefecture	4	3	7	17	20	24	28

very low starting point, and particular in the decades between 1960 and 1980. It remains to be seen whether approaching a third of the Chinese population living alone will take an equivalent time in China.

Europe and North America

Table 2.1 shows that in several European countries, even by 1950, one-person households were around a fifth (20 per cent) of all households (Sweden and Finland are at the top of the table but also Iceland and France). By 2010, in ten of the countries listed, people living alone make up a third or more households. If Scotland were shown, with 33 per cent it would be number 11 above Japan and several places above the United Kingdom. Note that in Sweden almost half of households involve people living alone and living alone has increased to around two-fifths (40 per cent) of households in Denmark, Finland, Germany and Norway.

Although Therborn's analysis of demographic patterns is the most ambitious and global schema, a number of scholars have produced classifications mustering European countries into different 'clusters' or regimes displaying similar characteristics. Several studies have drawn on Esping-Andersen's (1990) influential welfare-state typology;[5] however, others have argued that typologies based on religious affiliation or geography performs as well or better than one based on welfare regimes (see Iacovou, 2004). Therborn (2004, p. 220–223) distinguished three European variants and one American variant of the Christian-European family system from which we extract the implications for living alone:

- the north-western European pattern, the most favourable for living alone in earlier adulthood and across working-ages because of early youth independence, informal coupling and high rates of couple dissolution;
- the southern European pattern, which is less favourable since young people remain longer 'in the shadow of the parental household', are more likely to live with their parents until marriage and divorce is much less common;
- the eastern European pattern, in flux since the collapse of communism and which may diverge into several patterns, but which shared a previous history of young and near universal marriage, with limited youth independence and, in some countries, a history of co-residence with parents after marriage.

The United States forms a fourth 'Western' pattern that takes the legacy of the Christian-European family in a different direction characterized by a contradictory 'dualism of marriage and non-marriage': higher rates of young marriage, virginal marriage and young childbearing than in Europe, alongside high rates of youth independence, single parenthood and divorce. The joint effect of this dual pattern might place the American variant between southern and north-western Europe in terms of the proportions living alone. Therborn suggests that the other European settler societies of Canada, Australia and New Zealand are closer to the north-western European pattern than the American. All variants, with the possible exception of some eastern European countries, normally result in living alone in older age as adult children do not normally live with parents after marriage. However, it is not yet clear what the longer term effect of the recession affecting North America and many parts of Europe in the years following 2008 might be on patterns of residence.

With the exception of Italy, the ranking of European and the European settler countries on Table 2.1 is consistent with Therborn's classification. The north-western European countries, represented by the Nordic countries (Denmark, Finland, Iceland, Norway and Sweden), the Netherlands, Belgium, France, Germany, Austria, Switzerland and the United Kingdom, cluster together and are ranked within the top 15 on the table. With the exception of Italy, the southern European countries, Greece, Portugal, Spain and Cyprus are clustered together between ranks 30 and 36, but Italy is much higher up the league table at 18 and closer to the block of north-western European countries.[6] The unstable eastern European pattern is represented by Estonia, Hungary, Romania, Slovenia, the Czech Republic, Slovakia, Poland, the Russian Federation and Ukraine. Five of these nine countries are clustered with Greece, Portugal and Spain, between ranks 26 and 31, with Ukraine nearby at 23 but Estonia (9) and Slovakia (14), are within the ranks of the north-western European countries and Hungary (17) and the Czech Republic (19) are with Italy close to the north-western European bloc. The United States of America and the other European settler societies of Australia, Canada and New Zealand form one cluster between the north-western European bloc and the southern European cluster of Greece, Spain, Portugal and Cyprus.

The differences between regions of Europe involve different rates of living alone among both the working-age population and older people. Table 2.4 shows European countries combined by Therborn's categories and disaggregates living alone by men and women and by age groups using the European Social Surveys (ESS) conducted between 2008 and 2010, and comparative figures from US census data. It shows the proportion of women or men living alone in random samples of their age

Table 2.4 Regions of Europe: Percentages living alone 2008–2010, men and women by age groups

	Aged 18–29			Aged 30–59[a]			Aged 60+[b]		
	Men	Women	N = 100%	Men	Women	N = 100%	Men	Women	N = 100%
All ESS[c]	12	11	24,148	17	14.0	53,730	25	50	29,253
The United States	7	7	51,014k	12	9	103,966k	16	36	39,151k
North-western Europe	19	14	7864	22	17	19,757	27	50	10,719
Southern Europe	9	7	3575	12	8	7825	16	32	4644
Eastern Europe	7	5	8031	12	11	18,089	23	45	10,123

[a] For the United States, aged 30–54.
[b] For the United States, 65+.
[c] European Social Survey countries: Belgium, Bulgaria, Croatia, Cyprus, the Czech Republic, Denmark, Estonia, Finland, France, Germany, Greece, Hungary, Ireland, Israel, Latvia, the Netherlands, Norway, Poland, Portugal, Romania, Russian Federation, Slovakia, Slovenia, Spain, Sweden, Switzerland, Turkey, the United Kingdom and Ukraine.
Source: European Social Survey combined waves (2008–2010) and U.S. Census Bureau, Current Population Survey, 2011: Table A2 (authors' own analysis)

and sex. The working-age group is broken down into 18–29 and 30–59 to roughly map onto the biographical stages prior to and after a typical age at the birth of a first child in Europe at the survey date of 2008–2010.

Rates of living alone in north-western Europe are higher than other European regions for both men and women in each of the age groups. In eastern Europe, rates of living alone at older ages are almost as high as in north-western Europe but living alone in early and middle adulthood remains low and closer to the southern European rates. It has already been noted that high rates of living alone in older age in north-western Europe reflect the long-established preference for nuclear households over sustaining multi-generational households. However, there are traditions of co-residence in parts of eastern as well as southern Europe. Higher rates of living alone in older age in eastern Europe partly reflect high out-migration among young adults, a factor that has also been linked to higher rates of loneliness and deficits of care in older age (Vullnetari and King, 2008; Yang and Victor, 2011).

Men are more likely to be living alone than women below retirement age and women are more likely to be living alone than men above retirement age, and this is true across all the regions of Europe and in the United States. Across north-western countries, between a fifth and a quarter of men (22 per cent) aged 30–59 live alone and about one in six (17 per cent) women. The situation reverses in retirement. Indeed, around half of women aged 60 and over live alone in ESS countries overall. Living alone is the most common living arrangement for women aged 65 and over in most EU countries (Iacovou and Skew, 2010, p. 93), and for women aged 75 and over in the United States, almost half (47 per cent) of whom live alone (Administration on Ageing, 2011). Gender differences in older age reflect differences in longevity, while the differences across working age reflect differences in men's and women's biographical routes through adulthood.

The distribution of living alone between men and women, and between working age and older age is further explored by scrutiny of Sweden, the country that leads living alone by some distance (see Table 2.5). Unlike Table 2.4, Table 2.5 focuses on households and shows the contribution made by men and women living alone at different ages to one-person household as a percentage of all Swedish households. Men below age 50 make the largest contribution to one person households followed by women over 65 but the balance of working age and older age and of men and women has modified over time. The proportion of women living alone under age 50 is almost the same as the

Table 2.5 Sweden, 1991, 2001 and 2010: One-person households as percentage of all households, women and men, by age group

	One-person households								Both	All households
	Women				Men					
	18–50 years	50–64 years	65+ years	All ages	18–50 years	50–64 years	65+ years	All ages	All ages	All ages
1991	7.5	4	12	23	14	3	4	21	44	4141
2001	8	5	11	24	14	4	4	22	46	4393
2010	9	5	10	24	13.5	5.5	5	24	48.5	4660

Source: Statistics Sweden household finances sample survey: http://www.scb.se/Pages/TableAndChart___146284.aspx (accessed 11 December 2012)

proportion at ages 65 and over. Sweden, over the last 20 years, may show the direction of change in the north-western Europe.

Gendered biographies of living alone

Although some commentators in Europe and North America read the increase in living alone as a demise of conventional forms of family formation, differences in working-age men's and women's patterns of living alone reflect conventional gender differences in partnering, parenting and routes through adulthood (for example, see Billari and Liefbroer, 2010; Elzinga and Liefbroer, 2007 for an overview). Conventional gender differences in partnering and parenting persist alongside legal acceptance of gender equality, significant changes in women's levels of participation in employment and the demise in taken-for-granted acceptance of a breadwinning husband and childrearing wife model of family life (Casper and Bianchi, 2002; Crompton, 2006; Gerson, 2010; Pfau-Effinger, 2000).

Fundamentally, women are still the main carers for children, an important contributing factor to more men living alone than women in countries leading the trend, since when co-resident couples with children part, women typically become single-parent households and men often exit to living alone. Also, the median age of first co-resident partnership, first marriage and becoming a parent remains younger for women than men (Mensch et al., 2005). This is because men typically partner and have children with women who are younger than themselves and women with men who are older than themselves. This age difference also potentially contributes to more young men living alone than women since women exit earlier into co-resident partnership. But at the same time, there is also a pattern of women leaving home at younger ages than men across Europe and in North America (Mitchell, 2006), albeit sometimes in order to live with a partner. It is argued that sons have less need to leave to be independent because parents supervise and interfere with their independence less and expect less of them by way of contributions to household work (Goldscheider and Goldscheider, 1999, p. 139). Sweden has the youngest median age of leaving home and of first living with a partner in Europe, age 18.5 and 20.4 for women and age 20.2 and 23.1 for men (in the cohort born between 1953 and 1962), giving women 1.9 years of non-family living and men 2.9 years (Liefbroer and Golscheider, 2007). If women delayed partnership and parenting as long as men, as well as leaving home earlier than men, this would lead to women having a longer period potentially living alone than men. The slight narrowing of the gap between the contribution of men and women under the age of 50 to the make-up of one-person households in Sweden might indicate a modest change in this direction.

Conventional life course transitions

Statistics that are generated by the legally registered events of marriage and birth, such as those reported in Table 2.6, are the most widely available indicators of change at the level of population and individual biographies. They represent milestones that may be passed – first marriage, first child and completed family – when a conventional life course is being followed. While they are inadequate for mapping a social change that is not registered on this template, patterns of absence or delay in once conventional transitions provide some insight into the biographical space for living alone.

Countries are presented in Table 2.6 in the same order as in Table 2.1; Sweden has the highest ages of first marriage, just as it has the highest rate of living alone. The table shows the general trend of increase in age of marriage, age of mother at first birth and decline in fertility referred to as 'the second demographic transition'. What is not visible is how the typical relationship between age of marriage and leaving the parental home varies across countries (Billari and Liefbroer, 2010; Bynner and Pan, 2002; Holdsworth and Morgan, 2005; Iacovou, 2010; Kiernan, 1986; Reher, 1998; Yi et al., 1994). Where the gap between these two ages is large this is reflected in a high proportion of young people living alone, as in north-western Europe, and, conversely, where it is small, rates of living alone among young people are also small, as in southern and eastern Europe (Iacovou and Skew, 2010).[7] Leaving the parental home is neither routinely the subject of an official record nor necessarily a once-and-for-all transition (Heath and Cleaver, 2003; Holdsworth and Morgan, 2005). In north-western Europe, young people's first exit from the parental home is typically some years prior to marriage and the age of marriage does not normally reflect the age of first living with this partner, since the overwhelming majority of marriages involve cohabiting prior to marriage. In southern Europe the same increase in the age of marriage has more often meant a longer period living in the parental home. The north-western European pattern of earlier exit from the parental home significantly enhances the possibilities of living alone both prior to and on exit from cohabiting with a partner. Childless cohabiting unions that end in separation may result in both men and women living alone rather than a return to the parental home.

Table 2.6 Mean age of women at first marriage and first birth, total fertility rate and definitive childlessness for women, by selected countries and years

Country	Mean age of women at first marriage			Mean age of women at first birth			Total fertility rate			Definitive childlessness (%) women born in	
	1980[a]	1990	2008[b]	1980	1990[c]	2009[d]	1980	1990	2010	1940	1965
Sweden	26	28	33	25	26	28	1.7	2.1	2	13	13
Finland	–	27	30	26	27	28	1.6	1.8	1.9		20
Norway	25	28	31		26	28	1.7	1.9	2.0	10	12
Denmark	25	28	32	25	26	28	1.6	1.7	1.9		13
Germany	23	26	30	25	27	30		1.4	1.4	11	
Switzerland	25	27	29	26	28	30	1.6	1.6	1.5	16	
The Netherlands	23	26	29		28	29	1.6	1.6	1.8	11	18
Austria	22	24	29		25	28	1.6	1.5	1.4	12	21
Estonia		23	28		23	26		2.1	1.6		
Belgium	22	25	28	25	26	28	1.7	1.6	1.9	13	
Japan	25	26				29	1.8	1.5	1.4		
France	23	26	30			29	2	1.8	2	8	
Slovakia		23	27		21	27		2.1	1.4		
The United Kingdom	23	25	30			30	1.9	1.8	2	11	19
Hungary	22	22	28	23	23	28	1.9	1.9	1.3	9	10
Italy	24	26	30		27	30	1.6	1.3	1.4	15	15
The Czech Republic		21	28		22	28		1.9	1.5		
The United States	22	24	26	23	24	25	1.8	2.1	1.9	7	14
Canada	–	26	28	27	26	28	1.7	1.8	1.6[e]		
Australia						28	1.9	1.9	1.9	9	

New Zealand	24				28	2	2.2	2.2	9	
Ireland	27	30	25	26	28		2.1	2.1	20	16
Slovenia	24	29		24	29		1.5	1.6		
Poland	22	26	23	24	26		2.1	1.4		11
Greece					29	2.2	1.4	1.5	11	16
Romania	22	26		22	26		1.8	1.3		
Israel	23	29			27	3.1	2.8	3.0		
Portugal	24	28	24	25	28	2.2	1.6	1.3		4
Spain	26	30	25	27	30	2.2	1.9	1.4		13
China	22	23		26	26	2.6	2.3	1.6		
Mexico						5	3.4	2.1	5	
India					21	4.5	3.6	3.1[f]		6

[a] Data refer to 1982 for China;

[b] Data refer to 2000 for China; 2007 for Italy and Belgium; 2006 for the United Kingdom and Ireland; 2003 for Canada; 2002 for Spain;

[c] Data refer to 1995–2000 for China.

[d] Data refer to 2000–2010 for China; 2007 for Canada and Italy; 2006 for Mexico, the United States, Belgium, France and the United Kingdom; 2005 for Australia, Denmark, Japan and Korea;

[e] Data refer to 2009 for Canada;

[f] Data refer to 1981, 1991 and 2001 for India.

Sources: UNECE Statistical Division Database, compiled from national and international official sources (Eurostat, UN Statistics Division Demographic Yearbook, WHO European health for all database and UNICEF TransMONEE): http://w3.unece.org/pxweb/Dialog/varval.asp?ma=08_GEFHPrivHouse_r&ti=Private+households+by+Household+Type%2C+Country+and+Year&path=../DATABASE/Stat/30-GE/02 Families_households/&lang=1 (accessed 24/05/2012); UN World Population Prospects http://esa.un.org/wpp/Excel-Data/fertility.htm (accessed 03/02/2013); UN Data, World Marriage Data: http://data.un.org/DocumentData.aspx?id=212 (accessed 03 February 2013); OECD Family Database, compiling information from different OECD databases and databases maintained by other (international) organizations: http://www.oecd.org/els/soc/oecdfamilydatabase.htm (accessed 24 May 2012); Census of India http://www.censusindia.gov.in/2011census/hlo/hlo_highlights.html (accessed 27/07/2012); World Bank Indicators, http://data.un.org/Data.aspx?q=China+Fertility+Rates&d=WDI&f=Indicator_Code%3aSP.DYN.TFRT.IN%3bCountry_Code%3aCHN (accessed 03 February 2013). For statistical purposes, the data for China do not include those for the Hong Kong Special Administrative Region (Hong Kong SAR) and Taiwan province of China.

In the context of the United Kingdom, it is conventional to distinguish between 'leaving home' and 'living away', which encompasses an understanding of eventual return (Leonard, 1980). Neither automatically leads to living alone but both practices are implicated in the current trend.[8] Using census data, Michael Rosenfeld (2007) dates the beginning of what has been described as a new stage of youth independence in the United States (Goldscheider and Goldscheider, 1999) to 1960 and the growing proportion of cohorts of young adults in college, living apart from their parents outside of marriage. The young people themselves are likely to have thought of themselves as 'living away' from rather than having left the parental home, but Rosenfeld documents how attempts at exercising control *in loco parentis* over students diminished over time and 'independence' grew, including opportunities for experimentation and renegotiation of sexual and gender relationships (Rosenfeld, 2007). The year 1960 marked the beginning of world-wide acceleration in enrolments in higher education (Schofer and Meyer, 2005), and while it is likely that the United States was the world leader in a significant proportion of an age cohort adopting this particular 'living away from home' practice while going to college, the United States may not have led another significant practice of independence. In the 1970s, young women and, after 1975, men and women in Sweden left their parental home earlier than their US counterparts. Zeng Yi (1994) and his co-authors attribute this to 'the greatly increased popularity of cohabitation before marriage in Sweden' (Yi et al., 1994, p. 76). Subsequent literature on cohabitation continues to debate the extent of similarity or difference between cohabitation and marriage and whether in the pioneering stages of cohabitation it was more experimental and less 'trial marriage' (Manting, 1996; Prinz, 1995). This interpretation is consistent with seeing leaving home to live with a partner as a period of innovation involving renegotiation around sexual and gender relationships among the Swedish-led pioneers of the 1970s. In contrast, cohabitation in this region in the twenty-first century is often seen as a period of transition into 'settling down'. Research talking to young people about their cohabiting often finds element of both of these different understandings of its meaning being deployed (Duncan and Barlow, 2005; Jamieson et al., 2002; Sassler and Miller, 2011).

The countries in Table 2.6 with the highest rates of living alone do not have the lowest fertility rates. Only Finland of this group has higher rates of childlessness than other parts of Europe. In Sweden, Finland, Norway and Denmark, fertility is low but remains above the level of 1.5 per woman, which demographers use to distinguish 'very low' fertility.[9] Of the countries shown in Table 2.4, Germany, Austria, Japan, Slovakia, Italy, Poland and Spain all have very low fertility, and Hungary, Portugal and Romania have a level that has been labelled 'lowest low'. Rapid rates of fertility decline in countries with pronounced family-oriented cultural traditions, such as Spain, Portugal and Greece, have been described as 'the great paradox of our times' (Esping-Andersen, 1999, p. 67). Peter McDonald (2000a, 2000b) suggests this contradicts theories contending that low fertility is driven by freedom from tradition, enabling ascendancy of valuing self-realization and the satisfaction of personal preferences. Rather, McDonald emphasizes the importance of mismatches between women's expectations of gender equality and how they perceive social institutions, as facilitators or barriers to realizing their expectations if they have children. He argues that if women have educational and employment opportunities near equivalent to those of men, and they can see that gender equity is severely curtailed by having children, then, on average, women will restrict the number of children (2000a, p. 10, see also Chesnais, 1996; Esping-Andersen, 1999). Sweden, he would argue, offers women better possibilities for combining employment and parenting with a sense of gender equity than countries in southern Europe (see also Crompton, 2006). Aart Liefbroer and Frances Goldscheider (2007) note that Swedish men are strongly encouraged to contribute equally to home-making and child care and that welfare-state arrangements of state-subsidized child care and parental leave remain generous.

Heterogeneity by social class

In addition to differences in the incidence and pattern of living alone by men and women at different ages, detailed studies typically show diversity in the socio-economic characteristics of men and women who live alone. For example, Kaufmann's 1994 review of European data noted solo-living was most common among men at either end of the social class scale, a polarization evident in several subsequent studies using British data (Chandler et al., 2004; Glanville et al., 2005; Wasoff and Jamieson, 2005). This body of work also shows that professional women are disproportionately represented among women living alone.

De Vaus and Richardson's (2009) finely grained analysis of Australian census data identifies women living alone, especially those younger than 50, as 'educational winners', more highly educated than other women and men who live alone. This is reinforced by the picture of occupational status. In all age groups, employed women who live alone are more likely to be in professional occupations than other employed women, all men, and men living alone. Among men, especially middle-aged men, living alone is associated with educational underachievement. Nevertheless, both men and women living alone at working age tend to be clustered in either the lowest or the highest income groups (2009, p. 25). Wasoff and Jamieson (2005) note that a larger minority proportion of men and women living on their own in the United Kingdom have disadvantaged circumstances: for example, comparison of housing circumstances of those living alone with those living with others shows that access to home ownership is lower and use of social housing higher among working-age solo-livers (see also Hall et al., 1997).

Our analysis of Scottish Household Survey (SHS) data confirms these patterns of relative advantage and disadvantage amongst working-age men and women living alone, and in comparison with those living with others, in Scotland. For example, solo-living men are the most likely to be unemployed than all other adults of the same age. Solo-living women are much more likely to have tertiary qualifications than their male counterparts, as well as more likely than men and women living with others. Both solo-living men and women are more likely than those living with others to be permanently sick or disabled, and more likely to be in receipt of various state benefits, though the difference is more marked among men than women (see Tables A2.4, A2.5a and A2.5b in Appendix 2).

This polarization by socio-economic status doesn't match one common stereotype of people who live alone as occupants of smart expensive city centre apartments. Living alone is also not exclusively an urban phenomenon. In Britain, the Scottish Household Surveys show that around one in seven working-age people living alone are in rural areas. At the same time, British rural housing studies confirm that there are more opportunities for men to live alone than women, by demonstrating that childless unpartnered women are the most disadvantaged in rural housing markets (Jones, 2001).

Recession and transitions

Young people in many parts of Europe find themselves cut off from employment opportunities and economic security by the severe economic recession in the years following 2007. This in turn exacerbates fears of 'prolonged adolescence' and a 'generation on hold' (Côté, 2000; Côté and Allahar, 1996; Mayer, 1994; Schnaiberg and Goldenberg, 1989), young men and women choosing or simply unable to find the means to progress onto central responsibilities of adulthood. In some parts of northern Europe and North America, moving out of the parental home and living independently had become normative. In many other parts of the world, leaving the parental households to live independently happens without being the norm. In Japan, some young men were leaving home for higher education almost as early as in the United States, but living alone as a young adult continues to be treated as an aberration. However, in Europe and North America, living alone is increasingly accepted by young people themselves as a marker of adulthood. Some authors see establishing an independent household as one of a number of such markers of adult status, for example, educational attainment, employment, romantic partnerships and parenthood (Settersten, 2007), but living alone may be increasingly standing in lieu of other markers, experienced as sufficient to signify adulthood without the support of other transitions. Studies of young people living independently document their pleasure in managing adulthood (Arnett, 2001; Heath and Cleaver, 2003; Holdsworth and Morgan, 2005; Molgat and Vézina, 2008). Recession shrinks the possibilities for living alone, making this significantly more difficult for young people and it is not yet clear whether the trend will falter. At the same time, recession also makes other more conventional transitions to adulthood highly problematic.

The conditions of recession mean that governments may lack the political will or means to modify local conditions in ways that make a difference to young adults with 'futures on hold'. Much of the demographic literature emphasizes the influence of government policies in the spheres of post-secondary education, employment or housing on transitions. Educational provision varies considerably across national contexts, for example, being largely self-funded in the United States and fully state funded in Finland. Prolonged education delays the transition to economic independence, partnering and parenting (Alders and Manting, 2003; Kohler et al., 2002; Stone et al., 2011). In some national contexts, even tertiary education has not guaranteed the promised subsequent secure economic future (Jeffrey, 2010, 2011). In parts of Europe suffering severe recession, where education was a relatively safe route to stable employment, such certainties are undermined as the proportion of young unemployed people rises. There are fears of a retreat in the gains women have made, now forming more than half of the graduate/postgraduate students in a majority of European countries (Sobotka, 2004).

Housing policies are also known to influence the timing of leaving home, establishing partnerships and parenting; these often become less supportive of young adults during recession. In Sweden and Finland, independent living for young people is supported by housing provision and financial support through the welfare state (Liefbroer and Goldscheider, 2007; Schulenberg and Schoon, 2012). In Italy, on the other hand, the housing situation stands in the way of leaving home among the young: housing is rather expensive and rented accommodation is in limited supply (Alders and Manting, 2003). Comparative analysis of the age by which 50 per cent of young people were living away from the parental home in 2007 show an average age of 21 for men and 20 for women in Finland, compared with 30 for men and 28 for women in Italy (Iacovou and Skew, 2010, p. 90). Low wages, unemployment and tighter housing markets can delay leaving the parental home and forming relationships, while the higher the income of young adults, the more likely they are to leave the parental home and not to return to it (Ermisch, 1999). Sue Heath (2008), using data for England and Wales, highlighted the persistence of a strong social class divide determining young people's housing transitions, with the young middle classes enjoying 'privileged pathways' into independent living, while those from working class backgrounds experience more challenging transitions. She also noted a dramatic shift away from home ownership and towards the private rented sector. The European and North American economic downturn from 2007 has had a disproportionate impact on young people who may increasingly remain in (or return to) the parental home for economic reasons. Thus, a recent study in the United Kingdom predicts a considerable increase in the number of young people living with parents between 2008 and 2020 (Clapham et al., 2012),[10] while others suggest that patterns of shared living currently confined to the age group in their twenties will extend further into adult life (Stone, 2011). An increase in the private rental sector alongside falling home ownership in the United Kingdom has given rise to the neologism 'generation rent'. At the same time, the financial security of individuals in older age is increasingly premised on accumulating capital in the form of housing equity that can be used to pay for care in older age (Heywood, 2011).

Concluding remarks

This chapter has drawn on official statistics, census and survey data to provide a picture of the geographies of solo-living by regional grouping, attending also to age and gender. In general, national differences in trends of living alone cluster in ways that are consistent with Therborn's account of family–sex–gender systems, the legacy of the main geo-cultural systems of the globe. Leading the trend are countries carrying the legacy of the Christian-European family into a north-western family–sex–gender system. Its long-standing tradition of nuclear family households created the path to the normalcy of older people living alone in widowhood. Its particular trajectory of turning away from the patriarchal rule of father and male kin, relaxed approach to marrying and divorcing, and encouragement of youth independence paved the way for living alone in earlier adulthood as well as across all ages. India was discussed as an opposite example where patriarchal institutions remain relatively intact despite economic development, long-standing intergenerational tensions and a formal discourse of gender equality. Youth independence is absent or gained by means other than living alone. Older people in India generally rely on co-residence with and assistance from kin, and here living alone is not seen as the solution to deficits in delivery of kin care. Japan was also discussed as an exceptional case, with high rates of living alone separating it from the other countries within the East Asian Confucian family system. Here there are signs of young people adopting a stage of youth independence and older people increasingly accepting living alone as an alternative to deficits in respectful filial care. It is suggested that Japan will point the way for the other countries in this region in much the same way that Sweden has led the way for north-western Europe.

A more detailed analysis of the trend of living alone across Europe, broken down by age and gender, shows the divergent patterns within Europe. Statistics that chart family formation help to further document some of the complex interplay of demographic trends associated with living alone. Delay in partnering, increases in childlessness and decline in family size generally play out very differently for young men and women in southern Europe and in north-western Europe. In all regions of Europe, more working-age men live alone than women. Despite the fact that the pursuit of gender equality is often seen as associated with the trend of living alone, aspects of the pattern repeat conventional gender differences in family formation. Women typically partner at a younger age and tend to be left with the children when a child-rearing couple separates. Small family sizes, lack of partners and childlessness all increase the likelihood of living alone in older age, even within societies where the tradition is not one of nuclear family households.

As well as documenting differences between countries, the chapter notes variation within countries by age and gender as well as by socio-economic status. When the socio-economic circumstances of people living alone have been examined in Europe and Australia, both the multiply disadvantaged and the relatively affluent are over-represented, reinforcing the absurdity of thinking about those who live alone as a homogeneous population. The chapter ended with discussion of youth independence in the context of recession. There are some indications that the trend to living alone in early adulthood could be stalled by national and global recession as youth unemployment rises and the accessibility of affordable housing falls. However, if family–sex–gender systems have already been modified to make living alone seem normal and desirable then this is likely to be a temporary falling back, not a permanent retreat.

3
Solo-living with and without Partnering and Parenting

Introduction

People who live alone across the ages normally associated with child rearing are not necessarily turning away from couple relationships or parenting. Some have partners, some have children and those who are childless may not be making a lifestyle choice. This chapter explores the orientation of people living alone in early to mid-adulthood to partnership, parenting and the presumed intimacy that they bring. It is structured by comparison between men and women, across three different biographical situations: people living alone who have no partner or children; people living alone while in a couple relationship with someone who lives elsewhere; and parents living alone while their child or children's main residence is elsewhere. These biographical circumstances can overlap, since some parents are also in couple relationships and, exceptionally, those who are single and childless sometimes take up a parenting role to a child or children of friends or family.

The main subjects of this chapter are respondents in our study of those aged 25–44 years old, living in 'one-person households' in Scotland, the United Kingdom (see Appendix 1 for a more detailed description), but with reference to the wider research literature including the discussion of discourse about love in Part I. Unlike some women in Eric Klinenberg's North American study, respondents in our UK study had no affiliation with social movements that celebrate being single and childless. Also, unlike in South Korea (Song, 2010), solo and single women did not see themselves as pioneers. The chapter begins by exploring whether those who are without partners are avoiding or seeking an intimate partnership relationship. This is followed by exploring whether those living alone in couple relationships that are not co-resident are keeping intimacy at a distance.

Solo-living childless 'Singles'

Disavowing choosing to be single

Among our sample, more than half of the men and half of the women living in urban areas and slightly less than half living in rural areas described themselves as 'single' in the sense of being outside of any form of couple. The majority of these 'singles' had come to live alone in early adulthood without ever cohabiting, although some had been previously married or lived in cohabiting relationships without marriage. Many of them, both women and men, spontaneously made it clear that they regard choosing to live alone as a residential arrangement that was not a statement of resistance or intention concerning partnering arrangements. As the evidence unfolds, we ask whether, nevertheless, those who embarked on living alone in early adulthood as a temporary phase were taking a course that might complicate and weigh against their desire to 'settle down', live with a partner and have children in the future. Consciously setting out to be pioneering is not the only way of effecting social change.

> I chose to live alone in the respect that I don't really want to share with anybody, but I don't choose to be single'.
>
> (Jessica, 31, urban, never lived with a partner)

> It's not in a way a sort of chosen lifestyle, it's just that I haven't met anyone who I get on with and is single, well enough to get into a relationship that we would live together.
>
> (Neil, 40, urban, never lived with a partner)

Culturally accessible 'common sense' views about the process of finding a partner – the appropriate steps, the time needed to develop a relationship and the 'right time' in a biography – were part of their explanations of living alone.

For those living alone after the dissolution of cohabiting or marriage relationships, unplanned breakdown in the normative coupled trajectory was presented as their reason for living alone.

> I basically moved in with my girlfriend at that time. We'd bought a house, and then the relationship broke down, so I kind of moved out of the house, which she'd wanted to keep. And then I just bought this flat.
>
> (Sebastian, 35, urban)

Interviewees seemed to anticipate and wish to stamp out possible confusion of living alone with choosing a life without a partner. Unpartnered women had more experiences than unpartnered men of their family or friends expressing anxiety about their lack of a partner and stressing the desirability of couple relationships. For example, Eleanor (29, urban) felt she had to assuage her mother's anxiety by making a reassuring phone call everyday after work, while Annabel (30, urban) tried to laugh off her partnered friends' matchmaking campaigns, assumptions that any man she admitted to dating should move in with her, and comments like 'Oh, you don't know what you are missing'. However, not all single women's friends subjected them to such views of how their lives were less than ideal. For example, Lauren (37, urban) noted of living alone among her circle of women friends:

> It's as normal as being married and having children, you know. You get to like sort of late 30s and it's not uncommon for people to be living on their own either because it's the first time they've done it, due to separation of or a marriage breakdown, or because that's just what they've always done since they've left home.

But, beyond her circle of friends, she encountered gendered stereotypes paralleling research findings concerning single women (Reynolds and Wetherell, 2003, 2007; Sharp and Ganong, 2007, 2011; Simpson, 2009).

> If you are a woman who lives on her own and are happy to live on your own then there's something wrong with you. And that's an assumption made by both sexes. But if it's a man [living alone], then that's fine.
>
> (Lauren, 37, urban)

Men more often than women encountered envy of their situation expressed in comments like 'It's all right for you, you can do what you want' (Anthony, 40, urban), although women occasionally received wistful comments about their freedom from childcare responsibilities from friends with small children.

Living alone and 'Normal' life stages

Many interviewees who began living alone as young adults described this in terms of establishing themselves as independent adults. Their accounts fit with the academic literature suggesting that economic and residential independence have replaced marriage and cohabitation as key markers of adult status for many young people in north-western Europe and North America (Andrews et al., 2007; Arnett, 1997; Aronson, 2008; Benson and Furstenberg, 2007; Henderson et al., 2007; Holdsworth and Morgan, 2005; Orrange, 2003; Thomson and Holland, 2002). Interviewees who moved to living alone from their parental home or shared accommodation with peers had often made decisions about living arrangements quite separately from consideration of an imagined or anticipated future as a partner or parent. Among our interviewees, both women and men took it for granted that you reached an age and stage at which self-development and self-respect require res-idential independence from parents whether or not you have a partner. Some also talked of outgrowing shared housing and reaching an age at which they needed a 'place of their own'. As the previous chapter out-lined, this is a very different approach to leaving home to the majority of young people in other parts of the world, including southern Europe. In Greece, Italy, Portugal and Spain, many young people continue to combine leaving home, marrying and establishing a couple-household with a partner (Aassve et al., 2006). Ron Lesthaeghe (2010) suggests that there are recent signs of the take up of cohabitation in southern Europe, which may be the beginning of these transitions moving apart, as southern Europe completes the 'second demographic transition'. He also suggests that young people are moving in this direction in East Asia led by Japan. UK interviewees demonstrate the strength of expectations about establishing an independent household in young adulthood by expressing embarrassment about delay in leaving their parental home, acknowledging a risk of loss of face and vulnerability to accusations of stunted development once they were 'too old' to be living with their parents.

Within the United Kingdom, young adults' strategies for achieving residential independence from parents vary with class background, eco-nomic circumstances and local housing markets. The cheapest form of living arrangement independent of parents involves shared housing. Among our interviewees, many, particularly young men, had already passed through some form of shared housing before deciding they wanted their own home. Some interviewees had secured tenancies in social housing after long periods on waiting lists, some were privately renting and some, typically those with better paid jobs, were purchas-ing their own home, both men and women, seeing this as an investment and logical progression in becoming independent. Interviewees had generally gained mortgages prior to the near collapse of parts of the United Kingdom banking sector in 2007 and 2008, following which opportunities for borrowing money including a mortgage for a home purchase required higher levels of earnings and savings. While those who started living alone as never-married young adults did not see this as a deviation from a trajectory towards finding a partner, those who had exited from childless marriage or cohabiting relationships had a sense of starting again. The majority of childless interviewees in their twenties and early thirties wanted to have children. Despite advances in reproductive technologies, almost all of them took it for granted that a co-resident partner was a necessary precondition to becoming a parent: 'if the choice came to have a family of my own then I would like to be with the person' (Ailsa, 28, urban). In contrast to a relaxed attitude of 'everything is still possible' among the young never-partnered, some interviewees indicated fears about 'missing the boat' or being 'too late'. Not surprisingly, this was more common among many of the women in their late thirties and early forties; however, it was also evident among some of the men in this age group. For some, awareness of biological limits created a sense of a greater urgency about parenting. Some interviewees raised worries about the disadvantages of being an older parent.

While the dominant desire among the single and childless was to live with a partner and hoped for children at some point in their future, a minority proportion were much more ambivalent or had turned away from this. They included interviewees who had decided they would prefer not to have a co-resident partner, and some who were lukewarm about any kind of partner, although nobody expressed an emphatic aversion to such relationships. The perceptions and experiences of those in living-apart couple relationships are taken up in a subsequent section, suggesting that, for women at least, the desire for a co-resident partner may wane when having children are no longer part of the future picture.

About a third of childless respondents anticipated remaining so. Expectations of parenting were much lower among those oriented to same sex relationships; most of the men and the one woman we interviewed in this category did not expect to become parents. Consistent with the findings of attitude surveys, views concerning future children varied by age (Hird and Abshoff, 2000; McAllister and Clarke, 1998). Women respondents who were in their late thirties and early forties, approaching the end of women's reproductive capacity, unlike most younger interviewees anticipating becoming parents, were likely to view parenting as a transition that would be omitted from their life course. This age effect is more marked among women than men. More than half of childless women in this age sector had decided they were not going to have children, many saying it was already too late. Some had close relationships with children, through entertaining nieces and nephews or other child family members, acting as 'aunties' or god parents to friends' children or continuing contact with children of a previous partner. Only a very few indicated both that they had never wanted children and that they did not enjoy children. While the majority of men in this age sector still anticipated having children, some thought they were too old and that their best option was to acquire a 'ready-made family' by partnering a woman who already has children, some seemed less aware of age issues or explicitly referred to the possibility of partnering a younger woman and a few were unsure if they would ever want children. Setting aside the men who were fathers, who are discussed at greater length in a subsequent section, among our sample, men were less likely to have intimate relationships with children than women, but, nevertheless, some men were playing the role of favourite 'uncles' to children of family or friends.

Economic insecurity and/or ill health had put the idea of a partnership and parenting relationship very consciously on hold for a small number of mainly male interviewees and, sometimes, off the agenda. A minority proportion of working-age adults living alone in the United Kingdom do so in poverty and ill health (Table A2.5a in Appendix 2 shows a higher percentage of 'permanently sick or disabled' among those living alone than those living with others in the Scottish working-age population, 16 per cent of men and 14 per cent of women compared with four per cent and three per cent, respectively). The idea that a man is the main provider for a family still has currency, making an inability to earn seem irreconcilable with family life. For example, plans to marry were on hold for Nazeen (40, urban), a British Pakistani, despite the cultural emphasis within his family and the British Pakistani community on marriage as key to living 'a good life', and the unacceptability of cohabiting without marriage. He was underemployed, struggling to pay a mortgage on his two bedroom property on a very low income and had abandoned supplementing this by taking in friends as lodgers due to 'too much fight with friends!' Nevertheless, he continued to hope for marriage in his future imaginings despite being very uncertain that he could ever manage this financially. In contrast, partnership and parenthood were not part of the imagined future of Alistair, who was diagnosed schizophrenic and living on state benefits awarded on the basis of certified disability. He volunteered that he was not looking for a partner because his illness 'prevents me from forming meaningful relationships a lot of the time' and that his mental health also ruled out parenting: 'I don't think I'd be able to cope with the demands of raising children'(Alistair, 39, urban).

'Natural progression' versus seeking

The majority of 'singles' had a personal ambition, to 'meet somebody to want to settle down with' (Jessica, 31, urban), consistent with the valorization of romance in popular culture but, paradoxically, most were not proactively seeking a partner because their personal philosophies of love worked against this. Age, economic security, health, gender and cultural expectations were among the factors modifying the mixture of pragmatic and philosophical considerations at play in not actively looking. Younger interviewees communicated a lack of urgency, gesturing to the importance of 'establishing themselves' first, typically by having a footing in a job and/or career, sometimes through realizing other plans for self-development, and in the case of a migrant worker, resolving insecure residence in the United Kingdom. Rather more men than women had everyday practices that closed off opportunities for finding a partner. Men were also more likely to sustain relationships they categorized as unsuitable despite professing the wish for a suitable long-term partner (Jamieson et al., 2010). Across this variety of circumstances, men's and women's personal philosophies of love downplayed actively seeking a partner resonating with widely circulating cultural discourse.

Sometimes a mythic story of love (Swidler, 2003) was deployed as part of a fatalistic explanation of how no action could be taken to find 'the one' but one day it might happen. In our sample, more men took this approach. Anthony put it succinctly, 'What's for me won't go by me' (Anthony, 34, urban), and Andrew noted 'if it's going to happen it's going to happen and I can't force the issue' (Andrew, 43, urban). Women more often cited folk wisdom consistent with prosaic realism, for example, the idea that you have to 'get yourself sorted first' before embarking on a relationship. Both men and women, and particularly those who had been in previous relationships that ended badly, stressed the inadvisability of accepting an unsatisfactory relationship for the sake of having a partner. Consistent with previous research, being desperate to find a partner was seen as counterproductive and involving loss of face (Jamieson et al., 2003); hence advice against zealous 'going looking' for a partner was common. Ideals of gender equality, women's independence and the demise of the breadwinner/housewife model mean it is potentially degrading for a heterosexual women to be 'desperately seeking' a man for economic support. A heterosexual man 'desperately seeking' a woman can have his masculinity called into question if he 'needed to advertise' to find a woman since masculinity implies heterosexual 'pulling power'.

Both men and women claimed that building possibilities of meeting people into normal life is the best way to find possible partners, that relationships take time to develop, that it is important not to 'rush into things' and that 'natural progression' is a series of steps that can also be thought of as tests and trial periods. For Fiona, living with somebody was a 'next step' that tested the relationship.

> Well it's just a natural progression and if you meet somebody you are prepared to compromise, not compromise but share a life with...thats an important next step. You have to move in together to test the relationship.
>
> (Fiona, 31, urban)

In Fiona's account of 'natural progression' living together checks out mutual suitability for a life-time together. Sebastian's account of 'natural progression' emphasizes the pleasure of the moment rather than this ultimate goal but he, nevertheless, is also suggesting a sequence that builds on experience rather than an unfolding fate:

> If it had its natural progression...if it's right for both parties...it was a loving relationship it's a natural thing is, you'd want to spend more time with that person, so that's what you'd do by moving in.
>
> (Sebastian, 35, urban)

Meeting possible partners and Internet dating

With the possible exception of those oriented to a gay community, Internet dating was often seen as beyond normal ways of going about initiating relationships and 'natural progression'. About one in five of our interviewees said they had used some form of Internet dating, including some who met their current partner this way, and a few more thought that they were likely to try this in the future. The majority of those who lacked and wanted a future partner were not using or planning this approach.

Common reasons for not engaging with Internet dating expressed incompatibilities with gender identities and personal philosophies of love, but, sometimes reasons were mundane and pragmatic. A small minority had no Internet connection or lacked the means and skills to get online but most interviewees were routine users of email and Web services ranging from social networking, gaming and hobby communities to news, travel and shopping sites. Some respondents focused on the time, effort and costs involved for an uncertain return. The imagined effort was enough to discourage Julie (33, urban) who commented 'as my friend said it's a numbers game. I think she went on the internet and met about 80 men [laughs] and out of that she found one…but I'm not that go getting'. Some reactions blended pragmatic and philosophical elements including both 'mythic' and 'pragmatic realist' views of love. The thought of meeting and then having to reject a succession of people was sometimes philosophically unappealing because it is too far removed from understandings of normal 'natural progression'. Those who thought that using the Internet was fundamentally going about things the wrong way were inevitably doubtful it was going to produce the right result.

> The wedding that I was at earlier this year, I met a friend I hadn't seen for a while and she's at least ten or 12 years younger than I am, and she was extolling the virtues of the, I don't know, Match.com or something, one of these web dating services. […] she was extolling the virtues of this because it matches you up with people that are supposed to be on the same sort of wavelength, she'd been through three [possible partners] from that particular web site in a matter of a few months. And I thought, 'Well, you've been extolling its virtues but by the same token you're now onto the fourth person' […] I would rather meet somebody in the conventional way, but never say never, again.
>
> (Nathan, 40, urban)

Even within the gay community, although, and precisely because using the Web to find sexual partners is the norm, its value for finding a life partner was also sometimes questioned. Ray took this view when talking about the popular gay Internet site, Gaydar for Men:

> But to be honest with you that's really just meeting for sex basically…I think the bulk of people that are on these sites are not really looking for a long term relationship, because it's so easy to go and have anonymous sex whenever you want…I think that being realistic with what I know about the gay lifestyle and gay relationships I don't really have a terribly high confidence of meeting someone that is potentially wanting the same thing as I, which is to settle down in a monogamous relationship and to live together. […] I usually find out that they're either married or they've got a

partner they're not telling me about, or they want to have an open relationship or something like that.

(Ray, 44, gay)

Some women with experience of looking for male partners through the Internet also complained that the men they met were only looking for sex:

I didn't like the people I met. Even though you got on with them on the phone or whatever and I did meet people and I thought, oh, this isn't... they were just all out for one thing and I didn't... I find it very hard to trust these people and I never get anything out of it, other than just not feeling that good about myself.

(Julie, 33, urban)

Those who doubted the advantages of Internet dating often reiterated their own version of 'normal' ways of meeting people, through friends and family, sociability in pubs and clubs or participation in sports, hobbies or other activity groups. Nevertheless, Internet dating was not usually dismissed as 'desperately seeking' by women, even by those who did not do it, perhaps because it is seen as a form of action that is better than accepting a traditionally female role in mate selection of passively waiting. The British press reported that Kate Middleton, now married to Prince William, was teased by friends as 'waitey Katie'. Interviewees desiring partners typically neither wanted to be seen as 'desperately seeking' nor as 'in waiting' as if unable to get on with life without a partner. But for some heterosexual men, using the Internet threatened their masculinity, suggesting to themselves as well as the world, that they needed to advertise to find a woman. As Andrew (43, urban) put it, 'I've always felt – it may sound bad – if I do that, I've really become a failure'. Pervasive use of Gaydar meant there was no such implied threat to 'pulling power' among gay men. Heterosexual men who had not internalized such a version of their own masculinity nevertheless feared ridicule but sometimes found ways of successfully side stepping this. Jake (28, urban) neutralized possible discovery at work, by providing colleagues with an appropriately crafted commentary which informed them that he was Internet dating playfully, for fun and entertainment, and not in desperation: 'I was quite open about it in work, so I was able to keep people posted on what was happening because I found it quite funny. I thought that was the best way to deal with any potential stigma if someone spotted me.'

Cynicism about the quality of partners Internet dating offered was another argument advanced against it, particularly by unsuccessful users. Mark (33, urban), for example: 'You're only going to meet, like, sad, unhappy people, basically, that are quite lonely. So, yeah, that's my experience, yeah, I suppose I was maybe quite sad and lonely at the time as well'. Jake (28, urban), complained of 'weird' people and 'lack of decent stock' and that you 'turn up expecting one thing and you find something entirely different'.

Not surprisingly, the most upbeat accounts come from users who have successfully found a partner. Among our respondents, it was women living in rural areas who provided the largest stock of upbeat success stories. Paula, for example, not only saw the Internet as transcending the problem of the limited choice of partners that is characteristic of a small rural population, but saw the extra effort involved in travelling long distance as a form of quality control.

> I know people who've married through it you know, so it's, I think if you've got a sensible head on, and don't get swayed by every man who tells you you're the most beautiful sexy person he's ever come across, you know, then. And I also think that you live in such, you know, so out of the way, it helps in some ways. Because if you lived in a city there'd be like meet and the people who are just there for a quick leg over or whatever, they're deterred by the fact that it's a complete effort to get to meet you, you know what I mean. It's not easy to, it's a bit of a mission to go and meet somebody. And, you know, for me to go into [nearest city] and meet somebody, I would have to be really sure that I would want to meet them. You know, I've got a 120 mile round trip, so I'm not going to just do it on a whim.
>
> (Paula, 36, rural)

All using Internet dating have to make decisions about their willingness to pursue relationships at different degrees of geographical distance; those in rural areas generally have no hope of hitherto undiscovered local possibilities that their urban counterparts might entertain. For those who want a co-resident partnership, relationships that start at a distance inevitably must involve negotiations about relocation and place of residence, as is further discussed in Chapter 7.

Unlikely to partner and unlikely partners?

A small number of women and men seemed to be settled and content living alone and without a partner. Women and men in middle-class professions are typically involved in satisfying employment that not only fosters vibrant social networks, including opportunities to meet potential partners, but also encourages deferring co-resident partnership and children until their career is established. In their late thirties and early forties, professional women seemed more likely than professional men to anticipate remaining childless and continuing to live without a partner. It is possible that for economically independent women the desirability of a partner diminishes more rapidly than it does for men with whom they might partner once they reach the age of giving up on the idea of children, something that happens with greater certainty earlier for women than men. Since conventional gender roles allocate more of the domestic and emotional work of homemaking and sustaining a partnership to women than to men, the risks of future co-resident partnership may seem higher for women and the attractiveness less without the promise of the joint project of children.

Violet and Sophie are examples of women who gave up on (Violet) or never had (Sophie) the desire for children, who relegate couple relationships to a relatively minor part in their repertoire of life's pleasures and clearly did not anticipate the big relationship with 'the one' true love. Violet is a health professional working for a local authority and Sophie runs her own business providing a professional service.

> Well it was a two and half year relationship but I always knew, and made him understand, that it wasn't anything more than a companion/sexual friendship – social relationship, I called it – and that I didn't want it to be anything else; that he wasn't moving in, basically [laughs]. Although he would have [laughs] happily moved in.
>
> (Violet, 40, rural)

Sophie explicitly distinguishes between the acceptability of friends making demands on her and the unacceptability of a demanding partner.

> I'm fiercely independent. I do not like other people – oh gosh this sounds awful. I find myself saying this. I do not like other people making demands on my time – well no, there's something quite weird about me, because actually when my friends do it I don't mind it at all. I don't know what it is I'm thinking. But I don't think I ever – and maybe that's partly it actually, I have no strong urge, in fact I am disinclined ever to live with anybody and other people can't cope with that … I'm told I have a very male attitude towards relationships. (laughs). Yes. So I don't mind having relationships but they – I really

only want to have them on my terms, and my terms are not about buying joint properties and certainly are not about moving. My life, my career is up here, my career is very important to me. People want you to put them before your work and I don't.

(Sophie, 38, rural)

Some interviewees seemed to depart from a path to future partnership by behaving in ways that belied declared preference. There were interviewees, typically men, who professed faith in the mythic version of love as unalterable destiny while sustaining patterns of behaviour that seriously limited their prospects of such a romance. Their optimism about finding love sat alongside objective conditions suggesting this is highly unlikely, for example, everyday routines that shut out opportunities for meeting new people or almost any people of the appropriate gender. For example, Neil, quoted above as noting that he had not chosen to live alone as a lifestyle, went on to say: 'I suppose I'm an optimistic on that front and I just think, "Oh yeah, it'll happen." ' (Neil, 40, urban). However, his leisure time is focused on sporting activities predominantly peopled by men. He feels unable to engage in regular social commitments because his work involves unpredictable periods living away from home. Neither his friendship network nor his kin typically draw him into wider social circles. Finally, his home is always unavailable as a social space, because it is in a state of incomplete DIY (do-it-yourself) work, and, at the time of interview, had no furniture to sit on. When asked about whether he does anything, such as Internet dating, to meet partners, he said, 'No. Once I've decorated the flat [laughs]. It's been a great excuse. I've been decorating it for ten years'.

Andrew, also quoted above, made emphatic statements about wanting a co-resident partner with whom he will have children but described a life lived in ways that make achieving this very unlikely. For example, he maintained a sexual relationship with a woman who had a family and did not want any more children and was 'never going to be and never will be a permanent relationship'. He kept the relationship socially invisible by not telling others about it. Moreover, his sexual partner did not visit his house which, like Neil's, was never used as social space. He declared it a 'mess'. His leisure was focused on a club-based sporting activity where he was very unlikely to meet possible partners. In addition to reference to mythic ideas of fated love his interview contained much self-observation accepting incompatibility between his routines and a partnership relationship. His dismissal of Internet dating contained not only his reference to mythic fated love 'if it's going to happen it's going to happen' but also his unwillingness to invest the time, effort and expense when there was no guarantee of a result. He acknowledged that his general approach to life of trying to achieve what he wanted by his own idiosyncratic means of minimizing expense might be an impediment to partnership.

Finally, a few interviewees, men rather than women, expressed unhappiness at a self-assessment of no hope of a future partner. They were mindful of a list of circumstances that disadvantaged them including lack of resources, such as income, health, housing, employment and the undesirability of their area of residence. For example, Harry, a gay man troubled by depression and living on incapacity benefit in a 'rough' city area that his friends and family were reluctant to visit, was both very keen to have a long-term partner and very pessimistic about his prospects.

> They say the Internet is supposed be a good tool and made it easier, I don't feel it. I have profiles but I don't chat to anybody, I don't say...I look at profiles but I don't even have the confidence to say hello to somebody...I just seem to be totally lost. Because I don't even know where to try, and I'm not...I've tried to go out at night and I just don't like it. Part of it's a safety thing, part of it's cost as well. And then there's nowhere really that [sigh] I don't know, there's nowhere I really felt I belonged in the daytime, let alone at night'.
>
> (Harry, 35, urban, gay)

Relationships without co-residence: Keeping intimacy at a distance?

Irene Levin and Jan Trost (1999, 2004) were early advocates of recognizing LATs as a distinctive family form which emerged first in Nordic countries. In their view the social acceptability of cohabitation dissolved the normative link between marriage and co-residence. In other words, once living together without marriage was socially acceptable and just like marriage, so also 'marriage' without living together became a possible choice. Like Mary Holmes, they also note the growth of distance relationships and dual residence couples as the outcome of the difficulties in coordinating places of employment in fluid global labour markets without sacrificing gender equality of expectations about economic independence and the pursuit of a career (Holmes, 2004, 2006). It is generally observed that LAT arrangements are less conducive to beginning a family than co-residence, albeit that many men and women do parent across households following the dissolution of a co-resident arrangement (Maclean, 2004; Smart et al., 2001) and 'community' parenting across households is common in some ethnic minority communities (Reynolds, 2005). Levin divided her Swedish respondents between those who said they would like to live together but there were one or more reasons not to, including not only work or study in different places but caring responsibilities for others, and those who did not want to live together although they wanted to remain a couple. Different authors continue to put different emphasis on the extent to which living apart relationships reflect choice or constraint, while typically accepting that both are involved.

The extent and significance of contemporary Euro-North American living apart couple relationships remain debated but it is widely accepted that the trend is linked to the demographic changes associated with the growth in living alone (for example, delayed first partnering and high rates of relationship dissolution) and that gender equality and opportunities for economic independence are important preconditions. The implication of Levin and Trost's analysis is that as cohabitation becomes more common across a range of countries, so will LAT. The issue is being researched across a growing number of countries (for example, Beaujouan et al., 2009; Castro-Martin et al., 2008; Haskey, 2005; Reimondos et al., 2011; Strohm et al., 2010). While Levin's and Trost's research in Sweden points to an upward trend, analysis of demographic trends in Germany and the United Kingdom (Ermisch and Seidler, 2008) have not. John Ermisch and Thomas Seidler emphasize that for those under the age of 35 the pattern looks more like continuity with previous partnering practices than radical change. A period of building a relationship with somebody living elsewhere typically ends in co-residence or the dissolution of the relationship clearing the way to starting again. While accepting that LAT may be more common over the age of 35, the authors suggest that the arrangement remain very unusual, expect perhaps among highly educated groups. The relationship between LAT and high levels of education has also been found in Australia and Spain (Castro-Martin et al., 2008; Reimondos et al., 2011).

British research studies following Levin in combining large scale quantitative work with qualitative interviews have found that couples living apart are a heterogeneous population doing what they do for a range of diverse reasons (Duncan and Phillips, 2010, 2011; Haskey and Lewis, 2006). Some are constrained to live apart by circumstances, some prefer to live apart because of other caring responsibilities, and some are not (yet) prepared to take the risk of co-residence (Haskey and Lewis, 2006). Taken as a whole, the evidence suggests that very few couples living apart see themselves as pioneering new living arrangements. For example, few heterosexual couples seem to be engaged in a political act designed to avoid falling into conventional gender inequalities and divisions of labour, what Mary Holmes has called 'the normalizing, gendered processes that constitute intimate relating' (2004, p.180). The idea that LAT are de-emphasizing couple relationships (Roseneil, 2006) or seeking both intimacy and autonomy was found to reflect the views of only a very small proportion of couples living apart (Duncan and Phillips, 2010, 2011). However, debate remains. Duncan and Phillips question Haskey's and Lewis' conclusion that living apart together is 'characterised more by caution and conservatism than radicalism and individualism' (Haskey and Lewis, 2006, p. 46).

In our UK study, we conducted telephone interviews with 55 men and women who were in a relationship but living apart, and an additional nine who had recently exited from this situation to co-residence.[1] In the case of six men, this was a same sex relationship. The majority of our interviewees in living apart relationships described this as having been established for at least a year and as long term but one relationship was described as 'just starting up' and some were only a few months old.

Most of our interviewees had not consciously set out to develop a 'living apart together' arrangement over a co-resident relationship, which for many remained their preferred long-term form of partnership. On the basis of the qualitative interviews, we categorized people by what they said about the prospects of co-residence in their current relationship and this is shown in Table 3.1. Some were already planning future residence and their situation does not seem to merit a special label of 'living apart together'. Others were in relationships that they felt would be good as co-resident relationships and were thinking about this but uncertain, seeing factors against this as well as for it, practical obstacles or, in some cases, working on their partner's resistance. For many, the benefits of living alone and the risks of co-residence loom large. For them, co-residence is not off the agenda but it is on hold and certainly not a certainty. 'Caution and conservatism' are often appropriate adjectives for their approach. Then there is a separate group, where the question marks were more about the relationship itself; the relationship was not deemed as at a stage or of a quality where co-residence would 'naturally' be considered. In a few cases, this was because the relationship was never viewed as a potential partnership but 'just for sex' or a 'convenience' or doomed to be unstable, 'on and off'. Most,

Table 3.1 Orientation to co-residence among interviewees aged 25–44 living in one-person households in Scotland and in a relationship

	Already moved to or planned co-residence with partner	Considering co-residence but uncertainty or unresolved obstacles	Relationship not viewed as a partner or not yet proven as long term	Committed to partner and to living alone (LAT)	Total
Urban men	6	2	6	2	16
Rural men	6	1	5	3	15
Urban women	8	2	4	4	18
Rural women	5	5	4	1	15
Total	25	10	19	10	64

however, had doubts because it was 'early days' and 'too soon' to know whether it would unfold into a long-term relationship. Finally, there was the very small proportion of interviewees who were in settled relationships that they wished to continue as living apart together because they were enjoying combining living alone and having a partner as 'the best of both worlds'. The 10 respondents in this category, about 1 in 6 of those with partners, are the only people to whom the label LAT unequivocally applies. Some of those who were considering co-residence, and hesitating, might accept they are moving towards becoming LAT. If all of those were also classified as LAT, then a quarter of the men and just over a third of the women in some form of couple relationships would be classified as LAT.

The detailed stories that people tell sometimes suggest specific dilemmas for men and women, in urban and rural areas, and for gay men.

Following a 'normal' trajectory of co-residence

The interviewees in the first column of Table 3.1 saw themselves as following the conventional progress of a couple relationship, and co-residence with their partner was the natural end point of living alone. As discussed in the previous chapter, across northern Europe, co-residence now typically precedes marriage. The very small proportion of couples who marry without prior co-residence are usually devotees of religious faiths requiring chastity before marriage. Kapoor (29, urban), a professional migrant from India who had been working in the United Kingdom for six years, struggled to explain that he had never regarded himself as living alone because he always knew the timetable of his arranged marriage 'Usually the reason for living in, alone, it's not alone, actually, because they will marry around 28 or 29. That is usual in India. So here's the thing I'm saying, it's not living alone. OK'. For the majority, discussion of living together was not necessarily bound up with plans to marry. Agreement to move in together often followed a period of developing a relationship over years but some adopted co-residence after a relatively short time. Sylvia's boyfriend, for example, moved into her home seven months after their first meeting and despite fairly modest amounts of time together since it was a long-distance relationship. Her boyfriend's geographical move also meant they were both dependent on her modest salary until he found a job. Sylvia spelled out the possible risks by recounting the problems of a previous co-resident relationship, but commented: 'Life's too short. And I love him' (Sylvia 34, urban). Life was also short in the context of knowing she wanted to have children and wished to find a life-long partner to be their father.

Planned co-residence was sometimes interrupted or delayed by a partner temporarily working abroad (Charlotte, 31 urban) or in the armed forces (Tracy, 25, rural). Distance relationships are in a different category, however, if their ending in co-residence is uncertain. The table 3.1 separates out those who are choosing to be LAT, being committed both to their partner and to living apart and shows that they are a very small proportion of the total with partners. In contrast, about two-fifths of those with partners elsewhere saw themselves as definitely heading towards living together.

Considering co-residence but uncertainty or unresolved obstacles

On the other hand, those who were still weighing up the possibility of co-residence sometimes had a sense of being stalled. The experience of living alone was, in itself, sometimes cited as reason for caution. Particular subjectivities were linked to living alone and seen as inimical to living with others, such as being 'set in my ways', 'fiercely independent', valuing solitude or taking pleasure in total control of domestic space and things. Some factors weighing against co-residence were not unique to people living alone but, nevertheless, seemed more acute in that context. These included complicated practicalities such as the necessity of at least one geographical move involving loss of proximity to people and places of work, the difficulties of shifting jobs or housing, costs of house buying, trials of moving and storing accumulations of stuff. Interviewees also referred to the challenge of reaching arrangements that suited and were fair to both parties in the face of objective inequalities such as their different incomes, disparate sizes of homes and unequal losses likely to flow from rearranging connections to localities and employment. The intrusion of previous family and relationship histories were also complicating factors, for example, creating the need to wait for further recovery from a previous relationship, or to have regard for caring responsibilities for children, ill or ageing relatives. All of these issues have the potential to be compounded by additional sources of resistance for people who have lived alone for long periods. As Chapter 4 explores further, for some people living alone involves a sense of cherishing their own home and filling it with items of significance to them. As Chapter 6 explores, it can also involve building a social life and commitments facilitated by the combination of a home alone and the absence of a partner, or consciously developing self-reliance as an aspect of identity, a strategy often adopted following exit from a relationship. It seems that years living alone often create attachments, practices and states of mind with resistance to moving to a co-resident arrangement.

The experience of living alone creates routines that do not involving the sharing of time and space and adapting these was recognized as a source of resistance delaying co-residence by interviewees. In the United Kingdom, the practice of buying a home during the phase of establishing independent adulthood also complicated the process of moving to co-residence as the 'natural progression' of a relationship.[2] Owner occupation, and the difficulty of whose property, or giving up both properties in the risk of joint investment, is a hazard that most home owning interviewees mulled over in their accounts. For example, Campbell (34, rural) said about his year-and-a-half-long relationship when asked if they had considered moving in together, that they discussed it several times and decided against it for a 'stack' of reasons, including the size of houses indicating the need to sell and rebuy and resistance to adjusting to each other's habits, practices of hospitality and uses of space:

> Both our places are very small so it would probably involve getting another place, and then you know, the discussion sort of lends on, well, that's a much more permanent step and how, in some ways we're not hugely, we're quite different people and there are issues about how well either of us can compromise with the sort of things we like and the environment we'd like to live in. And, for example, a sticking issue is maybe my friends mean a lot to me so my ideal I'd love to have a place where I can invite them round and they could come and stay for a week, and they have small children and that's in some ways almost her worst nightmare (laughs). So we have sticking issues, and it's much more practical that we have our own space.

Campbell was interviewed twice and this theme appeared across both interviews. At first interview, he professed to having left the door open to the possibility of both co-residence and having children, although he was careful to emphasize he was not as sure about wanting children as his friends who have become fathers. At the second interview, he was pondering the fact that they had not yet explicitly discussed whether they had given up the trajectory to a 'normal' co-resident relationship.

> I think the longer it goes on the longer it becomes apparent this isn't like a normal relationship where two people meet, they decide, then they move in, they live together, I don't know, get married if they want to or don't. You know, the nature of living in two separate places is almost that it hangs like a bit of a reminder, I guess. So it would involve a process of accepting that that's, you know...but there has to be, I guess, a line drawn under that to say, 'Well, actually this is okay.' So a discussion, I guess, you'd need to have a discussion.
>
> (Campbell, 34, rural)

In their accounts, interviewees of both genders suggested that openness to living with another person became qualified the more they enjoyed total control over their domestic space and recognized the freedoms and pleasures of living alone. For example, Alexandra (41, rural), has recently started a new relationship and has not yet explicitly discussed whether they will live together although she has already been considering this issue:

> It's still, although we're both seeing it as a long-term relationship, it's still you know, early days to kind of like discuss those kind of things and well not discuss them but think about them but actually act on them because there's, it has, I can't think what the, knock on effect with kind of like my work, his work, where we live, who's house and I think I said you know, I've lived on my own for 20 years, I'm quite selfish now and also, his house is tiny. And I've got a bigger house. So it's kind of practical issues about where and ... Yeah lots of things that really you know, in the next year will be discussed and sorted but it's kind of scary thinking about them at the moment.

Alexandra fits into the category of 'undecided' in Roseneil's (2006) categorization of LAT relationships but it is clear that she see her relationship as in transition and it may become either a settled LAT relationship or co-residence. Euan, like Alexandra, illustrates how both the ease of living alone and risks of co-residence can accumulate over time. He is a divorced father and his child stays with him every other weekend. Although he highlights his employment as the reason for delaying co-residence, as found in other studies (Duncan and Phillips, 2010, 2011; Haskey and Lewis, 2006) these caring responsibilities are also a part of his sense that living together 'might not be great at the present time':

> It's okay having a relationship but it's actually living in the same space with one another might not be great at the present time. We've just got to get used to one another. I know seven years is a long time, but [laughs]. As you get older you can change as well. As your job situation changes you can change and my job situation changes and so has us. It puts you under different pressure.
>
> (Euan, 42, rural)

In addition to those who are undecided about whether they want co-residence, there are also a few cases of interviewees who knew they wanted co-residence but simply could not yet have it. Rhona (40, rural) would like to be married with children, and has been in a socially recognized sexual relationship with a 'stubborn' man who has continued to resist over the last seven years. It's not clear whether she is still hoping it may happen or whether she is reconciled to a LAT relationship.

Uncertainty about suitability of 'partner'

Some interviewees describe sexual relationships which were never perceived as potentially co-resident. Often such descriptions involve transient relationships, although sometimes lasting years. In the early stages of relationships, interviewees are often unable to say whether or not the relationships were transient or the kind of relationship which might become co-resident. Many of the respondents who offered a reason for not living with their partner said that it was too soon, suggesting that this co-residence might still be on the agenda. More men than women sustained relationships that they did not think of as having the potential to be long-term relationships. Graham (37, urban), for example, had been going out with somebody 'for about three months' and when asked if he thought co-residence might be possible in the future he confirmed this was a longer term aim but not with this person: 'I don't necessarily see the relationship going in that direction. I don't see the relationship progressing to that stage'. Similarly, Richard (31, urban), a gay man, looking for a long-term partner says: 'I'm dating someone. But I'd still say I was single right now. I'm just dating this guy'.

Living apart together: LAT committed to a partner and to living alone

Neither the term 'LAT' nor any other word has yet entered everyday use as a name for the practice of sustaining long-term couple relationship without co-residence in the United Kingdom; however, in our study, about one in six of the interviewees in relationships acknowledged this was their chosen and preferred option. These respondents fit comfortably into the definition of LAT as living apart together in settled committed relationships while planning to continue living alone. All had long-term socially recognized relationships with little or no expectation of or desire for co-residence. For example, Christine (43, urban) saw little reason to live with her partner of five years' standing, without ruling it out completely. She talked about having 'the best of both worlds' by living apart together and suggested that the only reason she might consider living with her partner was financial – alluding to living as a couple being cheaper than paying all her own bills. Callum (44, urban), was clear that he wanted a long-term gay relationship without living together, 'I think I decided that I function better on my own'. For another gay man, Cameron (39, rural), a LAT relationship had the additional advantage of avoiding high visibility as gay in a small community. Considerations external to the relationship were also important for Abigail (44, urban), a mother of dependent children who live with their father, her ex-partner. She was committed to not living with her current partner, mainly because of her children.

While it seems most appropriate to reserve the term LAT for living apart arrangements that are respondents' preferred and settled ways of living, arrangements and their meaning also change over time. For example, Brian (42, rural) described a relationship of ten years' standing which would have been classified as a settled LAT had they not now moved into a phase of planned co-residence. He and his partner have two children. They cohabited for a year and a half, followed by a period he described as living separately but splitting up before living separately but in a relationship. Like some other respondents, he suggests that separating co-residence from the relationship removed some of the stresses and strains and made the relationship easier to sustain. However, co-residence is now on the agenda with a timetable for realization: 'We're seriously contemplating looking at April next year to totally moving back together and having the whole family atmosphere, because the kids are now just starting school'.

When the categorization as LAT is reserved for those who see this as a long-term arrangement preferred to co-residence, no one classified in this way in our UK study was under thirty and most, including all the women, were in their forties with no expectations of future children. They were not all highly educated and advantaged as some authors have predicted (Ermisch and Seidler, 2009). Alison (42, urban), for example, has few qualifications, serious health problems and a low income in the form of state benefits.

Solo-living parents

About a third of the men and four of the women interviewed in our UK study[3] had a child or children. All of the mothers and just over half of the fathers were in regular contact with their children. Involved parents of dependent children often had them staying overnight, most often on the weekends and holidays. Some involved fathers not only spent time with their own children, but also with the children of friends and family and their own children's friends. Their experience is in marked contrast to most of the men interviewed who typically had very little contact with children and much less than many women living on their own in the same age group. It was much more usual for childless solo-living women to be involved with the children of relatives and friends although some women living alone also had very childfree lives.

For some of the involved fathers and one of the two mothers with dependent children living elsewhere, the time they gave to their children was prioritized over any other activity and a reason to keep potential partners at a distance in order to protect space for the parent–child relationship. Abigail (44, urban) had been in a relationship for five years and when asked why they did not live together explained 'I would say number one, my children, because they don't really get on with him'. Like a number of fathers, she said of her children 'they are the most important thing in my life', and went onto suggest that the possibility of living with somebody will be easier as they become adults. Abigail spends more time with her children than most involved fathers, two evenings a week going with the youngest from school to the children's family home and staying with them till they are asleep, as well as having the children overnight in her own home every weekend. This routine is facilitated by having her own business and being able to work her long hours (necessary because of debt problems) around seeing her children:

> My most extreme was very recently when I actually worked for 48 hours on the trot without any sleep, although I did nip out to do my children in between times... my children don't live with me, I go out and see them. So I'll work some days until about 2 pm, go out and get the kids, come back at 11 and quite often will work until maybe two in the morning or something like that.
>
> (Abigail, 44, urban)

Some fathers specifically mentioned the richness of their relationships with their children and sense of loss when they no longer had everyday contact. For example, Mike (36, urban) expressed this as the main disadvantage of solo-living: 'In my case being away from my daughter really. I am not a full father'. Some involved fathers spoke of the intimacy with their children as more important than a new partnership relationship or compensating for the intimacy they had lost with their partner, but at the same time recognizing that the period of intimacy may be fleeting since children grow up and have their own lives to lead without parents playing a central role: 'With [son] growing up it might well be that when he starts university that come weekends it's no longer part of his routine to come up here, and certainly any less contact with him, yeah, I would miss it, but I've also got to be aware of the fact that he's growing up and he's going to have interests in things that he wants to do' (Nathan, 40, urban).

Abigail also expressed a sense of loss and regret. As a non-resident mother, Abigail both gets more recognition and support from friends – 'I think they feel sorry for me also that I don't live with the kids. So I think there's a lot of sympathy there' – than any of the non-resident fathers reported. She was also aware that first reactions to a mother who seems to have 'left her children' are often very negative and, like very involved fathers, the extent of her involvement with her children was generally not recognized:

> People without meaning to hurt you make assumptions... They sometimes don't necessarily believe that I spend the amount of time that I do with my children... once they get to know me, they like me, so it transcends any thought that I'm just a selfish bitch that couldn't be arsed living with her children, but they still can't quite understand how I can juggle. I think a lot of them think, and I don't mean

this to kind of bum myself up here, but they wonder how on earth I manage to pack all the time that I do in with the kids and everything else, and probably sometimes don't quite totally appreciate just how much time [laugh] I do doing all that.

(Abigail, 44, urban)

Nicole (33, rural), the only other mother in the sample with a dependent child, expressed no such regrets, noting it was 'more convenient' that her son lived with his father following their divorce. She was a less involved mother with a much less regular routine of visits, a pattern that was also typical of several fathers. She was the only parent who thought it was possible she would have another child.

None of the fathers anticipated having more children, with those on low incomes typically often referring to the financial demands of providing for children. For example, Nathan said: 'Always, from when I was a young man I wanted more than one child, but again circumstances dictate that I would need to be in a substantially better financial position'.

No contact

The interviewees who had no contact with their children were all fathers, predominantly on low earnings or benefits, who sometimes also highlighted the issue of providing.

Would I like more children? Well I don't have contact with the one I've already got. I would love to have loads and loads of kids but unfortunately there's a thing called money. Do you know what I mean? I'd love to live like the Waltons, but they need to be provided for and when it all goes wrong there's a thing called the CSA [Child Support Agency].[4]

(Anthony, 34, urban)

The most often volunteered reasons for having no contact with children concern the nature of the relationships with the mother, particularly the circumstances of breakdown of that relationship and sometimes the circumstances of the birth. Tommy actively shut the door on his children the same day that he shut it on his wife when he found her with another man: 'I walked out! Simple as, you know what I mean? You go with my wife, I'm leaving bye bye, get lost. That was it, shut the door and never went back. Didn't even bother looking back' (Tommy, 43, urban).

William (41, rural) had children with three different partners and his lack of involvement with the children was a corollary of the casual nature of the relationships with their mothers. He described the first relationship as always precarious and he stressed that he made it very clear in the case of the second relationship that he did not want children: 'Basically away back at the beginning she'd said that she wanted a child before she reached a certain age. And I said, 'Well, you're with your wrong person'. Because I already had a son from a previous relationship that failed and I felt I was letting him down. So I certainly didn't want any more'. His, perhaps, third child was a recent revelation:

> And I did say I've got three children, I only found out recently about the other one and that was from even longer ago. So this other kid's twenty years old and I've not really had much contact with him . . . . I bumped into his mother on a train when I was on my way down to visit my folks. She said, 'Oh, by the way, you do realise that [name] might be your son?' Jesus! Okay, right.
>
> (William, 41, rural)

Fathers who had previously lived with their children but now have no contact with them often still remember their birthdays. For example, Tommy had not seen his children for 11 years and had no idea where they were but when asked their ages immediately said, 'My daughter now is 18. My son was 16 yesterday'.

Intimacy with and without partnering?

Even those who did not want co-resident partnership typically saw some benefits in this arrangement and, although the term 'intimacy' was not always used, when broadly defined (Jamieson, 1998, 2011), it was at the heart of the described desirability of couple relationships. The imagined benefits of living as couple were the practices that generate intimacy including everyday, routinely available, companionship, reciprocity in practical caring for and about somebody else and sharing the ups, downs and mundane details of life. Some referred to physical intimacy but more often affectionate touch and cuddles than sex. Some made reference to an intense dialogue of emotional disclosure, a practice that is taken as the essence of narrower definition of intimacy than the one used here (Giddens, 1992).

Most of those who had previously cohabited were keen to recreate the positive aspects of their experience in a future cohabiting relationship despite also having the experience of a relationship breaking down. For example, reflecting on the comparison between cohabiting and living alone, Julie (33, urban) said, 'I felt more settled. I suppose I felt as if I had a bit more of a life, you know, and I don't want to be on my own and have no one there to help or be with or to talk to, you know. That's not a long term plan. That's not what I want my life to be.'

Ray, who declared himself happy without a relationship, nevertheless remained mindful of the benefit of a co-resident relationship as well as the costs:

> I think from an emotional, human point of view it's good to have someone at home or in the house to talk to about things. [...] when the relationship is not going very well I don't really care for all the emotional involvement and upheaval that goes with all that. Towards the end of the relationship, when the relationship is breaking down it can be pretty uncomfortable emotionally and mentally.
>
> (Ray, 44, urban, gay)

Company or companionship was the most commonly mentioned quality sought from a relationship by both men and women. However, this concealed a more varied repertoire of views concerning the essence of company, ranging through the pleasures of having somebody to do things with or talk to, that seemed to focus on the convenience of somebody 'being there', to a stress on deep emotional closeness and connection. Mike and Leo express these extremes:

> Getting a pizza on a Friday night. Hill walking. So company to do these things with, company when you wanted to do these things company to do it with somebody else.
>
> (Mike, 36, urban)

> It's like saying what do you enjoy about a child? It's actually something much deeper than simply what you do. It's just the state of being connected to someone. Of itself. It's like just having a brother or sister. Even if you never see them, it is of itself extraordinary. And the same way; the state of being connected, you're being completely loyal to someone in that way. It just far transcends any individual thing.
>
> (Leo, 36, rural)

More practical sharing and caring were frequently mentioned by men and women in both general terms and with reference to specific themes such as sharing domestic chores, financial costs and decisions. Even those who professed pleasure in living alone typically identified benefits to co-residence including having help constantly on hand.

I was talking to a friend the other day who had to go into accident and emergency and had gone on her own and she was saying that she was sitting there and she was the only person there on her own and I said 'Well why on earth did you not call me? I would have come with you.' And she said, 'Well I knew you were busy and I felt bad disturbing you' and I suppose that's the thing, if you've got a partner sitting there at the other end of the sofa it's just expected, it's non-negotiable that they are going to take you wherever you need to be, you don't have to ask, you don't have to make arrangements. So I suppose that's the main thing. I have got a lot of good friends who are happy to help out but I have to ask them.

(Sophie, 38, rural)

Physical intimacy and various forms of emotional support were imagined as refreshing vitality. Nathan (40, urban) observed, 'probably one of the biggest misses for being on your own is basically the close physical contact, you know, there's somebody that's living with you, they're there to give you a hug if you need one, they're there to kick you up the butt if you need that too. But that's the biggest miss'.

Security or stability was also mentioned by a small number of respondents, rather more women than men. Several women talked of enjoying being in a couple and of the benefits this brought to their social life and/or social standing. One man (Hugh, 39, rural) acknowledged how his ex-partner had drawn him into a richer social life.

Concluding remarks

No available evidence suggests that those who live alone in north-western Europe across the ages conventionally associated with being partnered and childrearing are self-conscious pioneers deliberately celebrating their individualism or forging new individualized pathways across the life course. Our UK study found the majority of people living alone do not think of themselves as doing something remarkable or as standing outside the norm of partnering and parenting. Our research respondents would be as baffled by the idea of being a pioneer as they were irritated by the stereotypes of 'missing out'. The majority, particularly those in their twenties and thirties, continued to imagine a future of living with a partner and having children. Those in couple relationships were not typically settling for living apart together, a LAT arrangement, but rather on a conventional trajectory to co-residence or still searching for the right partner. The minority who were LATs had no name for this way of being a couple and were generally unaware that it might be seen as a new trend; yet, at the same time they were accumulating a particular practical knowledge of being a couple that is likely to contribute to ultimately shifting meanings.

The concept of 'missing transition' needs very careful treatment if it is to be of theoretical value without doing injustice to the subjectivities of those living alone and to the diversity of lives as lived. For most of those who are single and wish for a future as a couple, a partner's continued absence is not a subjectively self-defining form of 'missing out', nor does it undermine the possibility of contentment with living alone. Getting on with developing the pleasures of living alone while hoping for a partner is completely consistent with popular wisdom in Euro-American culture concerning how to become an independent adult and find a partner without 'desperately seeking'. For those who are living alone, doing so is, in itself, a demonstration of independent adulthood and 'desperately seeking' risks undermining the achievement. There is no inconsistency between irritation with the stereotype of unhappiness and emptiness implied by 'missing out' and acceptance that the partner they wish for is indeed missing along with the on-hand access to intimacy they are thought to bring. However, for some of our research respondents, living alone enabled everyday domestic and leisure routines that made finding a partner unlikely and living with a partner less and less imaginable. Some of the research respondents who had reached their forties without a partner or parenting acknowledged that they had missed these transitions, sometimes despite other intentions. Nevertheless, it was exceptional for this 'missing' to involve much regret. Regret was more often expressed by parents, some of whom lamented the loss of full-time co-residence with their children as the collateral damage of relationship breakdown. Parenting from a distance or across households was never presented as a desired new way of parenting. For fathers who had little or no involvement with their children, this was sometimes a cause of bitter regret and when recounted matter-of-fact, with no emotion, it was as if acknowledging a 'missing transition'. While most of the research respondents expressed unease at the idea of still being alone in older age when directly asked, reasserting the possibility that a transition to co-resident couple might yet happen, it was also clear that an old age alone was not a preoccupying threat.

While they may not be pioneers, those who live alone are contributing to changes in the structuring of the adult life course. The subjective experience of living alone can, in itself, create resistance to co-resident partnering and planned parenting. A prolonged experience of living alone in the years between the mid-twenties and forties heightens a sense of risk and hesitancy associated with co-resident partnering, and, in most cases, capacity to enjoy living alone. Despite unfulfilled desires for children and acceptance of the conventional script – committed partner first then children – co-residence is often delayed by the experience of living alone, which in turn makes parenting less likely. This additional hesitancy about co-resident partnering among the growing pool of childless men and women living alone contributes to low fertility and childlessness. Although there are very few people choosing to be LATs among those living alone, those living alone who have partners are living the separation of co-residence and partnership and contributing to the demise of sustained co-resident partnership across the adult years. Similarly, parents who mainly live alone and sometimes have their children staying with them are living out the separation of co-residence and parenting, a practice much more common for fathers than mothers. Although not celebrating or seeking a turning away from partnering or parenting, people living alone, nevertheless, contribute to the demise of life-long partnering and sustain low fertility. However, as Chapters 6 and 7 also show, this does not involve withdrawing their energies from family life or the wider web of relationships that sustain social life and 'community'.

The different partnering and parenting biographies of those living alone – in a relationship with a non-resident partner or without any such relationship, parenting a non-resident child or without parenting – result in distinctive sets of experience that are also inflected by differences of age, gender, socio-economic circumstances and health. Among the 'single' these factors influenced ideas about timing and strategies for finding a partner and among the 'partnered' they influenced ideas about the right time for co-residence. Perhaps those most likely to imagine a future life living alone and without a partner or children were working-class men with particularly disadvantaged circumstances and middle class, relatively socially and economically advantaged career-focused women. The barriers to co-resident partnering and parenting seem higher for the most disadvantaged, although accounts of unintended pregnancy and opting out of parenting formed part of the repertoire of experiences related by low-income men living alone. Not surprisingly, disinclination to find a co-resident partner or live with an existing long-term partner is highest among those who are happiest living alone. As the next chapter shows, relatively advantaged career-focused women were not the only people in this category but their presence is notable. On the other hand, dissatisfaction with living alone and a desire for a co-resident partner does not always lead to actively seeking change and philosophies of romance work against this. Men were typically more hesitant in seeking partners than women, being more likely to express disdain of Internet dating, to sustain relationships that did not match their ideal of a partner and to have lifestyles at odds with hopes of meeting 'the one'.

Part II
Home, Consumption and Identity

Introduction

The idea of home has multiple meanings in most cultures; Part II begins by exploring the interplay between the experience of being a 'one-person household' and normative meanings of home. Chapter 4 considers not only how people think about their home, but also how people use their home: for example, who visits, who is invited in, what entertainments and activities go on there, as well as how it is decorated and maintained. Discussion is organized by an overarching interest in the relationship between home, self and others expressed in notions such as the homely or unhomely home, the hospitable and inhospitable home and the home-from-home. While this chapter focuses primarily within the home itself, Chapter 5 brings together a set of social practices' some of which are outside the home. Nevertheless, their meaning and how they are experienced are utterly linked to the meaning of home. The practices are eating meals, celebrating Christmas and taking holidays. Each of these provides indications of how people living alone are embedded in social relationships and manage practices of consumption. They are all social practices that can become something of a trial for people living alone, particularly those who are outside of partner relationships, illustrating the efforts and learning required to meet the challenges of living alone well (Klinenberg, 2012, p. 58). Do the practices require the development of special subjectivity – a sense of self that feels, experiences and enjoys in particular ways? If so, can this be done similarly by men and women, and by those with more or less resources?

Identity and the meaning of home

Questions about the meaning of home dovetail with others about identity and subjectivity, including analysis of 'being set in my ways' and the extent to which living alone involves developing skills and practices that constitute the self in particular ways. Is there any propensity for people who live alone to develop a love of solitude? Is the home of a person living alone necessarily a site of growing inflexibility of the self expressed in unwillingness to compromise and accommodate others? Several alternative lines of argument seem immediately possible. Perhaps the least positive is the claim that such inflexibility would not render those who live alone exceptional, since those living with others also demonstrate this trend. Respected texts on social change in marriage relationships in the United States, for example, suggest an increasing proportion of couples leading parallel individualized lives (Amato et al., 2007; Cherlin, 2009). A leading authority on the impact of personalized computers, mobile phones and entertainment systems on children and their families in Europe (Livingstone, 2009) suggests an individualizing effect, as family members with their personal devices separate into their own spaces, undermining the previous function of TV as 'the family hearth' (Morley, 1986), a trend mothers seem determined to resist in parts of Asia (Lim, 2008). This latter example, however, also points to a counter argument, the idea that pervasive digital communication technologies create possibilities of connections, 'networked individualism', that transcend living arrangements (Wellman et al., 2006). Many people living alone inhabit homes that are hubs of electronic inputs and outputs or launching pads of comings and goings rather than sealed and silent fortresses with their drawbridges up. The balance of constructing the self in separation from others versus negotiated connectedness is an empirical question also taken up in Part III.

The concept of 'ontological security' derived from psychology has often been linked with the idea of a home, for example, in the field of architecture, housing studies and sociology (for example, Cooper, 1976; Cooper Marcus, 1995; Dupuis and Thorns, 1998; Hiscock et al., 2001; Silva, 2007). A person has ontological security when he or she has a secure sense of self and agency without constant crushing doubts about the continuity of his or her being, self-determination or place in the world; he or she has a basic trust in others and in a world in which people usually are, and the world mostly is, as it seems. Erik Erikson (1950) attributed the origins of ontological security to caring and predictable parenting in early childhood but it is also an ongoing accomplishment in a person's biography, requiring continued social and material support, particularly in times of rapid social change and where there is a heightened sense of risk (Giddens, 1984, 1991).

Different theoretical traditions within social science emphasize different ways of sustaining 'ontological security', but a diverse body of authors agrees on the importance, at least in Euro-North American cultures, of a sense of having a home and of following taken-for-granted routines. Houses as homes potentially create a sense of protection from the social or public 'outside', through enabling the experience of space as if entry is controlled by the occupier, and privacy is assured, enabling what happens there to feel under their control. A home offers a place, the relevant equipment and time for being enveloped in mundane social routines including around performing the biological necessities of self-maintenance, eating, washing and sleeping with reference to culturally accepted getting-up and meal times. Houses are constructed with layouts and furnishing that suit these cultural routines. From these routines, Chapter 5 identifies food and eating as particular challenges for people living alone.

Research across a range of disciplines, studying people in a variety of circumstances, itemizes the many meanings of 'home.'[1] Using the term 'home' often suggests the key site, whether geographically-fixed, mobile or imaginary, of a range of emotionally-charged, highly valued but intangible elements, as well as a material structure that is a place of human dwelling and, particularly in the case of home ownership, an asset with a monetary value. These emotionally charged intangibles are also widely shared normative notions attached to 'home' and include being one's self, privacy, refuge, sanctity, security, investment, ownership, control, domestic life, family, love, intimacy, belonging, origin/roots, community and nation, all of which potentially contribute to identity or sense of self, whether as an individual or through belonging to a larger unit. Some of the possible meanings seem much less accessible to people living alone, particularly the conflating of home and family and the idea of the home as a site of love and intimacy, but, perhaps, also the link between home and roots or community. But is this so? Should it be assumed that there is greater potential for individualized meanings of home for people living alone: being one's self (without family or community), privacy, refuge, sanctity, security, ownership and control?

The existing literature also indicates that extreme adverse economic and social circumstances work against a place of dwelling feeling like a home, precisely because those circumstances rule out too many of the emotionally positive meanings. Those who enjoy few of the emotional benefits of 'home' may invest the term with little more than the minimal sense of 'the place where I live' or say they have no home. Worldwide, this is the situation of millions of people who might be described as living alone, including many thousands living in rooming houses and single room occupancy hotels in the rich countries of North America where the quality of accommodation and relationships with tenants and landlords deny occupants a sense of privacy, security and control (Klinenberg, 2012; Mifflin and Wilton, 2005). Caravan and trailer park occupants in many of the richer countries of the world may fare better, but they too often contend with stressful circumstances that include chronic insecurity (Bunce, 2010; Newton, 2008; Verderber, 2008). In their comprehensive review of the meanings of home, the geographers Alison Blunt and Robyn Dowling (2006) suggest that homes may often invoke simultaneous feelings of belonging and alienation; moreover, places judged as unhomely may sometimes be rendered pleasingly or homely, and homely places sometimes experienced as unhomely. Nevertheless, this does not mean that whether a dwelling is pleasing or unhomely is simply in 'the eye of the beholder'. Some materials are more resistant to homeliness than others and very disadvantaged social and economic circumstances make the precariousness of homeliness and feeling 'at home' more acute. The very poor living in low-consumption poorer countries of the Global South occupy self-built insecure accommodation with little or no recourse to publicly-provided infrastructure or welfare (Dayaratne and Kellett, 2008; Kellett, 2005). The poor in rich high-consumption national contexts may benefit from systems of government regulation and enforcement by local authorities, ensuring a reasonable standard of dwelling supported by an appropriate infrastructure, affordable rents and security of tenure; those who are not acknowledged as citizens always remain outside any such provision and housing policies typically prioritize families over people living alone.

Consumer culture: Homes and stuff

Growing sectors of populations across the world have increasing levels of consumption including items for embellishing the home and for use within it, many of which are heavily marketed. For example, Yaunxiang Yan writes of China in the 1990s that 'most Chinese families had basically completed their 'family modernization'; they had already acquired all the 'essential' items, such as television sets, refrigerators and washing machines' (2009, p. 217). High-value household goods have often become part of the currency of traditional systems of exchange including dowries and bride wealth. Across many social contexts, the acquisitions of goods for the home may be primarily for display and used to make claims of social status and identity, whether of uniqueness or belonging to or distinction from particular social groups. Theorists of consumer culture have documented how even the most mundane use of objects reproduces particular ways of life, social relationships, identities and distinctions (Slater, 1997; Southerton, 2011; Warde, 2005). However, display might be self-referential in the sense of people ceasing to care whether anyone sees it other than themselves. Current definitions of practices of consumption extend beyond the purchase and use of physical objects such as houses and furniture to 'goods, services, performances, information or ambience' and the idea of 'use' encompasses 'utilitarian, expressive or contemplative purposes' (Warde, 2005). All of these forms of consumption can take place at home through the Internet, which enables listening to, viewing and downloading a seemingly endless set of services, performances, information and perhaps even ambience, as well as enabling somebody to order the delivery of physical objects through online shopping that can then be consumed at home. For people living alone, how is the home used as a site of consumption? What is the balance of self celebration, absorption and entertainment versus consumption geared towards promoting social life? Is it primarily a place of functional reproduction, retreat, meditation and recuperation that then enables an active social life conducted outside of the home?

Across the twentieth century and into the present, the ideal stereotypical 'Western' home represented in multiple art forms is a white middle-class heterosexual family home occupying a suburban house with garden (Coontz, 1992; Tyler May, 1988). It has arguably become a global icon. When the representation was produced in moving images, in its 1950s heyday, a manly father's repertoire includes using tools and equipment to look after the fabric of the house while the mother's uses fabrics, furnishings and flowers in the interior to make it pleasing with her 'feminine touch'. In many societies, the tradition of home is not centred on a couple, but the stereotypical Western home becomes less specifically 'Western' as other patterns of residential practices and family ideals take their own paths towards conjugal families. Many commentators from different perspectives have linked the conjugal family to individualization and the spread of market capitalism (Goode, 1970; Therborn, 2004, 2011; Yan, 2009, 2010) and to global discourses of romantic love emphasizing the intimate couple (Cole and Thomas, 2009; Hirsch and Wardlow, 2006; Padilla et al., 2007). The factors encouraging the centring of the family on the couple in turn also make living alone more imaginable. In China, as well as in Japan, ageing parents can no longer presume co-residence with their children and living alone in old age does not automatically signify failure to raise filial children (Xin and Chuliang, 2008; Yan, 2003, 2010; Zhang, 2004).

While contemporary European and European settler societies have moved far from the colonial and patriarchal roots underpinning the iconic home, class and gender divisions are still expressed in the making of homes. Daniel Miller points to research on council homes in London as showing how gendered divisions of labour in which men do 'DIY' and women 'home making' enable people to transform local authority housing into 'homes' they feel are their own (2010, p. 87–88). Miller refers to houses as 'the elephants of stuff' as 'huge lumbering beasts' that are enormously expensive and less readily orchestrated to the purposes of the self than more modest forms of stuff such as sets of clothes (2010, p. 81). Miller suggests that people living alone face particular challenges turning the 'elephant of stuff' of a house into a home. The iconic family home may be part of their difficulty. This chapter asks if it is, nevertheless, possible for a home, which is a home alone, to express personal relationships and even be engaged in 'displaying family' (Dermott and Seymour, 2011; Finch, 2007), rather than being exclusively focused on displaying the self. Given known gender differences in sustaining family relationships, this seems likely to be done differently by men and women, inadvertently giving off or actively projecting particular gendered or classed identities. Exploring this line of argument through the accounts of people living alone leads us to move from practices taking place within their household to beyond its thresholds, for example, to look at eating out as well as eating at home, and going on holidays as well as holidays at home. The consumption practices of people living alone have also begun to attract attention because of the detrimental implications of the growth of households for desired reductions in carbon footprints of populations. Studies in the United Kingdom document how a shift from multiple-person to one-person households may mean that the same number of people use more energy, land and goods (Williams, 2005, 2007).

4
The Meaning of Home Alone

In our UK study, a variety of approaches were taken in exploring the relationship between sense of self and home. Information about the meaning of home would inevitably emerge from more general discussion of the experience of living alone. One direct thread of study involved exploring how open the home was to visitors, cooking for others, encouraging friends or family to stay overnight and to generally making visitors feel at home. Another involved discussing whether interviewees felt they had put a personal stamp on their home and another, potentially in tension with this, explored the extent to which the home expressed the presence of others. The home may be used to sustain or develop intimacy with friends and family (children, parents, partners, siblings and other biological, legal or fictive relations) whether or not such persons are normally geographically distant or local. How important is it to people living alone to have hospitable homes? To what extent do people living alone who have long-term partners or who parent children with a residence elsewhere, wish to create a sense of shared home or a home-from-home for them?

Housing stock and the state control of housing in the United Kingdom reflects the shifting position of welfare regimes between the residual welfare system of the United States and the more generous social democratic systems of some parts of Europe (Esping-Anderson, 1990, 1999; Harloe, 1995). The private rented sector is much less regulated than in some other European countries such as Germany (Bone and O'Reilly, 2010) and although local authorities are obliged to house those who are 'unintentionally homeless', 'single people' living outside of family relationships are often treated as low priority (Reeve, 2011). In the decades following the Second World War, before the UK Conservative government Housing Act of 1980 which gave local authority tenants the right to buy, significant proportions of the population, particularly in Scotland, lived in local authority provided/socially rented housing, that is, housing allocated on the basis of a system of waiting lists and calculated need. Since 1980, publicly owned housing has shrunk across the United Kingdom and much of it is concentrated in stigmatized urban areas of multiple deprivation where trust in neighbours and satisfaction with the neighbourhood tends to be low (Feinstein et al., 2008). In the early twenty-first century, the majority of people in the UK are not reliant on publically owned and socially rented housing but, nevertheless, among working-age people who live alone, a larger proportion occupy such housing having less access to alternatives than their peers who live with others (see Appendix 2, Table A2.1a and A2.1b). In Scotland, the majority of family homes are terraced, detached or semi-detached houses but the majority of people living alone occupy flats, apartments or maisonettes (a housing style characteristic of a period of council housing and private housing estates at the lower end of the market) (Tables A2.2a and A2.2b). Among the working-age population in Scotland, living alone is slightly more concentrated in urban areas than living with others (Table A2.11) but remote small towns also seem to attract people living alone and even among remote and rural areas, about one in ten households is a one person household (Table A2.12). Research suggests some variation might be expected in the emotional benefits and meaning of home by housing tenure and the socio-economic character of neighbourhood (Hiscock et al., 2001). Our study conducted in Scotland included interviewees across the spectrum of housing tenancies, types of housing, urban–rural geographies and the range of socio-economic contexts. While all of our interviewees were housed, a small number had experienced homelessness, including two interviewees who described periods of 'sleeping rough'.

Home alone and pleasing yourself

When our UK research respondents were asked about the advantages of living alone, a sense of control that depended on being the proprietor of their own homes (whether or not the house was a tenancy or owner occupied) was raised much more frequently than solitude, 'enjoying my own company' or 'time to myself'. This is perhaps not surprising, given that a sense of control has been identified as central to 'ontological security'. Research respondents frequently raised control of time, space, money, domestic order and decisions about everyday life, often summed up as being able to 'please yourself'.

The advantages? Like you've got plenty. Just what you want, when you want. You're independent and you don't really need to rely on anybody. You know when you come home your house is going to be the way you left it like tidy-wise and stuff. And like your money, like you can budget yourself and stuff like that.

(Aileen, 27, urban, council tenant)

I feel it's kind of like…not a sanctuary but it's mine and it's yes it's somewhere to come home to and it's yours and that's what's really special, and you've made it – messy – but that's me and this [is] mine and this is how I wanted it to be. […] I know it's my mess.

(Alexandra, 41, rural, owner occupier)

The idea of a lodger was extremely unattractive for most people because it would compromise their control.

It's okay for me to make a mess but somebody else doing it [laughs], 'No'.

(Donald, 28, rural, owner occupier)

Living alone was often contrasted with previous experiences of lack of control over space, order and resources in shared living arrangements. However, the advantages of 'pleasing yourself', not needing to consult or share, was also recognized as the disadvantage, nobody else on hand to consult and share with:

Well, some of the advantages can also have their flip side. The fact that yes, you've got the freedom to go out and about but also no one to talk to, no special person to talk to about any day-to-day problems and such like. Like a lot of things in life, you gain one thing, you lose something else.

(Alfie, 41, rural, owner occupier)

It was also common to express concern that 'pleasing the self' had negative consequences. Sometimes this was the acquisition of bad habits such as domestic neglect and unhealthy eating. Alfie, for example, acknowledged he needed a co-resident to motivate him to keep domestic order:

You get into the habit of just doing things to please yourself. Which sometimes means not doing things like housework [laughs], because there's no one to tell you to tidy the house up or 'Isn't it time you hoovered the carpet?'

(Alfie, 41, rural, owner occupier)

Fears about reshaping the self as more selfish, inflexible and too 'set in my ways' to be able to live with a partner, seem to share the discourse of pessimistic social commentators:

I do worry that I'm getting too set in my ways [laughs]. That is my main concern, I don't know. I would think about living with somebody else but then could I cope with the compromise?

(Ailsa, 28, urban, owner occupier ex-social housing)

Some, more rural respondents than urban respondents, suggested that they had reached a point of no return. Those reaching this view include both relatively disadvantaged men like Harvey who had long-term health problems and was in receipt of invalidity benefit and Angela who was a relatively well-paid health professional:

I think I'm too set in my ways now. It's just one of these [things]. I've just accepted health-wise and money-wise I've accepted that probably this [living alone] is it.

(Harvey, 38, rural, council tenant)

No I couldn't live with anybody now. No, I'm too set in my ways. It's the little bit of selfishness in me.

(Angela, 44, rural, owner occupier)

Home for the self and home for others

As shown in Table A2.3a and 2.3b, about 60 per cent of people living alone in Scotland in the age group of our interviewees have more than one bedroom. For many interviewees, the spare room facilitated use of their home to sustain and develop family or friendship relationships; for some it was dedicated to creating a home-from-home for a visiting child and for many it was part of maintaining a hospitable home. Even interviewees who acknowledged that its primary purpose had never been hospitality, typically used their spare room for visitors. Catriona (37, urban, owner occupier), for example, said 'I got somewhere with two bedrooms so I would have a room for all my books! [laugh]' but she also noted 'Because I've lived in loads of different places, I've got friends who aren't close by, so I've got quite a few friends that might come over from the States or will come up from London or wherever they are now. Everybody I worked with are kind of all over the world some of them. So, yeah, sometimes they'll come and stay'. For the 40 per cent who have only one bedroom and very small homes, creating the hospitable home or home-from-home is much more of a challenge.

Hospitality to friends and family

British research on friendship in the late twentieth century suggested that entertaining friends at home was more typically a middle-class than a working-class pattern, but this class difference may not have been sustained. Graham Allan described working-class friendships as 'context specific', that is, friendships are contained in one setting (the pub, the club, the mother-and-toddlers group, or wherever they meet each other) and do not typically enter the home, which is generally reserved for entertainment of close kin. Middle-class couples, on the other hand, used hospitality at home to transcend the particular setting in which friends were first made and to further develop the relationship. Allan explains class differences primarily in terms of the time, energy and resources that people have to give to friendship as a consequence of their position in the labour market and the material and economic circumstances that go with this (1989, p. 35–38).

Many of our respondents, both middle-class and working-class, were consciously concerned to maintain a hospitable home for friends and family. Offers of food and drink are a common form of hospitality, and meals are discussed in more detail below, but Isobel illustrates how oriented to visitors she was through the stocking of her fridge.

> If you look in my fridge half the stuff in my fridge is not actually mine because I've always got stuff in for other people. I mean it's like there's copious amounts of Red Bull...I don't touch it, but it's purely because I know that everyone else that comes into this house does and I don't want them to come in and to not have anything...Just like my friends and my brother, just general people...And I don't drink milk but there's always milk in the fridge purely because they take milk in their tea.
>
> (Isobel, 29, urban, council tenant)

When maintaining a hospitable home was a priority, this could be an obstacle to living with a partner if he or she was perceived as less hospitable. For some who were contemplating moving to co-residence with a partner (for example, Campbell discussed in the previous chapter), whether or not their friends and family could be made equally welcome in the new arrangement was sometimes a major consideration.

Homes from home

The interviewees who were in couple relationships planning co-residence often had elements of a shared household and sometimes provided each other with a home-from-home. Those who were actively parenting dependent children (mainly non-resident fathers, but also two non-resident mothers and Isobel, as a godmother), wanted their home to be their children's home or at least a home-from-home. Isobel's pattern of creating a home for her cousin's children was very similar to that of the non-resident parents. The two children stayed with her almost every weekend, a spare room was 'their room' and each child had a range of clothes, shoes and toys in her house. The practice of keeping a room for a child whose main residence was elsewhere sometimes persisted beyond their school-age years.

> I wanted to keep it as their rooms. [. . .] I still kept bedrooms for them for when they came home.
>
> (Arthur, 43, rural, owner occupier)

Non-resident fathers with only one bedroom sometimes made do at the cost of their own physical comfort:

> When my son came to stay he just slept in my room and I would sleep on the floor or whatever
>
> (Nathan, 40, urban, owner occupier)

Welfare provisions can be hostile to such practices; the 2013 UK 'bedroom tax' reduced income support for parents with a 'spare room'. Limited space adds stress, undermining the possibility of creating a home-from-home

> It's difficult because I only have a one bedroomed flat. So I've got a, I've got a collection of blow up beds and I have, if I have like the kids staying over then, it's just impossible to move because it's quite a small flat [. . .]. Yes, it's like a war zone in here at the weekends sometimes.
>
> (Stephen, 41, urban, private sector renter)

Holiday visitors and overnight visitors

Interviewees who have moved cities and countries and consequently have dispersed social networks are the most likely to play host to non-local friends and family, sometimes helping them combine tourism with paying a visit (Larsen et al., 2006, 2007, 2008; Mason, 2004). In our sample, migrants with dispersed social networks were more commonly found to be men in urban areas, many of whom had moved to the city for work or education, and women in rural areas, some of whom were in-migrants who had come to take up professional positions. Some interviewees living in the area where they were brought up were returners rather than people who had never moved, so they too typically had non-local friends who might visit. Employed interviewees were generally working within easy travelling distance or had jobs that involved moving around the country and very few were involved in the kind of long distance commuting that necessarily stretches out social networks (Viry et al., 2009). In a study of the effects of geographically "stretched out" social networks on social life among particular mobile populations of workers in the United Kingdom, Jonas Larsen and co-authors note that, although the frequency of meeting is, in part, a function of distance, no matter how far away friends and family are, if they are identified as among 'the most important people' they typically meet up at least once a year. Interviewees hosting such visits often made considerable efforts to put people up in their home.

Janek is a migrant from Eastern Europe who is renting a two bedroom city flat through a private letting agency. He explained that the second bedroom is to encourage friends from his home country to visit without any consequent discomfort:

> I just didn't want to have one single bedroom just to confine myself in it, you know, living on my own I just like to have friends come over and being able to put them in a separate room rather than stay myself in the living room, you know what I mean, so I like my comforts a little bit [laughs].
>
> (Janek, 27, urban, private sector renter)

Jake works in Scotland having moved from elsewhere in Britain to London and then deciding he would have a better quality of life taking a job in Edinburgh. He estimated that he has a friend coming to stay in his spare room about every three months.

While friends coming on long-distance trips might stay several nights, interviewees also described regular patterns of hosting more proximate friends, sometimes including those who live in the same city. Abigail and Ailsa, for example, measured distances in terms of the ease and safety of returning home late at night after an evening involving alcohol when defining 'local':

> Usually because they're not local and they come for a wee drink and they stay over and I'll do the same with them.'
>
> (Abigail, 44, urban, owner occupier)

> A few of the girls that I went to school with, they don't live locally anymore so if we are going out in [town] or this area then they'll stay with me.
>
> (Ailsa, 28, urban, owner occupier, ex-social housing)

Complex dynamics are involved in whether homes are perceived as fit for visitors and, in some cases, visitors stayed elsewhere because the interviewee's home was regarded as less suitable than the alternatives. Those who have only one bedroom often regret not having more space because they would like it to be easier to have visitors. However, only some interviewees without a spare room said that this prevented friends and family from staying overnight. Some, like Geraldine (44, urban, owner-occupier) who had a sofa bed in the sitting room, had found ways round this. Willingness to host others, even in a small flat, partly reflects differences by age and social class in the acceptability of 'making do', ideas about inconvenience and appropriate standard of accommodation. The importance of the host-visitor relationship and estimates of how deterred from visiting or offended visitors might be if not accommodated are all factors at play. Even geographically distant and important visitors are not always hosted if other family nearby offer alternative higher quality accommodation or visitors are known to be willing to pay for available local accommodation. Sophie, for example, considered her very small dwelling completely unsuitable for visitors but partly because she could assume that friends in her middle-class social world would not be deterred by staying in the local bed and breakfast.

> It's just that very unfortunate thing that, as I say, when my friends say 'Oh', you know, 'We're heading to the north west coast for our holidays. Shall we pop in and see you on the way through?' You know, I have to say, 'Well yes, please do and I will book you into the local B&B.'
>
> (Sophie, 38, rural, owner occupier)

Neil could take it for granted that his middle-class parents would continue to come up from his former family home in England to visit
without worrying about the fact he had thrown out most of his furniture as part of his unfulfilled plan to decorate. He knew they would
follow their usual practice and book into self-catering accommodation
for a week.

> They know how small the flat is, so, my parents come once a year and
> stay but they stay in a holiday cottage. Well, it's a flat but it's found
> through the Holiday Cottage brochure.
>
> (Neil, 40, urban, owner-occupier)

Less hospitable homes

Several interviewees, all men, made it clear that their home was not a
suitable place for visitors. Four different scenarios emerged from their
accounts in different tension with the significance of home for the person living alone. They described situations that should not be inflicted
on others or that others might not be able to take: the uncherished
home that was more or less neglected and chaotic; the home over-
dominated by their struggles of personal survival; the home that was
so personalized that others felt excluded; and the home stigmatized by
an association with deprivation.

Unhomely or uncomfortable homes

Some people manage to sustain their sense of self with less reliance on
their home as their base than others and, for men, this sometimes meant
a rather unhomely or uncomfortable and inhospitable home. For them,
their home is certainly not cherished as a shrine to themselves and their
own pleasures since they have trouble spending time there and in looking after their home; keeping others out may not be about protecting an
inner sanctum for self recovery but, rather, sparing others from unnec-
essary exposure to a domain of minimal effort and varying degrees of
chaos. There is also a feminized version of this, which involves protecting the self from the shame of letting other people see a state of disorder.
Men can, of course, also be 'house proud' and then feel personally
embarrassed if others see their mess but in many cultures domesticity
remains associated with femininity and harsher judgements including
self-judgments are still made of women than men if their homes are
untidy. Among our interviewees women did sometimes keep visitors
out of their home because they did not want them to see the mess but

this was always a temporary state of affairs that was a lapse from normal standards and not an everyday strategy. Among our interviewees, the notion of sparing others the chaos of their home seemed to be the approach of Andrew and perhaps also Neil. Andrew is quoted in the previous chapter describing his flat as 'a mess'. When asked if he ever cooks for other people he suggested he would in principle, but it would be impossible because of the mess:

> If I did have people round, I would because I used to get complimented on certain things I made for people, but that's not, a handful of time, visiting my folks but, no, I would do if I had people round, which hopefully will happen in the future, if I get my flat sorted out.
>
> (Andrew, 43, urban, owner-occupier ex-social housing)

Neil's explanation of why visitors were impossible in his home was because there was literally nowhere to sit:

> No one comes round to my flat, no. Because I have no settee or chairs. Because I'm supposed to be decorating. It's a long standing joke. So, yeah. So that's an excuse at the moment in that I have thrown out the settee and the armchairs, there is actually nowhere to sit except for the floor.
>
> (Neil, 40, urban, owner-occupier)

He presented this as a joke, as if it was part of a deliberate ruse of DIY to avoid entertaining that had been running for ten years. His reported earnings indicated he could afford to buy in somebody to do the decorating but he had never considered this. At various points in the interview he made it clear that he wanted and still hoped to find a life partner; in final wistful remarks returning to the theme of DIY at the end of the interview, he refers to needing 'someone to nag me', the hoped-for-but-not-yet-found partner:

> But my friends keep pointing out that I do need someone to nag me about the DIY in my flat. Yeah, I think, it's just very personal. I find it a lot easier to do things, to get up and do things in life for other people than I do for myself.

At the time of interview, Neil was working conventional office hours on the premises of a local organization to which he was contracted as an independent consultant. He enjoyed sociability through his work and had evening and weekend commitments including volunteering, a programme of exercise and scheduled outdoor activities. He would have liked even more social contacts and saw meeting people outside his home as a higher priority than spending time on projects at home.

Home as a site of survival

Neil believes he can create a hospitable home if and when the right partner appears, but such certainty of capability feels beyond reach in more disadvantaged circumstances. Some interviewees struggled with misfortunes that create necessary preoccupation with survival, expanding the time and effort taken up by the basics of maintaining the self and the shrinking capacity to deal with others. Murray, for example, spoke as if both a partner and a hospitable home were now near impossible at least for the foreseeable future, regardless of what he might otherwise have wanted. Like Neil, he had problems finishing a decorating project in his council flat and the additional problem of a garden he was not managing to maintain, but these were minor issues in comparison with his struggle with his main preoccupation, combat stress, the legacy of his service in the armed forces. His weekly routine, and its occasional interruptions by emergency hospital admissions, revolved around the management of this condition and included four 2-hour home visits from care workers, and periods working with a voluntary sector organization providing support. His care workers had encouraged him to take on home decorating:

> I've papered half the bedroom and it's been like that for eight months [The plan was to do the rest in a different paper that was not yet purchased]. Once I pick the colour then it will probably lie for another three months until I get around to papering it. It's just, I'm not in a rush.
>
> (Murray, 43, rural, council tenant)

Old furniture, a bed and a settee, items he replaced when he finally won his fight for financial compensation, were lying in the garden in three feet high grass. Murray himself acknowledged that it was his mental struggles that created the major barrier to relationships and to creating a home that others would find comfortable and not its decorative order. For a small number of interviewees struggling with health issues, home is a space preoccupied by exhausting self-maintenace; for Murray there is currently little possibility of sustaining hospitable space for anyone other than those whose job it was to provide him with support.

The exclusively personalized home

Another circumstance of the less hospitable home is the one devoted to celebrating the preferences of the sole occupant to an extent that makes visitors feel unwelcome. It was only possible to explore this indirectly and there was only one clear indication of such a home. William reconstructed an interaction with his ex-girlfriend in response to questions about his home:

> My living room is full of computer gear. I've gotten rid of furniture to get more computer gear in, so all I've got is a couch and a coffee table. […] To me it's an Aladdin's cave. It's a great place. It's a den. It's a playroom. But to a woman, it's like, 'God, what's all this computer stuff?' [..]. She [ex-girlfriend] used to walk in and go, 'Oh, PC World.' [he replies] 'Yeah. You know what it's like, you don't need to come in and have a wee fucking dig at me every time you come into the house.' She was going, 'Yeah, but look at it, there's computer stuff everywhere. There's only one place to sit.' I go, 'Well, how many places do you need to sit? You know, you've only got one backside'.
>
> (William, 41, rural, council house tenant)

As well as describing his home as expressing his personality and having many positive words for his living-room, William later called his home a pigsty, acknowledging it is sometimes neglected. Despite considering a pigsty suitable for his male friends, he also noted the absence of visitors of any sort:

> Friends would come round because they live in pigsties as well, so it doesn't really matter. … blokes live in pigsties and women take a bit more pride over their environment. But yeah, I'd quite happily have mates back but I just don't seem to. I don't know, I can't remember the last time I was in someone else's house and I can't remember the last time someone was in mine.
>
> (William, 41, rural, council tenant)

He emphasized that his home was unequivocally more important than any relationship with a potential partner or friends. This was made clear in various ways during his interview including his account of how he came to live on his own. He told a story of a now over on-off 15 year relationship with a girlfriend with whom he had a child. The story is of long-term uncertainties and unsettled commitments, residential mobility away from and with the girlfriend, changes of occupation and unemployment, renting an unsatisfactory 'bolt hole' in the form of a room in private rented accommodation at the same time as partly cohabiting with his girlfriend in her home. The end of the relationship coincided with when he was offered a council house:

> Because just as it turned out, that was round about the time that the relationship with my ... with the woman who's the mother of my sixteen year old son, that's when that sort of hit rocky ground. So if I hadn't moved into this council house and sort of put a lot of energy and effort into sorting it out as a home of my own, things might have actually gone slightly differently. I might have been more inclined to try and ... I know how terrible it might sound but I might have been more inclined to try and make the relationship work.

> Interviewer: If you didn't have an alternative option of somewhere to live?

> Yeah, kind of. Although it's not like I didn't have a roof over my head, but the roof I had over my head was a privately rented flat with no sort of aspect of my personality about it.

The stigmatized home

Harry was also living in socially rented housing but rather than enjoying his home as William did, he felt ashamed of and stigmatized by it in a way that was similar to the how some tenants in single occupancy rooms in North America feel (Klinenberg, 2012; Mifflin and Wilton, 2005), despite much better circumstances than theirs. His illness, chronic depression, and the fact he desperately wanted to be partnered rather than living alone, obviously had a bearing on his feelings about his home, but it was his class position and sexuality that made him particularly vulnerable to stigma. He categorized himself as a middle-class professional who was now downwardly mobile, and trapped out-of-place in a rough area, describing his neighbours as Neanderthal: 'they don't say 'hello' to you, they growl'. While William fostered the identity of somebody who does not care what others think as a badge of honour he could take to his local pub, Harry kept to himself and felt unable to be openly gay, as this might result in hostility and abuse. The rough reputation of the neighbourhood as the place where ex-convicts were housed meant that his gay friends and his family would not visit him: 'when you're living somewhere that friends and family don't want to visit, you're kind of lost'. Although on a home-based interview, his flat was pleasant and orderly, he spoke as if stigma undermined his own desire to cherish it. Of decorating he said: 'it feels, for me, pulling a tin of paint out a cupboard and trying to do it, when, you answer yourself, you tell yourself that, well, 'Nobody visits, nobody comes, so why bother?" (Harry, 35, gay, urban, council tenant). Other interviewees occupied homes in equally deprived neighbourhoods, sometimes also struggling with illness or in more direct contact with trouble, for example, dealing with antisocial and abusive neighbours, or trying to mobilize the police to see off drug dealers. They did not share the same sense of stigma because their class position enabled them to recognize people like themselves within their neighbourhood, which did not seal them off from friends and family, nor were they dealing with the self-censorship of being gay in a feared homophobic environment.

My touch, love and the presence and absence of self and others in the meaning of home

My touch: Home as materializing the self

The idea that the home is an expression of the self was sometimes put directly to the interviewer:

> Someone coming into the house immediately gets an idea of your tastes and things. It's almost like an extension of your, you know, your taste.
>
> (Catriona, 37, urban, owner occupier)

Some interviewees, but particularly the more affluent home owners, who were mainly but not exclusively in middle-class occupations, spoke emphatically and eloquently about their 'personal touch', liking, aesthetic or taste and could talk at length about how this had been materialized in their home. Henry, whose occupation is linked to the building trade, had the vision, practical and managerial skills to make very significant modifications to his house:

> It's my personal touch that's on the house, you know. Because obviously, someone buying a new house your touch isn't on it, but when it's been converted and it's to my standard and my liking so yes everything in the house is the way [I want it] because if I don't want it I'll alter it to suit.
>
> (Henry, 40, rural, owner occupier)

Matthew also had experience of buying a property needing considerable renovation but he started with no particular expertise: 'But I had to learn how to do things and I did it myself because I couldn't afford to pay other people to do it. So the first time I had a leaky roof, you know, I had to climb up on the roof and fix it'. At the time of interview he had moved up the property ladder to his next home and was very clear that he had 'a particular aesthetic':

> I kind of like things how I like things. And I've got a particular aesthetic, you know, there are things that I like and how I like things to look and, I don't like clutter. But no, I do have a sense of how I like things to look, and it makes a difference to how I feel if things are tidy and ordered and the colours that I want them to be.
>
> (Matthew, 41, rural, owner occupier)

The pleasure of indulging personal taste without the moderation of others was expressed by a number of interviewees. Some who anticipated residential mobility explicitly resisted this, fearing an over personalized home might be more difficult to sell. Others, Henry, for example, took it for granted that their own taste could only enhance the value of the property. A few who were concerned with taste 'loved' their home and resisted the idea of ever moving on although not everybody who loved their home in this attached way was primarily focused on its look.

Presence of absent others

For many interviewees, pleasure in being in and looking at their home was not primarily about seeing their own personal touch, aesthetic or taste, but rather involved seeing their home in terms of expressing relationships. For example, Annabel's enjoyment of home drew on the memory of how her friends worked with her to create its look.

> I love my house, I absolutely love my house, I've worked hard and when I first [unclear word] it as well, and I do have a really good group of friends, it took us two weeks to strip the hall and get the lining paper down.[...] I think the hall, it's somewhere I like to just go and sit and chill because it took so long to actually do it, and then, when it's done, I think I just love my hall and I think I wish my hall was actually in my living room or my bedroom and I could sit there even longer. Do you know what I mean? Because there's so many good memories, because it did take us so long. And that really adds, to me, [to] the character of the house as well, you know.
>
> (Annabel, 30, urban, council tenant planning to buy)

For many interviewees, but particularly women, aspects of the look of their home were created with help from, and always reminded them of, their parents. As Alexandra (41, rural, owner occupier ex-social housing) put it 'there's a lot of dad in here as well', recounting how her father helped her commission and install a fireplace that was what she wanted and 'helped me decorate everywhere', adding 'Oh, and mum did – things like curtains and stuff'.

A small number of interviewees had inherited a family home. Angela described her home as a sanctuary: 'It's my home, it's my sanctuary and it's the place I can come and I can shut the doors and just have peace' and when asked to say more about why she chose that word she said:

> I think it's because it was my parents' home, I had a house down round the corner and then when my mum died I just moved in here and it's the longest home that my parents ever had, because my dad was in the [military] so we travelled everywhere. So this has been my family home since [year omitted for anonymity] and there's probably something to do with that and the memories.
>
> (Angela, 44, rural, owner occupier)

Previous work on material culture and displaying personal relationships has documented the ways in which objects within the home can express relationships and bring significant others who are absent into the home. The most obvious example is the use of photographs, portraits and representations of events celebrated or enjoyed with friends and family; other examples include the display of artefacts that are gifts or inherited or represent a place of family origin (Chevalier, 2002; Dermott and Seymour, 2011; Finch, 2007; Miller, 2001; Rose, 2003). Most of the research documenting the use of photographs and objects has focused on couples or families, but photographs of family and/or friends were common in homes of people living alone in our UK study. Ray, for example, a gay man who hinted at some lack of ease with the genre of family photographs, made it explicit that he began to display photographs because he wanted to show his visiting family how important they are to him:

> I never used to have photographs out and that's [pointing to the display] just because I've been given photographs of the family and I'm very fond of my nephew. I love my sister and my mother and that's the only photographs I've got. I mean two years ago I didn't have any photographs out. And yeah it's just, you know, I'm just fond of

my little nephew, I mean he's a lovely little guy and, you know, he's obviously fond of his uncle Ray. I think it's nice for my sister and me and my mother and him when they arrive and they see photographs there.

(Ray, 44, urban, owner occupier)

Parents who are in contact with children living elsewhere invariably displayed their photographs. When we asked what people would try to grab if they could only save one or two things from a fire in their home, the most common answer was photographs for both men and women because photographs that predate the digital camera were identified as irreplaceable. The same was said of inherited artefacts and keepsakes from deceased relatives. Some important items expressing relationships, like letters and cards, were not display items: 'the letters that people have sent me, like from aunts that are dead now and people that I've known in the past and just I've got a big box of things that I collect. Aye, I would save that' (Isobel, 29, urban, council tenant). Many of the items identified as things that had to be saved were gifts or inherited objects used as display items. This was the case, for example, with the blue ornaments in Harry's house: 'The blue collection was my mother's, that's there. Yeah, they've moved from flat to flat with me and moved from window to, well they've moved from room to room.' More interestingly he went on to explain why he did not display photographs.

I do have photographs but I don't have them on display, I find that too painful, because I do feel alone, wrong word, lonely let's be honest, call a spade a spade. And when I do see them, they do remind me that I am, that I feel isolated.

(Harry, 35, urban, council tenant)

Isobel also had a policy of not displaying photographs but presented a very different account:

if you look about there's no photographs or anything like that because that's not me. To me, photographs are in here and in here [pointing to head and heart], they're not like physical things like that. And I don't need, I don't have ornaments and things. To me I don't need that sort of stuff because the important things are people and they're not these items.

(Isobel, 29, urban, council house tenant)

The majority of people living alone are in regular contact with family and friends, and, unlike Harry and Isobel, take pleasure in visual evidence of relationships around their home. Photographs, gifts, things parents or friends have helped with and family keepsakes are common. Those creating a home-from-home typically have a whole room or part of the house expressing an absent relationship.

Rational security and irrational love?

Expressed intense 'love'-of-home was a shorthand for many complex feelings and factors heightening their intensity. Those who had lived in stressful or traumatic situations with other people were, not surprisingly, particularly likely to emphasize the security of their home. Some women interviewees expressed a 'love' of their specific home that was so strong they had difficult in imagining ever giving it up completely, even if desiring co-residence with an imagined future partner.

Geraldine bought her own home after her co-ownership arrangement with a friend had become very unpleasant. She decided to take a financial loss in order to gain a speedy exit.

> The decision to buy was because I had jointly bought a flat many years ago with a friend who I came over with [from Ireland] and it didn't work out and we fell out and I came out with nothing and I just wanted my own home [...] I was just relieved to have my own space...
>
> I could never imagine myself leaving this flat. I just love it so much. You know, I don't want to be in a big mansion house or something [laughter]. A millionaire would have to prise me away, but I just love it, and I think even if I met somebody and moved in with him I would always keep this rented. Because it's always, it's got a place here in my heart, but maybe because it's my first real home.
>
> (Geraldine, 44, urban, owner occupier)

The idea of a first home being a particularly significant attachment parallels the popular discourse of romantic love 'the first cut is the deepest'. This is a view that is completely at odds with more prosaic and functional understandings of property ladders in which a home, and particularly a first home, is an asset that, if circumstances permit, ought to be cashed in for something bigger and better or at least of higher value. The right to buy a council home on favourable terms and then sell it five years later opened up the possibility of climbing 'the property ladder' to council tenants and at least one interviewee had made the transition from council tenant to owner of a council property to owner of a home that had never been council owned. However, some interviewees, including some council tenants, professed an attachment to their current home that was 'love'.

Julie makes clear the potential confusion of love, where her 'heart' is, and security, which she identified as a particular issue in the absence of a pension.

> I would say my heart's in this house, just because of everything that I've done to it. I mean because the guy that I was with, he wanted me to sell it and, you know, us to buy a new place and I can understand that, when you move in with somebody, but the thought of it was just, 'No'. [...] I don't have a pension and I don't think I'll ever sell this place. You know, if I do eventually, you know, move in with someone again, or you know, I would, you know, or they moved in here, I still wouldn't sell this place. I think I would keep it as mine. Hopefully I'd be able to do that financially but I would keep it as mine and, you know, because it's daft to get rid of it, you know. Because you never know what the future is. I mean you could go and live with someone and then, like I was being when we split up like that, so then I would have had nowhere and I wouldn't be able to afford to get a new place. So, no. I'm going to keep hold of this for as long as I can.
>
> (Julie, age 33, urban, owner occupier)

The security of a home is an issue for men as well as women and some men among the research respondents also rehearsed calculations about keeping property as security against things going wrong when entering cohabiting relationships. Fewer men, more often council tenants than owner occupiers, professed the same intense attachment to their specific home. When seen primarily as an economic asset, an owner-occupied property may not be a barrier to a co-resident partnership, if ways of protecting against economic loss can be found. However, it is more difficult to protect against loss of a council tenancy, which is not an asset that can be translated into cash. Given the years it can take to get to the top of the housing queue and the known problems with much of the housing stock, a liked council house is not something that can be given up with any certainty that another giving equivalent pleasure will ever be on offer. Council tenants had particular reason to be wary of moving for a relationship.

A home is never just an economic asset and a home alone always involves exclusive control of space and place, which many people experience as a benefit. Thomas, one of the interviewees who had already moved in with his partner by the time of interview, was rational and matter of fact about his home as an asset, yet his deliberations over purchasing the new joint property not only focused on fairness in ownership of the asset, but issues of territoriality and equality of control.

> We felt it was important to buy a new property and, you know, to start on a, like an equal footing as it were, as opposed to one of us moving into the other's, you know, property. Because we felt that was always a very skewed, because it had been someone else's house and you were in their territory. So we decided to – and also the kind of, the value of the two properties differed quite dramatically. My partner's property was worth a lot more than mine. So we were able to sell up and kind of arrange things so that we moved in and were, you know, kind of – things were reasonably balanced, so. It sounds very cold and very fiscal but it was more to do with feeling that we, you know, we jointly owned a place.
>
> (Thomas, 28, urban, owner occupier)

Annabel described how her passionate feelings about her home meant that she could be enraged by the behaviour of a lover when he did not treat her home and her boundaries with what she regarded as due respect; a lover's failure to appropriately interpret her relationship to her home seemed to signal, if not the end of the relationship, very serious doubt about their suitability for the longer term.

> One of the guys I was seeing he had bought a vase thing for in here [living room] and I was outraged by it because I was like, 'This is my house', do you know what I mean? Everything that's in this house I've bought and paid for and I've worked for. 'And who do you think you are to?' And it was a really nice thought but it, I was just like, 'No'. And then certain things would get left like a razor and a toothbrush and it was 'No, that's it, stop it now!' Do you know what I mean? It was again, you know, very strange because, then, if I was there [at his house] I would leave some deodorant there, and then, that way, I know I've always got some deodorant and my toothbrush and all the rest of it, but it would be in a wee bag that you wouldn't notice. But it would just seem that everything was everywhere, and, you know, it was like, 'What are you doing?' I was outraged by it.
>
> (Annabel, 30, urban, council tenant)

Some aspects of Annabel's territoriality and sense of boundaries parallel those of William whose home was described as exclusively personalized; although he does not literally say he 'loves' his home, he makes clear it is more important than any relationship. William saw his home as expressing his masculinity and loner personality. For Annabel, home materialized her friendships as well as herself as a hard-working, independent women. The contrast between Annabel's very intense reaction to a lover populating her home with a few things as a colonizer and her treasured memories of how her friends helped her create the look of her hall indicates the unhelpfulness of categorizing her as if turning her back on others, or too 'set in her ways' to be adaptive. Annabel did conflate her home and herself; she clearly wished others to treat her with the same degree of respect with which she treated them. If this is individualism, it is more plausible to interpret it as of the moral type (Santore, 2008) than a selfish or narcissistic variant.

Gender and functional rather than personal homes

The idea of giving up or losing a home entirely generally carries a very high level of threat, but many interviewees were more matter of fact about the idea of moving from *this* particular home to another. Some who emphasized their personal stamp on their current home presumed they could replicate their look again, should they happen to move on. However, the possibility of replication was less taken for granted when the pleasure of a home relied on relationships expressed in the fabric of the building and impossible when the absent others were now deceased, as in Angela's inherited home. It is not the case that women were always more emotionally attached to their homes than men or more likely to see them in terms of relationships while men were more matter of fact and functional but, of course, there were men and women who behaved true to such stereotypes.

Some interviewees who were more matter of fact about their home focused on location and social and physical surroundings, rather than its interior (attachment to place is discussed further in Chapter 7). For Sophie, for example, the most important aspect of her home was the rural idyll of its location, which included room to grow vegetables, and having friends in the village, not the house itself, which she complained was too small, nor the stuff in the house.

> I was watching something on television the other day, it was slightly unnerving, it said something about your house is the ultimate reflection of your personality or whatever it is. And I found myself looking

round and thinking, oh dear. Because I'm not one of life's – I'm not a nester. I don't care about, you know – the location obviously is very important to me.

(Sophie, 38, rural, owner occupier)

Another form of being very matter of fact about a home was to deny that there was anything particularly personal about a home, as if any wind and water tight shelter was as good as another and nothing much was needed to make it comfortable. Struan's denial of any personal touch involved normalizing this by implying that across social class, in the kind of remote rural area that he lived, nobody was interested in expressing themselves through the aesthetics of their home. However, this view was contradicted by other elements of our conversation not quoted here, in which he described expensive and complex interior design projects he had been asked to undertake in his building trade.

> Even the richest farmers out here, you go in their house, they are very basic, they are just sitting there, like myself, tatty old furniture, old flagstone floor and that. But they are wealthy. If they wanted to express themselves they could. They could well afford it, but they don't bother.
>
> (Struan, 44, rural, council tenant)

The accounts of Alice and Andrew seemed to take a similar tack, emphasizing the 'house' rather than the 'home', focusing on the storage offered by their dwelling and the physical 'shell' they inhabit. They are also expressing differences that might be recognized as gendered, in the sense of calling on experiences and scripts that are more accessible to one gender than the other. This use of gender intersects with difference in social class positioning, rural versus urban locality and divergent histories of mobility in their view of the meaning of home.

> To me, actually a house is just somewhere to store all my rubbish. You know, it's just a shell that keeps me sheltered and cosy and that. I mean I, I don't really care what I've got round me. And I certainly wouldn't go out of my way to buy posh stuff and, you know, splurge on a big leather suite.
>
> (Alice, 36, rural, council tenant)

Honestly I wouldn't say anything [makes it personal to me], it's just it's really a place to stay. The place is an absolute midden most of the time. In fact that's a lie, it's all the time. It's a mess, and family members when they visit have to give quite a number of weeks notice [to make space in one of his three bedrooms] there's just stuff piled up all over the place. You see, there's no need, there's no requirement – as long as I stay clean and healthy and I know where stuff is – there's absolutely no need to [keep them clear].

(Andrew, 43, urban, owner occupier ex-social housing)

Andrew's account highlighted the volume of his 'stuff', suggesting hoarding, while assuring the interviewer he was 'clean and healthy' as if that might be called into doubt. The 'all my rubbish' of Alice's account seemed to refer to the fact that her furniture is second hand and of no significant monetary value rather than volume and her denigration of 'posh' distanced her from certain class positions. Unlike Andrew, she put emphasis on homeliness by suggesting a particular sort of comfort in being 'sheltered and cosy'. Cosiness is, of course, a culturally-specific notion with room for idiosyncratic interpretation. Marianne Gullestad's study tells us that the standard way of achieving cosiness in the homes of working-class Norwegian families in the late 1970s and early 1980s was by 'abundance of furniture, small lamps, green plants and orna-mental pieces (many of them some kind of souvenir) in the living room' (2001, p. 99). For Alice it meant furnishing through providing comfort, but without the distraction of mess or clutter. Alice emphasized order: everything must be in its place. The details of Alice's and Andrew's inter-views reveal that in terms of being 'house proud' and approaches to DIY, like many but not all interviewees, they conformed to certain gen-der stereotypes. Andrew denied any need for things to look orderly and sidestepped the trouble of impressions management by mainly keeping people out. He never entertained at home and, apart from relatives occa-sionally wishing to stay, never had visitors. As a tenant, Alice did not have responsibility for repairs but when it comes to DIY jobs like assem-bling flat pack furniture she said, 'That's what fathers are for.' Andrew took it for granted he will mainly do renovations himself, using male acquaintances to acquire the pieces of how-to-fix-it knowledge he knew he lacked.

The differences in how Alice and Andrew acquired and used their homes are about much more than gender: they express slightly dif-ferent class positions and contrasting local connections reflecting their rural versus urban contexts, combined with divergent mobility biogra-phies as returned-from-the-city-local and town-to-city migrant. Alice is a council tenant in a skilled manual job in the rural community where she grew up. Andrew migrated as a graduate to a modestly paid job in the city where he purchased a three-bedroom ex-council flat in a predominantly working-class area 'to get on the property ladder'. His background did not make buying a house a taken for-granted certainty. It was a choice informed by bad experiences with lodging and the view that as a single male 'there was no point even me going on the council waiting list because I wouldn't have stood a chance of getting a council house'. He chose his area of residence by the price range he could afford and described himself as managing a significant amount of debt. Alice's lower income (around £11,000 a year plus the earnings from a second five-hour-a-week cleaning job compared to Andrew's £20,000), meant she could not afford to rent or buy privately rented property and she lived with her parents while waiting years for her council house. The few shops and amenities in her village meant she 'has to have' a car and the bankloan to pay for it. Andrew had never learned to drive. Alice's 'one bedroom bungalow' was near family and friends who 'pop in' to see her, and are sometimes invited for meals and Alice 'pops in on' a retired women neighbour who doesn't get out much. Her mother and the friend who feeds the cat both had keys to her house. Andrew, on the other hand, had few local connections since his area of residence is neither where he works nor plays. There is considerable churn among the mostly tenant occupants of his block of flats and he has now been there longer than anyone else. Nobody local held his keys. His social life was organized around a competitive club-based hobby, which he picks up wherever he goes, and on which he spends many hours not only working on his own skills but also in service to the club. This pattern of devotion to a particular leisure activity is much more common among men than women.

Despite these considerable differences, when asked about whether they would ever consider having a lodger and putting up a friend for a few months as a stopgap, both agree on the significance of exclusive use of their home as a site of recovery and restoration for the self that would be seriously undermined if they had to share with anyone else. When Andrew originally bought he presumed he would get a lodger but considerably more progress with renovations would have been needed to realize this idea and over time it became unattractive. For both Andrew and Alice, their home was a barrier to geographical mobility. Andrew would like to move to a 'better' area but he cannot afford to move up the property ladder and will not give up the value he attributes to having his own home. Alice's retired parents are moving back to the area of their roots and would like her to move with them. She has said no. Her home, particularly the security of her council tenancy in interaction with her local social network, albeit reduced by the exit of her parents, is why she had too much to give up.

Among a small minority of our sample of people living alone, the home does not feel like a place for the recovery and restoration of the self. For a very few, even basic routines of self-mainenance go awry as people struggle for energy to cook or eat proper meals or have trouble managing wakefulness and a night's sleep. The most unhappy and socially isolated are exclusively men, and for some the pub is their main source of sociability, and self-medication:

> I don't want to stay staring at the four walls myself every day in life, so that's why I'm out and I end up, seem to end up going out and you end up kind of in the pub after work, things like that. Could I come home? No problem, like just now, yes, but I sort of get ants in my pants, sort of itchy feet, I don't like staying in all the time.
>
> (Anthony, 34, urban, owner occupier ex-social housing)

Concluding remarks

Our UK interviewees, living alone at age 25–44, identified the core advantages of their living arrangement as having control rather than solitude – over space, time, resources and decisions. This individualized, emotionally charged and intangible benefit of their home was often summed up as being able to 'please myself'. But, as Chapter 3 illustrates, the route to being able to 'please myself' is culturally prescribed since a person inevitably becomes too old to respectably live with their parents or share with friends and, in the absence of (or as a result of the collapse of) co-residence in a couple relationship, they have to take responsibility for creating a home as a base for their self if they are to demonstrate independent adulthood. In a society in which home ownership became a pinnacle of socially-accepted ways of establishing this conflated self and home, a home was purchased to 'get on the property ladder' by those whose economic circumstances persuade them to borrow and financial institutions to lend, with barriers to lending set low prior to the recession beginning in 2007. Tasks and costs, which sometimes feel burdensome, are involved in taking sole responsibility for a home as a base on which the self's independence depends (paying rent or mortgages, cooking, cleaning, conducting maintenance and the like). Unshared burdens are the 'disadvantages' flip side of the 'advantages', 'pleasing myself'. Interviewees not only recognized this but also feared that being able to 'please myself' carried the risk of becoming 'set in my ways'. Some accepted that the longer they lived alone the more difficult the compromises would be if they moved in with a partner. A few felt it was already too late and they were already 'too set in my ways'. But this took years and, as Chapter 3 showed, most of those living alone still hoped to live with a partner.

The home for the self can also be a home for others, and self-conscious efforts to sustain an open and friendly home to which family and friends could come and go were the norm among research respondents. Most disliked the idea of lodgers but enjoyed visits from friends and family. The spare room made both hosting visitors and creating homes-from-home easier but its absence was overcome by 'making do' or routing guests into commercial visitor accommodation nearby, depending on resources and conventions of age, class and gender. Those with emotionally close friends and family living at a distance encouraged visits and residence for holidays, having sometimes sought out properties with a spare room with this purpose in mind. Some interviewees in established couple relationships and those who were actively parenting tried to create a home-from-home for their partner or children. Some with mainly local friends used their home to facilitate gatherings. The majority of research respondents lived in comfortable and hospitable homes.

On the other hand, a minority proportion of our research respondents, all men, lived in inhospitable and sometimes uncomfortable homes. For some men with preoccupying health problems, hospitality to others was beyond possibility as life was an unabated struggle for self-survival whether at home or elsewhere. Some men with unhomely homes might be described as outgoing and socially engaged, seeking succour for the self in places, people and activities elsewhere, sometimes anywhere other than their home, which was a site of neglect, everyday domestic disorder and abandoned uncompleted projects. An inhospitable home was not necessarily damaging to a sense of self because sources of social engagement, identity and self validation lay elsewhere. However, ontological insecurity characterized some with thin social worlds and inhospitable homes. A small number of men were unhappy in themselves, at home and also in the world. But note that, with only one possible exception among our research respondents, those who lived in unhomely and inhospitable homes were not seeking to make others unwelcome by creating shrines to the self; rather, they themselves did not feel at home in their homes.

It should not be assumed that for people living alone the more individualized meanings of home (being one's self, privacy, refuge, sanctity, security, ownership and control) drown out the more obviously social and collective meanings of home (conflating home with family, love, intimacy, belonging, origin/roots, community and nation). The home was a visual expression of the self for some more affluent home owners, but others were less focused on the aesthetic of their home and more concerned about the way it expressed and facilitated their relationships. Many homes of people living alone display family and friendship relationships through photographs and objects, or gave material expression to relationships through the memory of assistance rendered in DIY projects, furnishings and fabrics. And for some who live alone, it is not the dwelling that makes their home but its location near family and friends, in a friendly neighbourhood or a particular landscape and community. A small number of interviewees, more often women than men, spoke of a deep 'love' of their home, an intensity of attachment which meant they could not imagine letting go and moving on and which made future co-resident relationships seem less possible. In contrast, some interviewees minimized the personalization of their home, seeing one home as much like another, but in both cases a home could function as a site of recovery and restoration for the self. The subjective experience of living alone varies; an interplay between characteristics of a person, biographical events and socio-economic context inflects how people feel about their home. It is clear that while living alone may encourage practices of 'pleasing myself' that sometimes create resistance to living with others, it does not result in one type of home, and certainly not in the dominance of inhospitable homes or shrines to the self.

5
Living Alone, Consuming Alone?

The previous chapter indicated variation in whether and how people living alone consciously express themselves through their home and showed that practices of 'consuming' the home often remember and display relationships to family and friends. This chapter extends the discussion through a focus on the consumption of food and holidays, topics that provide particularly interesting insight into the interdependence of the self and social relationships, as seen and managed in the subjectivity and social practices of people living alone. The environmental consequences of consumption were not explicitly raised in our study, but the interlinking of high carbon-emitting systems, food and holiday consumption were occasionally spontaneously acknowledged and this is also noted in the chapter.

Across cultures, eating is a fundamental necessity for nurturing the self and is used to sustain and celebrate relationships; for this reason, how people reflect on and manage eating in the context of living alone is both a personal challenge and of particular theoretical interest. Frustrations with 'learning to shop and cook for one' were identified in Eric Klinenberg's study in the United States of living alone (2012, p. 58) and in a large survey conducted in three English cities, 75 per cent of people agreed with the statement 'I dislike eating alone' (Warde and Martens, 2000). The authors of this UK study, Alan Warde and Lydia Martens suggest that the main satisfactions derived from eating 'arise from being in company and sharing food or the occasion' and that the pleasures of eating in company outweigh the satisfactions of being able to choose what to eat, when and where, if eating alone (Warde and Martens, 2000, p. 206). The researchers were particularly interested in 'eating out' in restaurants and cafes, a common leisure practice in most affluent societies: a 'situations where the enjoyment of each person is dependent upon the enjoyment of all' (Warde and Martens, 2000, p. 211). Eating out alone swaps the challenge of shopping and cooking for exposure to the gaze of others, a particular challenge in commercial eating places that are structured to cater for couples, families and groups (Heimtun, 2010).

A research focus on holidays similarly allows insight into how people living alone experience and manage the interdependence of the self and social relationships. In contexts where workers receive paid annual leave from employment, the English language use of the term 'holiday' often refers to this time away from work but it can also mean a more specific form of trips away from home. Workers in Europe typically have more generous paid annual leave than the rest of the world (Mercer, 2011). Full-time workers in the United Kingdom are entitled to 28 days of paid holiday a year and are mass consumers of the main products of the global tourist industry, the 'package holiday'.[1] The neologism 'staycation' emerged in the affluent English-speaking world to suggest practices generating a sense of being away from home on holiday while not actually going far. Advocates of 'staycations' include environmentalists encouraging consciousness of the carbon footprints created by air miles but, in the United Kingdom, the term is more strongly associated with economic recession and government-led campaigns to encourage consumers to spend money in their local economy. Holidays and holiday travel, whether at home in the imagination, locally or long distance, have historically been associated with withdrawal from normal life to enable relaxation and restoration of the self but not necessarily solitude. The contemporary ideal typical image of a 'good holiday' is not a solitary experience. The target market of the conventional package holiday is a family or couple, and research suggests that eating alone in the holiday resort is the ultimate challenge of negotiating such a holiday alone (Heimtun, 2012).

Holiday travel is often dependant on high carbon transport systems, typically car driving or air travel. In many car-dependent societies, people living alone are less likely to have access to a household car than people living with others. In Scotland in 2011, about half of solo-living working-age men had at least one car compared to 85 per cent of the households of men living with others (see Appendix 2, Tables A2.15a). The figures of car ownership for solo women are slightly higher. Car ownership varies significantly between urban and rural areas in the United Kingdom (Table A2.15b). In terms of cars per head, these figures indicate that in urban areas, as a group, those living alone are likely to have a lower carbon footprint for transport than those living with others. However, this is not the case in rural areas where a car is more typically regarded as a necessity. In the United Kingdom, cost is the main explanation offered for not having a car, but, as our study of people living alone illustrates, environmental considerations can also be a factor.

> I don't want to drive. It's all the extra cost. I couldn't afford it. I couldn't afford to charge my customers...the level that I charge them, I would have to put up my prices so much I would end up losing business. So it's counterproductive. So that's why I use public transport, and I've been doing that ever since I set up. So it's worked okay, and I get taxis when I need to. And I really think there's enough cars on the road as it is and I've always had that in my head.
>
> (Geraldine, 43, urban, owner occupier)

The availability of cheap flights radically transformed travel and holiday practices and again this is illustrated in our sample of people living alone, notably without any indications of concerns about the associated carbon footprint or anticipation of this option coming to an end. For example, cheap flights made it possible for Paula to develop the relationship she started through Internet dating (Chapter 3) with a boyfriend living 400 miles away. When explaining this to the interviewer, after remarking 'Thank goodness for BMI Baby' (a cheap flight airline) she added that cheap flights had also transformed her pattern of visiting her mother, a British migrant to southern Europe: 'it's completely changed you know, how I get about but I can get, well I can get a return flight for between £60–70.'

For many people across the globe, holidays are spent with others. In some cultures, holiday and festival are almost synonymous, particularly in poor global south contexts where people have little other claim on holidays; although festivals are religious, community and national celebrations, traditions around them typically also make them days for spending time with and celebrating family, kin and personal relationships. The tourist holidays of citizens of the rich global north often also involve time with family, kin and personal relationships. As Jonas Larsen and co-authors note, twenty-first-century travel that is called tourism now 'often involves connections with, rather than escape from, social relations and the multiple obligations of everyday social life' (Larsen et al., 2007, p. 245). For many people, part of their social life is conducted at a distance and, for some, biographies of mobility mean that their emotionally 'nearest and dearest' do not live near enough for the casual visits that are captured by such phrases as 'popping in' or 'dropping by'. With the very high levels of adoption of mobile phones, both local and distant relationships often involve mediated communication but relationships at a distance also require travel in the reciprocal process of hosting and visiting partners, friends and family at home (Mason, 2004; Urry, 2002). Being on holiday with friends or family potentially intensifies intimacy through constant co-presence and mutual availability, away from routines that normally create separation.

Meals alone, in company and as social events

Living alone, of course, does not typically mean always eating alone. In our UK research, some interviewees described regular meals with friends and family, including standing arrangements visiting another home or entertaining at home on particular days. A small number of research respondents had a pattern of eating that blurred household boundaries through their frequent presence at the table in another home. For example, Ailsa a working-class woman in her late twenties who, after a divorce, returned to live and work near her parents and sister said, 'I can eat out three, four times a week', referring to meals mainly at her parents' but also her sister's house. Research respondents with partners usually eat meals together on the days they are seeing each other. Most research respondents went out for meals with friends or family at least occasionally and sometimes regularly. But living alone typically involves eating alone at least some of and often much of the time. Some of the interviewees in our study found pleasure in cooking for one but most saw this, at best, as a necessary chore and some declared it a lost cause.

Experiences of cooking for one

Many respondents in the UK research itemized difficulties in cooking for one and eating alone. These included complaints about shopping for one when supermarket bargain offers and packages of perishable goods were designed for multiple-person households making them difficult to use without waste. Several also noted the expense of cooking for one. For some respondents, the difficulty of using up fresh ingredients without waste was an added attraction to the processed microwave-cooked meal, a form of food that often also has a high carbon footprint.

I don't like seeing food go to waste either, so I think, 'if it's, you know, a processed dish and it's all in the one dish, then it's easy enough just to chuck in the microwave and then you just eat it and that's it.

(Annabel, 30, urban, council tenant)

Many remained exasperated by the difficulties of scale, unintentionally producing more than they could eat: 'I can cook for huge numbers, everybody, I've had dinner parties for like 12, 14 in my tiny little house and everything, yeah. I can cook for big numbers no problem I just can't cook for me.' (Paula, 36, rural, council tenant)

Some research respondents had developed strategies for what was generally regarded as 'proper cooking', starting 'from scratch' with raw ingredients rather than heating up pre-prepared meals, and a few took pleasure in creating attractive meals for themselves. How people shopped and cooked occasionally also took on board wider political and ethical concerns.

I shop locally. I do try to use the smaller shops round about. There's some particularly good local produce shops nearby which I feel that I should support.

(Megan, 25, urban, owner occupier)

Most of our research respondents felt that 'proper cooking' is more problematic for one person than for a joint meal; there was a general agreement that 'proper cooking' needs less effort or produces a better return for effort when it is a social activity or in the service of others. Some came closer to feeling and acting on the idea that cooking for one is not worth doing. For example, Emily and David relied heavily on the non-cooking options of takeaway hot food or ready prepared food that can be heated up or eaten cold:

It's just heating stuff up...a takeaway is usually chip shop or whatever.

(Emily, 34, urban, council tenant)

I go through times where I can not be bothered. I'll buy...like I'll buy like a mince pie and instead of having potatoes and vegetables and stuff, well I'll just have the mince pie with some bread.

(David, 33, rural, tied housing – a farm cottage owned by his employer)

Making very easy minimum preparation dishes or using an element of prepared food (such as pizzas, or boiling pasta and combining it with a ready-made sauce) was a common strategy and again usually reserved for the self and not when cooking for others.

> I hate cooking for one. I am quite lazy, if I'm cooking for myself it will be the basics but I do have people round for dinner and do do the full Sunday roast.
>
> (Ailsa, 28, urban, owner occupier, ex-social housing)

Minimizing preparation time often also meant minimizing care over what is eaten. For example, Frank compared his experience of eating 'quick' and 'nasty' when living alone with a better quality of food when living as a couple:

> Because you cook for each other. You generally tend to take a bit more time over dinner, rather than just getting in, having something quick and maybe nasty and watching the TV.
>
> (Frank, 36, urban, owner occupier)

Interviews contain many examples of both men and women expressing difficulties in maintaining a healthy diet or a healthy weight because of cooking only for themselves and attributing unhealthy eating habits to living alone. Andrew refers to what health professionals describe as a problem of 'portion control'.

> I always cover my plates like Mount Kilimanjaro sort of thing...I tend probably to eat more, because I eat by myself, where if I was in a, if I was staying at home with my parents or I was in a relationship, I don't think I would be eating as much.
>
> (Andrew, 43, urban, owner occupier)

For a few respondents, eating alone was the epitome of what they did not like about living alone. Harry has already been identified as an extreme case in his unhappiness at living alone; he quickly moved from practical issues to emotionally charged questioning of the value of ever cooking for one.

> You can't shop for, you can't cook for one. You buy trays of meat and then you have to split them into single bags and then freeze them. And when I do go into a downer, when you're trying to cook

and, you feel, well, 'What's the point? What's the point in cooking a meal?' You know, there's nobody there to share it with.

(Harry, 35, urban, council tenant)

However, the potential negative emotions and difficulties of cooking and eating alone were set aside, some or all of the time, by most research respondents. Some had developed strategies for overcoming the sense of disproportionate daily effort in 'proper cooking' for one. Several interviewees used their freezer to store portions of batch cooked 'proper cooking'.

I'd say the last year or two, my focus has been more on buying the ingredients to make something, rather than pre-packaged meals. And making a curry or a chilli or something like that and freezing it as well.

(Brian, 42, rural, owner occupier)

Focus on the difficulties for cooking for one and eating alone seemed to fade when a weekly routine involved a blend of cooking for and with others as well as eating alone. Such a blend was more common for those who had regularly visiting partners and/or children. The practice of 'proper cooking' was often more established in these circumstances. Among the few respondents who had achieved the enjoyment of cooking for one, Sunil (38, urban, private sector renter), regularly cooked as part of his job and on days off would enjoy making the same sorts of food at home. Julie, on the other hand, had used cooking as a way of detaching herself from her work:

I had a really stressful job when I worked at [previous employment] but I'd always come home and cook my dinner because it took my mind off of the stress.

(Julie, 33, urban, owner occupier)

Cooking for others

Entertaining at home was often regarded as an occasion for 'proper cooking' and making 'from scratch' and was, therefore, associated with having or developing cooking skills. Cooking for friends was often reciprocated, which further reduced eating at home alone. Patterns of eating with parents and siblings were sometimes asymmetric with family homes more often acting as host. The frequency of cooking for others varied from several times a week, among those with such regular arrangements as children staying for weekends or routinely visiting partners, or through several times a month entertaining friends or family to the very occasional or never. Consistent with the pattern described by Graham Allan (1979, 1989, 1996), some of the more affluent research respondents were more likely to regularly entertain groups of friends for 'dinner'. Both Jake and Megan, for example, are in the same profession:

> I like hosting people for dinner. It's not always a huge success but I do try. And similarly my friends are like that, especially my friend who lives nearby.
>
> (Jake, 28, urban, owner occupier)

> I quite like to cook, and I often have groups of friends up for dinner.
>
> (Megan, 25, urban, owner occupier)

Many research respondents, including some in middle-class occupations, restricted their dinners to a smaller inner circle.

> I mean if I'm cooking something new I always like doing that, I always like having people round for dinner, try something new...Just my mum and dad mainly, and my pal [name]. We like cooking for each other. We're both Taureans. I think we quite like our food. [Laughs]. So we cook for each other as well.
>
> (Julie, 33, urban, owner occupier)

When everyday life involved only occasional and sporadic 'proper cooking', as was the case for many interviewees, not surprisingly this sometimes also meant either lack of confidence in or rudimentary cooking skills or both. Rachel attributed her lack of confidence in entertaining to not doing 'proper cooking' for herself: 'it's a confidence thing. I don't really like...because I don't cook a lot for myself and I just kind of think "Oh I don't really..." I'm probably not a very good cook, but...sort of occasionally I'll try things out on my friends, but it's got to be my close friends that will...I feel comfortable with'. She also reported another solution, entertaining that did not involve proper cooking, her friendship group circulated between each other's houses for evenings of easy cook food like 'pizza night' or 'nacho Mexican night'. However, this practice had not been sustained: 'I think it's just with lifestyles, and we've just been busy doing things, you know' (Rachel, 31, rural, owner occupier).

David acknowledged he has not yet 'mastered getting the timings right' in his cooking:

> You go to the potatoes after twenty minutes and they're still hard in the middle and you think, 'Oh, turn them up a bit more, right, the potatoes will be another five minutes', by which time everybody's here [his parents] and sort of 'Are the tatties not ready yet?'... And then you'll open the oven and the pie'll be starting to go black on the top and you're, oh (groan).
>
> (David, 33, rural, tied housing – a farm cottage owned by his employer)

For some, the feeling that cooking involves huge amounts of time and effort meant that going out to eat with friends was strongly preferred to entertaining at home, particularly if this could be done 'just as cheaply' with each person paying for herself or himself, rather than the host bearing the cost of the meal: 'the year when I first moved in I had friends over. But I find it such a faff. It's like just, and it's probably just as cheap now to go out and eat' (Alexandra, 41, rural, owner occupier ex-social housing).

Eating out alone

Like the Norwegian women reported in the study by Bente Heimtun, research respondents reported that being alone in cafes and lunch time venues was not as difficult as eating out alone in the evening and that going to a restaurant alone is not something they would choose to do.

> At lunchtime it's not so bad. I don't know you don't feel so strange at lunchtime eating alone but for like dinner it's very strange. You get weird looks. [laughter] Or pitiful looks, it's like 'Oh what a shame'.
>
> (Alice, 41, rural, council tenant)

Whether the feared looks of pity are imagined or real makes no difference to the feeling of being socially excluded from the normal clientele and pigeonholed into an identity of 'sad and lonely'.

As UK survey data has suggested (Warde and Martens, 2000) both men and women found eating out alone difficult. Ray, a gay man, enjoyed sitting alone over a coffee and reading the newspaper if he was out shopping during the day but if he wanted food in the evening when he was in town then he would restrict himself to a gay café: 'I'd just go there. Just maybe grab, you know, a burger or macaroni cheese or something like that' (Ray, 44, urban, owner-occupier).

The main gender difference was in the use of pubs. Evening pub eating might have been an option for some men but was not such an easy option for women; it is still relatively remarkable for a woman to spend time in a pub alone and quite unremarkable for a man to do so. Rachel's account suggests that this remains as true of the rural pub acting as the main social hub for a community, as it is for anonymous urban pubs, even if men's control of the pub as a social space is more muted than it was when Ann Whitehead (1976) wrote her famous article about gender relations in rural Herefordshire.

> Dad asked me about that because he thought I would go to the [village pub] myself quite often, just because it's a local, you know, walk up and the food's great, and you just sit there and it's quite a cosy place. You don't feel as if everyone is watching you, but I just don't feel comfortable doing that. I feel like a bit of a loner, that people must think 'Oh, she's got no friends and she's sitting by herself'. But, it's not the case, it's just that that's ... I would sort of think that other people are ... would find it peculiar, do you know, that a single girl's sitting by themselves. So I don't.

She contrasted this with having learned to quash the fear of the pitying gaze of others when she was staying overnight on a business trip. The work purpose of the trip provided the script she needed to reply to the question and assumptions she 'heard' in her imagining or observing of the gaze of others.

> I don't mind it then, because I know I've got a purpose, but I guess going to the local pub I feel a bit kind of like, you know, Billy-No-Mates sitting there. So ... but on business I'll, you know, I'll go and have dinner and just take a book with me, or a magazine [...] in my twenties, I used to worry about that in the same way that I worry about going to the local pub. But now I just kind of think 'No, I'm a business-person and I'm', you know, 'I'm going to sit and have a nice meal and enjoy it', you know. So it's not a problem there.
>
> (Rachel, 31, rural, owner occupier)

Holidays and travel

For those in employment, periods of annual leave are blocks of time that can be 'spent' in multiple ways. Recreation, leisure and sociability might compete with neglected domestic jobs at home that are solitary rather than consolidating social relationships. A minority proportion of interviewees spent all of their annual leave at home and many spent some of it at home. Nobody used the term staycation and it seemed that time spent at home was more often a mix of catching up on domestic and DIY chores and whatever form of relaxation was normally enjoyed at home than planning extraordinary daytrips and happenings. Some had particular reasons to stay at home, including the need to advance DIY projects or the desire for more time to take pleasure in relaxing in their home. Elspeth (43, urban, owner occupier), for example, said she liked to stay at home because 'I don't get home that often!', and that going away would be 'like a busman's holiday' since her job involved travelling all over the United Kingdom, often being away for several nights in the week. Some stated that they could not afford a going-away holiday in the year of the interview or, in some cases, that such holidays were generally unaffordable.

The typical form of going-away holiday was not based on spending time alone but involved either going alone to visit friends or family or going to a tourist destination with friends or family. Jake describes such a typical mixture of visiting, for him, contained within the United Kingdom and Ireland: 'I will basically use up my holidays by visiting the family, or taking a long weekend to visit friends in Dublin or London or whatever.' (Jake, 28, urban, owner occupier) But many people's travel follows the paths of transnational relationships across larger distances. Thus Christine's (43, urban, owner-occupier) typical holiday was to 'go and see my sister in Canada', and Hannah's (44, urban, owner occupier) to her sister in the United States. For those with partners, their holidays were typically with their partners or with their partner combined with friends or family, and partners widen the web of transnational relationships: 'My girlfriend takes me to America because obviously her, her family are in America' (Stephen, 41, urban, private sector renter). While the visit is typically about sustaining relationships combined with tourism, sometimes the diaspora is the tourist destination, in Megan's case turning them into effective kin:

> I went and met up with family that I've never met before ... who had immigrated and often third generation from those original emigrants and it was very interesting and I met lots of different types of people within my own family, but we've kept really close links with one family in particular and they came over this year in October and spent time here which was really, really nice. So, you know, there's a sort of reciprocity now established.
>
> (Megan, 25, urban, owner-occupier)

Annabel (30, urban, council tenant) exemplifies the possible mix of friendship-based holidays: she described a visit to see friends in their home setting in the United Kingdom, a short break away with friends to a UK holiday resort and a planned longer overseas trip to a tourist destination.

> My holiday time I'll catch up with other friends as well, I've got friends up in [a part of rural Scotland], so I'll tend to go up there. Yeah, that's a good opportunity to go up and see them when I'm off on annual leave and plus it gives me a wee break as well. [...] a group of my friends, we went to Blackpool, I think it was last year a wee psychic weekend! We all got extremely drunk and it's actually the ones that I'm going to Egypt with now.

Involved parents typically prioritized holidays with their children: 'It's almost always going away either with ... well, predominantly it's with the children, and I have gone away with my partner, and I guess I go down and visit friends who are maybe down south and stay with them for very short holidays' (Abigail, 44, urban, owner-occupier).

For most research respondents some standard forms of holiday, visiting a beach resort or travelling to tourist destinations, are not contemplated as a possibility alone. They would only be undertaken if it was arranged to go with friends or family or they had a partner to go with or children to take. Several interviewees had reflected on why it was that they had never 'been on holiday' alone. Mark commented:

> Do you know, whenever I was single I always tried to find holidays to go away on, on your own, and they're actually really hard to find, so any time I've been single I've just not went on holiday. So, yeah, I always go away with other people, basically.
>
> (Mark, 33, urban, owner occupier)

It was only a minority subset of people who said like Alistair 'I like to go away myself', and most had consciously worked at developing ways of enjoying going away on holiday alone. Like Mark, some who had never done it felt they perhaps ought to be able to. Some expressed the view that they ought to be sufficiently self reliant or that it might be somehow 'good' as if for strength of character to go away alone. And, indeed, 'a sense of achievement' was the phrase used by one woman who had done it: 'going on holiday on your own actually has a real sense of achievement, you know, it's quite liberating' (Lauren,

37, urban, owner occupier). However, although agreeing that it was 'brave' and 'good' to go alone, for some, it was an experience not to be repeated.

> But the reason I went on my own was me and [name – ex-partner] were kind of going through a bad patch and he had left and I was just fed up and I wanted to go to Florence. So I booked to go away for a few nights. And I did it because I felt, well I'm going to be on my own anyway and I don't, I shouldn't have to rely on people to go away. And when I was there, you know, it felt brave and stuff and it was good. I enjoyed it because I went. There was lots of galleries and things. But I wouldn't choose to do it again.
>
> (Julie, 33, urban, owner occupier)

The most common strategy involved identifying a way of going alone while feeling assured that the time would not be spent alone. Craig (43, urban, owner-occupier) had had the unusual practice of always going back to the same place and hence had built up a social network that he returned to each year: 'so it wasn't really like I was holidaying on my own'. Gay men had an advantage because they could choose destinations with a known gay scene. Ray had skipped having a holiday in the year he was interviewed because of 'financial constraints' but he recalled his last holiday:

> I went to Grand Canaria, typical gay haunt which I quite enjoyed. I'd been there before, I'd been there with my partner but I went by myself... Yes. I mean I know the haunts and, it was a bit sad in a way because sometimes, you know, when I was there I sort of, I ended up in places I'd been with my partner and that was, you know, bringing things a little bit home to me and thinking, oh it's quite sad, but I soon got over that, you know, it's just, you know. Yeah I mean it was nice to, yes, I mean it was again, it was quite a selfish holiday on my own and I enjoy my own company, and I don't, some people just would not contemplate going on holiday with themselves, that doesn't faze me at all.
>
> (Ray, 44, urban, owner-occupier)

While the gay scene offers possibilities of casual sexual encounters and friendly sociability, a degree of social effort and presentation of self is necessarily involved. How much social contact Ray actually had on holiday is not explored in any depth but it was sufficient for him to consider the holiday a success, albeit given that he 'enjoys his own company'. Harry, also gay, had tried an overseas holiday apparently without seeking out the scene and declared it a disaster. His identification of 'the Greek night thing' as the low point echoes other descriptions of the evening meal as the pinnacle of feeling alone and excluded in the tourist resort setting.

> I did try. It was a week's holiday to Corfu at the end of the season. And because you were getting no single supplement, it was a twin room with en suite and a fridge and a balcony, and I thought 'oh, this is luxury'. But it was the longest week. I actually lost a camera, as well, because I was just so stressed out. I went on the evening, the Greek night thing, but I just felt so... [Pause]. I like the safety of another person.
>
> (Harry, 35, urban, council tenant)

Commercially organized group holidays were used as one way of going alone but not being alone, by those who had sufficient resources to pay. Club-based activity holidays and activity holiday hotspots offered variants of this strategy. Neil (40, urban, owner-occupier) described himself as going 'by myself on group holidays' either sailing or mountaineering. Geraldine (43, urban, owner-occupier) went on holidays through her walking club and Lauren (37, urban, owner occupier) had made the switch from going with her diving club to going on a tour guided holiday alone: 'the Dive Club I joined went to Egypt as well and I really thought I should actually go and see Egypt properly you know, with they pyramids and the whole, all that kind of stuff and so in November I went on my own again, just joined up with you know, one of these companies that you go and you can be on your own or with somebody else and just join in basically.'

Some interviewees went alone with no organizational support but, because their destination was a socially organized activity hot spot, like the ski-resorts that were Andrew's (43, urban, owner-occupier ex-social housing) destination, they provide a structure that enabled meeting and having a common basis for communication with others. Hobby activities that are predominantly solitary often also have such hotspots. Alfie (41, rural, owner-occupier ex-council house) participates in motor cycle rallies and when he goes holidays and weekend trips alone on his bike he is on the lookout for other enthusiasts. A campsite could be described as a camping enthusiasts hot spot, and Alexandra (41, rural, owner-occupier ex-council house), who felt she should be able to go on holiday alone and had had other failed attempts, found she enjoyed camping holidays alone in Scotland.

The kind of commercially organized holidays that enable meeting other people are unaffordable for many people living alone. But there are free or low cost alternative forms of organization like the website sofa surfing movement and Tommy (43, urban, council tenant) was using his friendship network to identify ways of having a cheap holiday: 'Well I went [to Amsterdam] for my birthday and a friend here has a got a friend who lives over there, so I went and stayed with him.' Simon was one of the very few interviewees who presented himself as an 'independent traveller' who sets off with guidebook and language skills as his key aids:

> Well, I'm going to actually be starting next month learning German through the OU, and I do like reading the Rough Guide Books and I do like having to get other places to go to, a wee bit kind of off the beaten tracks. So I do like my old travel.
>
> (Simon, 31, urban, owner occupier)

Christmas as the 'family holiday'

In countries with a Christian tradition, Christmas is an annual child-and-family focused holiday that all are aware of. The phrase Festive Season is typically used loosely in everyday speech not to refer to the specific religious calendar dates but to mean the period from a day or two before Christmas Day until the beginning of January shortly after 'seeing in the New Year'. However, Christmas is typically seen as the main event, even in Scotland with its now much marketed New Year traditions that once seemed more collectively respected than Christmas.[2] Media pronouncements of the number of shopping days to Christmas, the practice of adorning public spaces with Christmas decorations and the playing of Christmas themed musak in shops and shopping malls, creates constant visual and aural reminders of the expectation of participation. Christmas is also a festival with a global reach which the anthropologist Daniel Miller (1993a) suggests is facilitated by its complementary relationship to the New Year and its syncretic mix of borrowed traditions and inventions (Barnett, 1954). Miller notes that in Trinidad, Christmas is celebrated with equal intensity by Christians, Muslims and Hindus, with the latter treating it as a continuation of Divali (1993b); another essay in the same collection describes the take up of Christmas by young adults in Japan (Moeran and Skov, 1993).

Much Christmas imagery conflates Christmas with home, family and the family meal and, at the same time, the Christian Christmas is a time when the charitable spirit is supposed to reach out to the homeless, those without family or alone. For those who are living alone, the charitable messages suggesting pity of those who are alone express their problem with Christmas as an inescapable version of the challenge few take up of eating out alone under the gaze of a restaurant full of families and couples. One much repeated fictional ideal-typical representation is the home of Bob Cratchit's family gathered together for a meal on Christmas day that solo-living, Christmas-despising Scrooge is forced to observe and learn from in Charles Dickens's *Christmas Carol.* The dominance of home, family and gendered domesticity in how living people celebrate Christmas was documented in detail by sociologists in the third study of 'Middletown', a Midwestern city in the United States, in 1978 (Caplow et al., 1982). Gift giving was overwhelmingly from older to younger kin and women did much more of the Christmas shopping and wrapping. At least two thirds of social gatherings were home and kin based and the authors note that 'there was remarkably little interaction with unrelated friends and neighbors' around Christmas with the exception of 'office and shop parties' (Caplow et al., 1982, p. 384). Several decades later in the twenty-first century and despite considerable change in family life and gender, Christmas is still frequently referred to as a 'family time' and particularly a time for children and domestic divisions of labour mean it still involves much more work for women than men. The pattern of women doing most of the work of Christmas cards and Christmas shopping as 'kin keepers' (Di Leonardo, 1987) has persisted and is consistent across a number of national contexts. The authors of a Belgian study conclude, 'as part of the work of kinship, gift giving is (still) women's labour' (Sinardet and Mortelmans, 2009, p. 139). Do people who are living on their own take part in the family Christmas, and particularly people living alone at ages more conventionally associated with the stage of bringing up a family? How is this then experienced? For those who remain alone at Christmas, is this a welcome escape, social exclusion or social isolation? Is the pattern different for those who are living alone because they have never partnered, from those who are divorced or separated from a partner or living apart from their children? Do the kin-keeping aspects of Christmas mean that women living on their own have less leeway for opting out than men living on their own?

A sentimental focus on family and domesticity is not the only story of Christmas in frequent public circulation. Social science and popular commentary routinely document as inevitable contradictions, tensions and disappointments of 'family time' at Christmas. Some commentators note that the mythic or sacred version of happy families created by Christmas cannot be matched in reality (Kuper, 1993); that the role playing and memory making of the moment is incompatible with any depth of intimacy, other than nostalgia (Gillis, 2004); others document the ambivalence, stress and conflict emergent from enforced ritualized time together, and the associated financial strains, burdens of domestic work, and bodily discomforts of overindulgence (Bittman and Pixley, 1997; Löfgren, 1993; Searle-Chatterjee, 1993). Writing about domestication and women's work in household organization at Christmas, Sheena Vachhani and Alison Pullen (2011) suggest that 'paradoxes of domestic oppression and dreams exist hand in hand. Christmas becomes a space of both idyllic connection and oppression' (2011, p. 813). Does the alternative discourse of the unreal, over-commercialized, exhausted and quarrelsome family Christmas create more room for a merry Christmas at home alone?

The dominant picture that emerges from talking to our UK research respondents about Christmas is the pervasive and unquestioning acceptance of Christmas as time to be spent with 'family'. For most, this meant going to their parent's or parents' household for the Christmas day family meal or whichever other family household was hosting their parent or parents for the Christmas meal. For those living some distance away this meant a holiday visit of several nights away from home. In some families, the locus of the Christmas family meal had moved down to the respondent's own generation, usually, reflecting continuity in gender patterns, to the family household of a sister but in the case of a few women research respondents, to their own household. The Christmas meal event was largely orchestrated by female kin and the meal most often cooked by them. In some cases the Christmas meal cycled around a small number of family households in turn. The day sometimes incorporated wider kin but the parents and siblings, nieces and nephews and, if they were alive, grandparents, were the key respondents. There were, of course, many variations on this theme that continued to exemplify the general rule of spending time with close family. Emily (31, urban, council tenants) had no living parents or siblings and she spent Christmas with her cousin. Jake's (28, urban, owner occupier) brother was absent from the Christmas family meal with parents because he now had 'his own family'. Interviewees who were active parents prioritized being with their children as the focal point to their celebration of Christmas and for some this meant going to their ex-partner's house for a block of time, which might or might not include participation in the Christmas meal. Those with partners might go separate ways and prioritized time with their own family or organized their time doing family visits as a couple. There were different ways of breaking up the day, sometimes clearly segregating the day into parts and allocating one part for 'the whole family' to be together. In Daisy's (30, urban, owner occupier) family, Christmas dinner was not the centre piece of what she described as 'a family routine', which consisted of gathering at 'gran's house' for the morning until lunchtime when people dispersed to have Christmas dinner at their own houses. Nevertheless, the majority pattern among the interviewees living alone, across class backgrounds and regardless of sexual orientation, was to participate in upholding the normative view of Christmas as 'family time'.

The obligatory character of being with family at Christmas was occasionally remarked on. Neil followed up saying 'I go back to my parents' in reply to what he did at Christmas with 'I have no choice in that by the way.' Referring to the period after he graduated he added: 'No, no. When I was unemployed my mum used to send me the money for the train' (Neil, 40, urban, owner occupier). However, there was no obvious will to rebellion against the weight of expectation and the conventionality of the particular family 'tradition'. Only a very few of the already small minority who spent Christmas alone or working were exceptions who were trying to do something other than a family Christmas. Ray liked the idea of having Christmas on his own and considered opting out of the family Christmas but rejected this because he did not want to disappoint his nine-year-old nephew:

Christmas I would normally go to my sister's and my mother would be there, so there's a small family get together. Yes although this Christmas funnily enough I didn't really want to go. I would have, I've never really spent, well apart from when I lived with my partner, I never really spent Christmas in my own home alone and this Christmas I just thought, look I just want to spend Christmas at home by myself doing my own thing maybe having some nice food, chilling out, nice wine, watching the television or a DVD and just having a nice relaxing time alone because sometimes Christmas with the family can be a little bit fraught. However, my little nephew, who's nine, for some bizarre reason is very fond of his uncle Ray.

(Ray, 44, urban, owner occupier)

When Christmas is seen in the context of the whole festive season the emphasis on family is balanced by New Year as the time for friends. Again there are variations on the theme and there is often no equivalent

New Year's Day meal of friends that is as honoured as the Christmas meal but making particular efforts to 'catch up with' friends was a part of the holiday for most.

> Christmas, I generally spend Christmas just with my sister, and visit family and friends, you know, right round the holiday period. And New Year everybody comes here. I have seventeen for dinner...It's mainly friends actually, that come – my sister comes, and the rest of it is my sister-in-law, my brothers and the rest of it's friends. It's just friends locally.
>
> (Elspeth, 43, urban, owner occupier)

Also, when the parent generation had been residentially stable, the visit back to the family home for Christmas created the possibility of catching up with school friends also paying their visit. Jake describes this:

> Well it's always the same pretty much. I go home and stay with my parents and we sort of do the same sort of stuff. My parents cook, my mum cooks Christmas dinner. And my brother has his own family now so they do their own Christmas. Then we do the rounds and visit [interruption here] Yes. I mean I spend my kind of week or so living with my parents and just visiting friends and family around home, and a lot of my friends who are from home, we all live all over the place, but we generally co-ordinate our holidays to spend time so we can visit each other at that time. We can see each other at Easter, one week in the summer and Christmas, we always make a point of being home so we can all socialise with each other, and catch up.
>
> (Jake, 28, urban, owner-occupier)

The interviewees who spent Christmas day alone were not necessarily opting out of the family Christmas. Most either had no local family and considered it impractical to get to wherever family lived or had seriously fractured relationships, which meant that those who were local might as well not be. Men who are fathers and have no contact with their child or children were over represented in the latter category. Anthony (34, urban, owner occupier ex-social housing) for example said his ex-partner would not allow him to see his son: 'She doesn't want me to see him in his life'; and of his mother: 'She's about quarter of an hour walk away, but it's sort of the relationship we've got, she could be at the other end of the world.' He did not see himself as celebrating Christmas because 'I see it as a family thing', and he had no family he was able to celebrate with.

Men with very fractured family relationships sometimes also had very few friends. This was not typically the case of those who had no local or easy-to-travel-to family. Nevertheless, the family focus of Christmas can make it difficult for even the friendship rich to feel socially included. Sunil, a migrant with no local family, chose to work on Christmas day. As well as explaining that he was happy to do this, that workmates were grateful that he and not they were working that day and it gave him double pay, he also explained that he felt unable to take up an invitation to intrude on somebody else's family: 'I would rather be working than being home on my own you know...My friend invited me, a few of my friends are invited me, but it's a family time you know, I don't want to be in the way' (Sunil 38, urban, private sector renter). Most of the interviewees who were working at Christmas had no choice and would rather be celebrating a family Christmas. Geraldine was one of the very few respondents who enjoyed her Christmas on her own without having the experience framed by absence of or longing for a family day. An important pleasure was cooking herself a delicious meal, which she could still remember and describe in detail. Nevertheless, her day involved significant amounts of family contact through phone calls to Ireland and America as well as social contact through going to church.

Concluding remarks

Those who live alone should not be caricatured as hyper consumers or celebrants of consuming alone; people who live alone exemplify a wide range of consumption practices, including the frugal and modest. While not wishing to deny that if people living alone were to become increasingly affluent as well as a growing population, the consequences are likely to be in the wrong direction in terms of carbon footprint, but even this cannot be taken for granted (Williams, 2007). Among working-age adults, the larger incidence of living without a car among those living alone contradicts the assumption that an increase in this living arrangement will necessarily escalate an average per capita carbon footprint. In this age group, people living alone are more concentrated in urban areas than their peers living in families; they are also more likely to occupy flats and rely on public transport or walking for mobility. As Eric Klinenberg has noted (2012), densely populated urban environments with amenities and services within walkable distance provide more environmentally sustainable ways of city living than living in the suburbs and commuting for many daily activities, common practice of many family households. It has been suggested in the United

Kingdom that with appropriate planning intervention the growth of one-person households in or near to city centres might help regenerate deprived inner city areas (Bennett and Dixon, 2006). Although those living alone in rural areas are only marginally less likely to have a car than those living with others, and environmental politics are not typically a motivating factor for the much larger proportion desisting from urban car ownership, if the United Kingdom were to follow the United States in developing politicized movements of resistance to stereotypes of singles and those living alone, perhaps environmental politics could become their ally. It would both debunk stereotypes of living alone and encourage pro-environmentalism, if those who do so without a car were celebrated for the lower carbon aspects of their lifestyles in the cultural imagery of living alone.

The inappropriateness of stereotyping those who live alone as self-absorbed, self-pleasing consumers is illustrated by the difficulties those without regularly visiting partners or children report in finding pleasure in meals and holidays. Most people living alone do not diverge from cultural norms designating the practices of eating and taking holidays as sociable activities that can only be really enjoyable with others. Not all who live alone are 'single' or childless, and those with partners and/or children living elsewhere often had regular arrangements of cooking for and eating with their partner and/or children and saw holidays as opportunities to spend time with them. Lack of success in cooking for one tended to reinforce lack of confidence in cooking for others; those who frequently cooked for and ate with others were often less troubled cooking for one. Outside these circumstances, few cultivate the pleasures of eating alone. Many conceded that they could not find joy in cooking 'proper food' for one, that they would never eat out alone, except perhaps at lunchtime or in a cafe, or go on holiday to a tourist resort alone. Scholars of domestic consumption document that, for most householders, many routines of everyday domestic life are integrated into high carbon systems, such as practices of heating and washing (Shove, 2003; Shove and Ward, 2002). However, there are possibilities of lowering environmental impacts while living alone suggested in interviewees' self-conscious accounts of the struggles over food and meals. The exceptional few who have learned how to enjoy a daily routine of cooking themselves 'proper meals' from fresh ingredients are likely to have lower carbon footprint food than the majority unhappily eating 'quick' and 'nasty' meals. Yet their situation is one that more people living alone might be more motivated to achieve if they were convinced that a socially important 'more' was at stake than feeding themselves.

The discussion of Christmas illustrates the conventionality of the majority of people living alone, men and women, straight and gay, in prioritizing family at Christmas. If there was leeway to opt out it was not generally taken up and escape from the family Christmas did not seem to be attractive to either men or women. Some interviewees were engaged in paid employment through the Christmas holiday but most were not deliberately seeking escape from the family Christmas. Very few of the respondents spent Christmas day at home alone and the overwhelming majority adhered to the script that Christmas day is a family day and spent time with family. In many cases this still involved going back to the parental home but, even when interviewees' parents had explicitly communicated that this was an obligatory requirement, rather than being burdensome, this was accepted without resentment or a sense of being infantilized. Gender differences in the practical work of Christmas persist and meant that women interviewees were more likely to be practically involved. The core group who spent Christmas alone were socially isolated men, in disadvantaged circumstances of ill health and low income. For them, it was not an opting out but a reflection of a more general absence of intimacy with family. The image of a pleasant day of private pleasure at home alone, enjoying some delicious food and perhaps a nice wine, was occasionally articulated as an alternative ideal to the acknowledged stresses of the family Christmas, but only very exceptionally was this actually taken up.

Part III
Networks, Community and Place

Introduction

The rise in living alone is often treated as if it is symptomatic of a dislocation from moorings to place and people of origin, exemplifying social processes of individualization. Part III addresses the evidence concerning the attachments of solo-living men and women to such moorings. Those who live alone are at risk of being caricatured as disconnected from others, with weaker links to family, friends and community networks, and higher levels of social exclusion. Indeed, the proportion of one-person households is sometimes used in academic research as an indicator of isolation and lack of social cohesion: Reher's (1998) analysis of family systems in western Europe, for example, uses this as a proxy for loneliness, identified as one of the most important social problems in 'weak-family' societies (see also Dorling et al., 2008). Yet, to date there has been relatively little empirical attention paid to the social networks and relationships of working-age men and women living alone, a population that overlaps with but is not exactly the same as those who are 'single' (but see Bien et al., 1992; Jamieson et al., 2009; Klinenberg, 2012; Wasoff et al., 2005). Chapters 3–5 have presented evidence of working-age people living alone while playing a part in the lives of others and with an interest in family life, as well as demonstrating heterogeneity and some counter narratives. Many, for example, are oriented to partners or potential partners and children, have hospitable and friendly homes, have people-oriented holidays and family Christmases. Part III looks more broadly at relationships within localities of residence and wider social networks, whether local or geographically dispersed, across a range of evidence, including our UK study. Are the social networks of those who live alone distinct from those who live with others, and if so in what ways and with what consequences?

A sense of isolation or inability to sustain durable and meaningful relationships is also often central to media representations of those living alone.[1] What are the impacts of such representations on those who are living alone, and how are their views shaped on continuing to do so over the longer term? We have already emphasized that such representations fail to address the heterogeneity evident among those who live alone. Chapter 6 begins by considering empirical work on older people living alone, prior to exploring various factors that shape the diverse range of social networks of the working-age men and women living alone in our UK study.

Those who live alone exemplify the separation of living arrangements and social worlds, enabling focused consideration of the factors that shape social integration and social isolation. Contrasting stereotypes of solo-living as either the domain of highly mobile careerists, implying fleeting instrumental relationships, or the socially isolated, suggest different factors that underpin the patterns in their social networks. Research on relationships over distance (Holmes, 2004, 2006) mobility (Kaufman, 2002; Kesserling and Vogl, 2008; Larsen et al., 2006; Lück and Schneider, 2010; Urry, 2002, 2007; Viry et al., 2009; Viry, 2012) and on transnational families (for example, Baldassar et al., 2007; Goulbourne et al., 2010; Wessendorf, 2010) provides evidence that casts doubt on the former stereotype. But is there a genre of personal community among those living alone that can be understood as distinct in ways that are consequential at either the societal or individual level? Might living alone be understood as indicative of a preference for solitude, now more of an option for those so minded? Does the lack of companionship 'on tap' mean that those living alone are likely to be more proactive in seeking it out? And are there constraints that limit possibilities for social interaction for those who wish for more? Gender has long been considered an important factor that shapes social interactions, with women's identity particularly associated with the expressive functions of managing relationships, traditionally in the family setting (see Widmer, 2004 for a review): does this still apply to men and women not living in co-residential partnerships?

In the subsequent chapter we consider attachment to place and relationships with proximate others and their potential to create a sense of belonging or embeddedness in a particular locality. Here we develop earlier discussion in considering the role that type of locality plays, whether urban or rural, in shaping the social networks of those living alone. We also consider mobility and residential history. Both the tradition of community studies and new studies of mobility suggest the complexity of being 'local' and the variable salience of being an established or recent migrant, a returner or someone who has never left the locality (Allan and Phillipson, 2008; Crow, 2008; Larsen et al., 2005; Savage et al., 2005). There is also a long-established sociological literature documenting class differences in the extent and character of personal networks (Allan, 1979, 1996, Taylor 2012). We consider the interplay between and influence of gender, class and residential history on social connectedness and their relationship to place. As we note in previous chapters, a body of social commentary suggests that place loses significance with rapidly expanding access to mobile phones, internet technologies and rapid transport, facilitating new ways of interacting across constraints of distance, including the formation and maintenance of social relationships that are not tied to a particular place. Indeed, Eric Klinenberg (2012) has suggested that this has been a factor enabling the increase in people living alone in the United States, although it is important to remain mindful of geographical, generational and socio-economic differences in access to such technologies. In this chapter we address the significance of relationships 'at a distance' for the social connectedness of people living alone.

Social capital

Social capital as a concept has been used to refer to people's social networks and relationships as a resource, engendering trust, norms of reciprocity and social solidarity (for example, Coleman, 1988; Putnam 1995, 2000; Putnam et al., 2003). The concept is given a more critical inflection by Pierre Bourdieu (1997) drawing on a Marxist intellectual tradition to analyse the deployment of social capital along with other forms of capital in repertoires of domination and the reproduction of class inequality, an analysis extended to discussions of gender (see Edwards et al., 2003; Fine, 2001; Franklin, 2004, 2005, 2007). Robert Putnam distinguished 'bonding' and 'bridging' social capital, echoing an earlier distinction between strong and weak ties (Granovetter, 1973); the former tends to bind people into close-knit groups but the latter makes links between groups, giving people access to more diverse social worlds. The concept resonated with policy-makers interested in how social connections and participation might deliver public benefits: across economic performance, reduced crime, improved health and well-being (Halpern, 2005). Political emphasis on the importance of social participation in economic recovery was evident in the policy idea of the 2010 UK Conservative Party manifesto, the 'Big Society', and in the Obama administration 'United We Serve' scheme to foster volunteer service in the United States.[2] An OECD working paper on healthy ageing, for example, links increasing social capital to enabling older people to remain longer in the labour force and delaying their need for longer-term care (Oxley, 2009). There is a risk of over simplifying, however, as if any or all 'social capital' is of equal worth; research on older age, for example, shows that social networks vary in their resilience and ability to sustain support to older people in ways that might not be easily reduced to recipes for 'bridging' and 'bonding' (Wenger, 1984, 1997; Wenger et.al., 2007).

Recent years have seen an extensive range of empirical studies addressing the relationship between social networks and individual well-being across various disciplines. Living arrangement, however, has generally not been fore-grounded as a category of analysis in research on social connectedness. An exception is the focus in social gerontology on the associations between living arrangement and well-being in later life.

Capturing social connectedness

Attempts at assessing social connectedness seek to understand the impact of changing social conditions, including waves of urbanization, migration and new possibilities of virtual connectivity that modify people's social relationships to and within localities, addressing recurrent concerns about social disengagement. Barry Wellman and his colleagues (2001, 2006) and Raine and Wellman (2012) describe 'networked individualism' as emerging from shifts over time from 'door-to-door' (spatially compact and densely knit) communities, to 'place-to-place' (household to household via landline phone calls and emails) to 'person-to-person' (personalized mobile wireless worlds in which each person engineers his or her own ties and networks) communities. Putnam's work focused on civic engagement, based on evidence from the United States on declining trends in participation in membership of clubs, voluntary associations and community organizations. While participation in such organizations may be an important way in which people can develop supportive social networks, Putnam had less to say about the processes of development of social capital within more informal associations, though he made claims about the 'loosening of bonds' within the family, both extended and nuclear (1995, p. 73). Attempts at researching social integration have typically shifted focus away from community studies focusing on social relationships within specific localities to tracing the informal social networks of samples of the population. There are, however, still arguments for studying locality-based organizations and relationships (Allan and Phillipson,

2008; Crow, 2002). A social networks perspective emerged from the concern to develop an 'a-geographical' or trans-geographical approach, that both allowed for the systematic collection of representative data and encompassed virtual connections across distance as well as face-to-face relationships. A body of work has demonstrated that digitally-mediated communication is overwhelmingly used to supplement, rather than substitute for, direct personal contact, countering fears that ICT developments threaten face-to-face interactions (Baym, 2010; Mesch and Talmud, 2010; Miller, 2011; Miller and Slater, 2000; Tyler, 2002). At the same time, studies are seeking to understand the implications of dispersed rather than localized, social networks (for example, Larsen et.al., 2006; Lück and Schneider, 2010; Viry et al., 2009; Viry, 2012).

It is easier in large-scale quantitative social network analysis to focus on readily measurable features of networks such as the number of individuals and levels of contact between them, rather than exploring the nuanced meaning of the relationships to the individuals concerned. By contrast, researchers in the sociology of family life and personal life have often focused in detail on the meaning, quality and content of relationships from the perspective of those taking part in them. Knowledge of the subjective and qualitative dimension of relationships, combined with detailed information about what people actually do for and with each other, has further enriched understandings of the social connectedness of individuals. An influential example is Ray Pahl and Liz Spencer's approach to mapping personal communities (2004, Spencer and Pahl, 2006). Here, a typology of personal communities was devised to capture the range, repertoire and meaning of different kinds of relationships with friends and family across the life course (see Pahl and Spencer, 2004, p. 210). David Morgan (2009) notes that personal communities also include acquaintances, people who fall between intimates and strangers, yet who, nevertheless, are of individual and social significance. Some researchers have sought to blend quantitative and qualitative approaches. Clare Wenger, another UK-based researcher, has used a range of methods to map aspects of relationships in order to capture their potential for providing levels of support to elderly people. She subsequently developed a typology of networks showing the ones that are more or less likely to deliver sufficient practical assistance to enable older people to remain in the own homes, including living alone, at higher levels of impairment (Wenger, 1984, 1992, 1993, 1997; Wenger et al., 2000, 2004). She found that the most supportive networks either have local kin as the main source of assistance, or an older person who is active in their local community and engaged with local family, friends and neighbours. Networks that involve no local kin and are restricted to the household, or that rely only on local neighbours, are much less effective in delivering practical assistance. Subsequent research focusing particularly on elderly people who are geographically distanced from kin in transnational relationships, notes both the possibilities of feeling cared-for and the limits of orchestrating practical care across distance (Baldassar, 2007; Burholt and Wenger, 2004; Harris and Shaw, 2006; Mason, 2004; Vullnetari and King, 2008; Zontini and Reynolds, 2007).

In summary the literature highlights the importance of considering relationships that take place at a distance and locally, and the value of understanding the nature of ties and the subjective importance that various relationships hold for individuals. Measures of numbers and types of relationships are insufficient to understand the meanings and likely consequences of different types of social connectedness. As Klinenberg (2001) observes, having limited social ties is distinct from being lonely, the subjective state of feeling alone – a point overlooked in pessimistic readings of increased loneliness from statistical trends in one-person households. We address below the importance of distinguishing between social isolation, broadly the number of contacts and interactions between individuals and their wider social networks, and the subjective experience of loneliness and negative feelings about levels of contact with others. In analysing data from our UK study, our main focus is on the informal personal ties of men and women living alone and the significance these relationships have for them.

The move to 'chosen' relationships?

Since the 1950s, a recurrent element in sociological debate about change in personal life in North America and the United Kingdom has been the contention that there is increasing emphasis on individualized personal choice at the centre of familial and personal life, with some authors highlighting negative consequences and others seeing mainly positive outcomes of gender equality, democratization and increased intimacy.[3] At the same time, various empirical studies have sought to demonstrate continuity in aspects of the functioning of family relationships over time. For example, the North American research by Bengston et al (2002) used a large longitudinal study, to show continuity in processes of socialization and inter-generational transmission (see also Brannen, 2006) and diverse bodies of research document continuities in gender inequality, particularly women's caring responsibilities (for example, Bianchi et al., 2006, Hochschild, 1990; Oinonen, 2008; Ribbens et al., 2003). In the twenty-first century, such discussions about 'choice', individualization and change in personal life are as likely to be centred on Asia as on Europe or North America (Liu, 2008; Uberoi, 2006; Yan, 2010) and here too the trend of living alone is seized up on as if it sounds alarms about the future of family life and about the continued willingness of women to care (Ronald and Hirayama, 2009; Song, 2010).

More recent research in the United Kingdom suggests that social change in personal life should not be characterized by the decline of families of 'fate' and their substitution by elective affinities of 'choice'; rather, it demonstrates what Pahl and Spencer (2003) have described as 'social suffusion', a more 'fluid interchange of friend-like and family-like relationships' and the increasing irrelevance of labelling family relationships as 'given' or friendship relationships as 'chosen' (2003, p. 129). Both family and friendship relationships can feel chosen and voluntary, or take on an obligatory character experienced as binding. This is demonstrated, for example, by empirical research that focuses on the subjective meanings attributed to family and friendship relationships and the everyday practices of conducting both. For many people, their close 'family' relationships extend beyond a nuclear or household-based definition of family to encompass more diverse relationships. Given high rates of couple dissolution, families sometimes comprise relationships formed through previous marriages and cohabitation, as well as extended kin, while friends are sometimes family-like (see Gillies et al., 2001; Jamieson et al., 2006; Maclean and Eekelaar, 1997; Ribbens McCarthy et al., 2003; Silva and Smart, 1999; Smart, 2007; Smart et al., 2001; Smart and Shipman, 2004). Friendship relationships can also feel obligatory, being difficult to end even when they are no longer pleasurable (Allan, 2008; Gullestad, 2001; Smart et al., 2012). We discuss whether the meanings of relationships and the practices of those living alone are consistent with this suggested suffusion of 'given' and 'chosen' relationships in social networks or with a turning away from relationships. Is there any evidence that people living alone are predominantly avoiding any sense of obligation to friends or family, being more focused on the self, as some of the negative stereotyping suggests?

Place and 'community'

Jonas Larsen and his colleagues comment that much research on social interactions is 'overly focused upon geographically propinquitous communities' (2006, p. 12). Debate about the relevance of place to identities in the context of globalization and increased mobilities has intensified (Larsen et al., 2006; Raine and Wellman, 2012; Savage et al., 2005; Urry, 2007) with the rapid developments of Internet and Communications

Technologies (ICT): 'Technological revolutions in transportation and communication, it is said, have all but eliminated the drag once imposed by location and distance on human interaction and on the flow of goods, capital or information. Social life now moves through nodes in one or another network, through points of power or convergence or translation but not anchored at any place necessarily' (Gieryn, 2000, p. 463).

For Putnam (2000), social capital required the proximity of residents within a geographically bounded neighbourhood and increasing mobility is one amongst various factors identified, with declining social integration, that threatens strong families and strong communities (see Coleman, 1988; Donovan et al., 2002). Yet the possibilities of socially integrating 'communities' that are not place-bound were proposed decades ago; Bell and Newby's (1976) concept of 'communion' described a community of affect characterized by close personal ties, 'belongingness' and emotional wrmth between members, yet not necessarily fitting with any particular settlement type and existing even where 'members' do not dwell in close physical proximity. Some theorists associate the age of rapid transport and multiple forms of virtual communication with positive capacities to sustain relationships over distance and to maintain connectivity with a large number of individuals without the need for spatial co-presence (Giddens, 1990, 1991; Raine and Wellman, 2012; Urry, 2007; Wellman, 2001). Yet such developments are also met with pessimistic assumptions about the effects of disembedding relationships from place, including the presumption that geographic distance necessarily results in emotional distance and less-dense social networks. Zygmunt Bauman has written at length about 'liquid relationships', associations that are doomed to be frail and to produce a sense of anxious impermanence (see Bauman, 2001, 2007).

Opportunities for mobility remain structured by socio-economic circumstances. For example, research in the United Kingdom demonstrates that young people growing up in poor neighbourhoods remain rooted through the social support they need to survive their difficult local circumstances and their lack of the necessary resources that might enable them to build a supportive environment elsewhere (Macdonald et al., 2005). Mobility is a socially selective process (Champion and Fisher, 2003). Certain groups – the young, those without children, highly educated or in professional occupations – have higher mobility propensities than those with lower levels of education, in social housing or mortgage holders, in couples or with families; living alone is also associated with higher mobility (Andrews et al., 2010; Boyle et al., 1998; Hughes and McCormack, 1981, 1985; Rabe and Taylor, 2010). One common stereotype of solo-living is the young urban professional, whose mobile lifestyle results in more fleeting social ties that can be easily chosen or disregarded when no longer needed. For several theorists, this is the archetype of individualization in the context of modern market economies, giving rise to market subjects unencumbered by personal commitments tied to specific locations, a 'fully mobile society of singles' (Beck, 1992, p. 122). Studies in the north of England by Savage and colleagues (2005) suggest a category of residents who are not oriented to conventional attachments to their locality. Rather than wishing to engage with local people or the specificity of place, they see themselves as 'electively belonging', inhabiting a suitably blank canvas for their own life project. Their enthusiasm about the place involves its redefinition as special because it feels chosen by and belonging to them.

As Wang and Wellman note (2010), anxiety about the decline of social connectivity is an old story. Fischer (1982), in his classic study comparing the social relationships of those living in rural and urban locations in the United States, describes similar long-standing concerns about the impact of urbanization on social connectedness. Fischer also notes longstanding rebuttals of such notions, citing Bertrand Russell from 1930 in illustration: 'The idea that one should know one's immediate neighbours has died out in large centres of population but still lingers in small towns and in the country. It has become a foolish idea, since there is no need to depend upon immediate neighbours for society. More and more it becomes possible to choose our companions on account of congeniality rather than on account of mere propinquity' (Bertrand Russell, cited in Fischer, 1982; p. 103). Calhoun (1998) draws attention to Melvin Webber's 1963 essay countering the tendency to imagine that modernity and the metropolis could only be sites of impersonal anonymity. Here he wrote about 'community without propinquity': as Calhoun notes, 'his grasp of the importance – and transcendability – of spatial dispersion reminds us that we knew something of time-space distanciation even before Hagestrand and Giddens, and before the Internet' (1998, p. 374). Claims of declining social connectivity persist alongside a large body of empirical evidence on the enduring nature of social ties such as those of family, kinship and friendship (Crow, 2002; Hansen, 2005; Jamieson, 1998). Such arguments can be seen as a continuation of long-standing anxieties about the social impacts of modernity, a storyline that, as Vanessa May (2011) describes it, since Marx and Engels, has 'depicted the evils of social change, wreaking havoc on individual people and communities alike...fast forward to...theorists such as Riesman (1961), Lasch (1978), Sennett (1998), Putnam (2000) and Furedi (2004) who have all offered similarly gloomy accounts of modernity, warning us of the dire psychological consequences of the loss of traditions and old certainties that is turning us into other-directed, self-obsessed, helpless and fragmented persons, which in turn is eroding trust, social cohesion and community' (May 2011, p. 364).

As Allan and Phillipson (2008) argue, there is still much to be gained from studying residents' attachments to their locality, including their local face-to-face social relationships, but without neglecting the totality of their social networks including their non-local and mediated social ties. If place attachment, emotional or affective bonds and a sense of identity tied up with place is salient, this may manifest itself in a sense of 'hereditary attachment' related to a person's generational links to a locality, a partiality for the area related to distinctive characteristics such as particular landscapes or a 'social attachment' constructed through people in the area. Mulder (2007) emphasizes the importance of family ties as a factor in 'location-specific capital', binding people to a place (see also Blaauboer et al., 2011; Mulder and Cooke, 2009). But just as relationships to people can shape feelings about place, so too can place shape social interactions. Claude Fischer's (1982) classic study demonstrates that social relationships are, in part, determined by the rural or urban character of where they take place. Fischer noted the larger part played by kin and neighbours in the social networks of small-town dwellers and the contrasting larger part played by friends who are not kin or neighbours in the social networks of urban dwellers. However, he argued that this does not reflect different moral or social principles but the greater choice and possibility of specialization enabled by the population size and density of urban areas. In rural areas with populations small enough for all to be acquainted with all of the inhabitants, most people, nevertheless, rather than being equally sociable with all, sustain an inner circle of closer intimates, just as city dwellers do. However, for long-term rural residents, kin and neighbours are for pragmatic reasons more likely to feature in this inner-circle. Friendly relationships with them must be maintained in any case, because they are kin or neighbours, and the pool of others who could be friends is limited. Although adoption of the mobile phone and Internet connectivity has diminished this difference between the pool of available social contacts for urban and rural dwellers, differences in local social life are not likely to disappear. Rural residents of small sparsely populated places will continue to negotiate being recognized and hailed or at least 'known' by most people they meet and potentially, therefore, are more enmeshed in face-to-face relationships, while urban residents negotiate the anonymity and possible lack of social recognition by the physically co-present others they encounter.

Theorists sometimes portray the essence of modern friendship as private, dyadic and idiosyncratic, suggesting something very different from the socially integrative qualities implied by the concept of 'community'. However, Jamieson has argued that a sense of belonging to a 'community' is a state of mind that can coexist with private exclusive intimate relationships (Jamieson, 1998, p. 85–89). The types of personal relationships most valued by 'locals' who feel part of a community are not necessarily markedly different from those who feel no such sense of community: 'for the majority of people, wherever they live, including 'the community local', their main sociability is with an inner circle of friends and kin. The 'local' does not share his or herself equally with all other self-defined locals. Their general sense of moral responsibility to the community may be rarely put to the test and their community spirit may involve little daily effort beyond friendly exchanges of pleasantries and carefulness not to offend others who may remain neighbours for life' (Jamieson, 1998, p. 83). Rural dwellers frequently maintain both private exclusive intimate relationships and general 'community' friendliness, and some urban dwellers may do the same if they inhabit an urban enclave they perceive as having a sense of local community. Research on the social networks of older people, such as that of Wenger and her colleagues, suggests that in times of need and vulnerability in older age, feeling encompassed within community friendliness has to be accompanied by a circle of closer relationships providing practical care to sustain an older person's 'independence' in their own home. However, for a working-age population living alone, it is less clear what value and investment might be placed on a local 'community' versus the personal community of the private inner circle of significant others who may or may not be local.

In these chapters, we draw on our UK data to consider the role locality plays in the sense of 'belonging' of men and women living alone, and the extent to which 'place' matters to their social relationships and sense of identity. Alongside this, we consider whether 'community', which necessarily delineates those who do and don't belong, may be experienced as exclusionary by those living alone: Wardhaugh refers to those who either reject or are unable to conform to conventional ideas and expressions of gender, sexuality and class who therefore 'might be both symbolically and literally 'excluded from any notion or semblance of home" (1999, 1997, cited in Mallett, 2004, p. 73). Is solo-living a marker of identity that leads to people feeling 'out of place'? If so, how is this shaped by factors such as gender, type of locality or residential history? Chapter 7 encompasses consideration of how particular localities enable or inhibit the social inclusion and moral acceptance of solo-living.

6
Solo-living and Connectedness

We begin this chapter by looking at existing research on the relationship between living alone and individual well-being at older ages. Recognition of the importance of social embeddedness to the well-being of older people has led to a body of research which considers the role of living arrangements alongside marital and parenting histories. We consider what this literature may indicate about the likely futures of those living alone at older ages in decades to come. We then move on to data from our UK study on the social connectedness of men and women living alone at working age. Looking across the diverse circumstances of the lives of those living alone, the data allow consideration of different dimensions of respondents' social networks, including frequency and type of contact, the relative weight placed on particular relationships and the extent to which interviewees felt they could rely on others or be relied on for support. Evidence of considerable variation in the social networks of those in our study counters simplistic generalizations about the social connectedness of those living alone.

Those living alone at ages conventionally associated with co-residential family life are often depicted as at the forefront of social changes in personal life, whether transforming intimacy by prioritizing other types of relationships over co-resident partnership and parenthood or by signifying diminishing ability to maintain intimate personal relationships in the context of modern market economies. Evidence of how working age men and women living alone 'do' social connections is put against prior assumption about their profoundly 'individualized' lifestyle.

Living alone and well-being in later life

Chapter 2 noted increases in the proportions of older people living alone across industrialized and modernizing nations, and estimates that this

157

is likely to continue. A trend of older people living alone is observed with much greater dismay in Asia than in north-western Europe and North America because of a different emphasis on multi-generational and joint family units and different understandings about the ideal old age. One factor facilitating older people living alone is their improved economic resources which have enabled them to act on their preference or their children's preference for independent living (Klinenberg, 2012; Kono, 2000). Nevertheless, access to the economic means of living alone remains uneven and population ageing is an international concern, in part because of the anticipated negative economic consequences of predictable age-structure changes (OECD, 2005; Oxley, 2009). The living arrangements of older people have been identified as a key determinant of well-being and, as such, the focus of considerable policy attention, with concerns about the potential resource implications of a decline in available family support, given that informal care is generally provided by family (for example, see CGA Canada, 2005; European Commission, 2011; Kono, 2000 on Japan; Weiner and Tilly, 2002 on the United States; Xin and Chuliang, 2008 on China).

It was noted earlier, that in the context of rural China the phrase for 'living alone' or 'living separately' is applied to elderly parents, whether a couple or a widow or widower, who are not living with and being taken care of by their adult children. This co-residence arrangement is still widely regarded as the moral ideal and in some contexts 'living alone' is shaming for both parent and adult child. However, a number of studies have questioned whether co-residence is always in older people's best interests, having found very unhappy older people living in the households of their children, and the research literature documents a changing preference among older people for living alone if they have the economic means to do this or if their children will provide them with the economic support they need to do so (Unger, 1993; Yan, 2003; Zhang, 2004). Meanwhile, an extensive body of gerontological research associates living alone with negative outcomes in terms of physical and psychological well-being amongst the elderly in European and North American contexts, but this also glosses considerable variation (Dean et al., 1992; Glaser and Grundy, 1998; Greenfield and Russell, 2011; Hays and George, 2002; Mui and Burnette, 1994; Speare et al., 1991; Wolinsky et al., 1992, Young and Grundy, 2009). Tomassini et al. (2004) refer to the excess deaths attributed to extraordinarily high temperatures of 2003 in France and 1995 in Chicago to illustrate the potentially greater risks of living alone for adverse health outcomes. Klinenberg's in-depth 'social autopsy' of the Chicago heatwave, however, identifies these heat wave decedents as isolated and reclusive seniors, rather than a representative sample of older Americans living alone (2002, p. 249). He notes also the methodological difficulties in researching the extent of isolation and reclusion among the general population. We emphasize throughout this book that those living alone are not a homogenous group, thus the need for attention to the diverse circumstances and experiences of those categorized by living arrangement. As we argue further in this chapter, this includes recognition of diversity in social connectedness.

Young and Grundy (2009) note a number of studies from England, Spain, Canada and the United States that indicate that older people living alone are more likely than those living with others to report poor health status, and low levels of psychological health and quality of life.[1] In part, this is attributed to the lack of potential benefits in financial and social resilience, as well as the absence of companionship and care that may otherwise be available at the household level (De Jong Giervald et al., 2001). Yet the results of such studies are not consistent or clear-cut. Lower levels of mortality have been reported among those living alone compared with those living with others in Japan and Italy (see Murata et al., 2005; Pizzetti et al., 2005; Walter-Ginzburg et al., 2002), while there are studies from the United Kingdom and the United States which find better subjective ratings of overall health and quality of life among older persons living alone compared with the unmarried living with others (see Gustavson and Lee, 2004; Michael et al., 2001, and Netuveli et al., 2006). Young and Grundy note these findings may in part be explained by the fact that the majority of people living alone are not isolated and have extensive social contacts and support from family and others beyond the household (see Daatland and Heroson, 2001; Silverstein and Bengston, 1994; Ulbrich and Warheit, 1989).

The associations between living arrangements and the health and well-being of older people are complex, and the underlying factors difficult to disentangle. There is likely to be 'health selection' into and out of living alone, with those able to live alone less likely to have serious ill health. National studies often demonstrate a strong association between changes in health and moves between different types of household. Murphy et al. (2007) note that the common exclusion from survey data of those living in institutions may help explain apparently inconsistent results concerning the consequences of living alone for health and well-being. Local, national and regional contexts vary in the extent to which they provide older people with support which enables them to live alone, and in the type of older person most likely to receive support. Factors such as gender and marital status also impact upon the likelihood of living alone in older age, as well as how that is experienced. Clare Wenger's (1992, 1993) typology of social support systems showed the importance of local kin, activity in the local community and engagement with local family, friends and neighbours, with networks involving no local kin or relying only on local neighbours much less effective in delivering practical assistance. This typology of social support systems has been applied to data from a number of other countries, including a comparative study of Australia, Finland, the Netherlands, Spain and the United States with some data also gathered on Germany, Israel and Japan (Wenger et al., 2007) and a separate study comparing Beijing, China and Liverpool, England (Wenger and Liu, 2000). The former study looked across countries at variation in levels of older people's weekly engagement with kin, friends and neighbours, highest in Japan, in patterns of attendance at religious services, highest in Spain, and in membership of clubs and voluntary organizations, highest in the Netherlands. Such differences have implications for distributions of types of support networks. Across all the countries where the typology was applied, childless older people were less likely to have the most supportive types of networks than those with children and childless men were the most likely to have the least supportive networks. Childless formerly married men were shown to be at greater risk than the childless never married or currently married, indicating reliance on their lost partner for their social contacts. The contrast in support networks between older people with and without children was most marked in the United States and the least marked in Australia. In Australia, a type of network offering modest levels of support (neither best nor worst) which Wenger labelled *wider community focused*, was very common, more so than in any other country. In this network, older people are in touch with distant kin but their main local involvements are with friends and voluntary groups.

This overview of the literature on living alone and well-being in later life suggests living arrangement per se is an inadequate explanatory variable in the absence of other information about circumstances and context. Thus, while numerous studies suggest living with a spouse at older age is associated with better health, especially for men, living with someone other than a spouse does not seem to confer the same advantage. Grundy and Murphy (2006) cite several studies that have found that those living alone are healthier than those living with adults other than a spouse, or even, in some cases, than those living with a spouse (see Cafferata, 1987; Glaser et al., 1997; Hébert et al., 1999; Magaziner et al.,1988).

The quality as well as type of social ties is clearly important for well-being. For example, a study of Swedes aged over 75 that took into account marital status, living arrangement, frequency of contact with children, other relatives and friends, and satisfaction with these contacts, found after a three-year follow-up that individuals living alone, those without any close social ties, and those with unsatisfying contacts with children, had increased risk of developing dementia (Fratiglioni et al., 2000). The authors concluded that an extensive social network seemed to protect against dementia and noted that groups such as the childless and those living alone could compensate by having other close ties. While many studies have shown that measures of social isolation – the number of social contacts and the amount of social engagement – are associated with poor health outcomes, these quantitative measures of relationships may not adequately capture the distress that an individual feels. The concept of loneliness is only starting to be recognized as a separate entity from social isolation and depression, with few studies to date examining it as an independent risk factor (Perissinotto et al., 2012). Several studies have identified differences in level and type of social contacts across countries (Walker, 2005; Wenger, 1997; Wenger and Liu, 2000; Wenger et al., 2007); A comparative study of life satisfaction amongst those aged 60 plus across six European countries notes however that it was not the *extent of* but *satisfaction with* social contacts that was associated with life satisfaction in all countries (Fagerström et al, 2007) .

The significance of the quality of social ties as distinct from quantity is also relevant to the distinction between social isolation, having limited social ties, and the subjective experience of loneliness that is addressed in some of the gerontological literature (see Andersson, 1998; De Jong Gierveld, 1998; Victor et al., 2009; Weeks, 1994; Wenger and Burholt, 2004). A recent US study using longitudinal data that investigated the effect of loneliness on older people found that it is a risk factor for poor health outcomes. However, they identified no connection between loneliness and living alone, observing that of the 43 per cent of subjects who felt lonely, only 18 per cent lived alone (Perissinotto et al., 2012). While loneliness and social isolation may be associated, they may also be distinct: loneliness can exist independently of social isolation, and social isolation in the absence of loneliness (Burholt, 2011). There may be wide variations in the size, diversity *and importance* attached to personal social networks, and we consider this distinction in analyses of our own data on the social connectedness of working-age adults living alone below.

As our discussion of research on different types of support networks already suggests, the extent to which individuals living alone have social ties and support outwith the household is mediated by various cultural and socio-economic factors. Numerous studies from various countries demonstrate the significance of gender and partnership and parenting trajectories across the life course for social connectedness. A review of the literature on living arrangements and health status in later life (Hays, 2002) reports that older women who live alone appear to be protected against functional declines and to enjoy better mental health and vitality over time than women living with a husband, due largely to more social engagement (Michael et al., 2001). Murphy et al. (2007) also observe that, despite research indicating that, in general, married people have better mental and physical health than the never-married and 'ever-married', studies in American and British populations have found that never-married women at older ages have as good or better health than their married counterparts (Gardner and Oswald, 2004; Goldman et al.,1995; Grundy and Sloggett, 2003; Murphy et al., 1997), interpreted as reflecting stronger non-marital social networks among never-married older women (Goldman et al., 1995, cited in Murphy et al., 2007, p. 287). One stark indicator of social isolation–requiring state burial – is also gendered: a survey of funerals carried out by local authorities in England for people who died without friends or family to make arrangements or cover costs reports that men are more than two and a half times more likely than women to die alone, 'a stark picture of isolation, loneliness and, in many cases, impoverishment' (Burstow, 2005, p. 2). Klinenberg (2012) also notes the sex differential in burials by state government in the United States, observing that this demonstrates the 'paradox' that older women are far more likely than elderly men to live alone but significantly less likely to be cut off from social ties.

Reading across studies also demonstrates the significance of national and cultural context. Comparative analyses of survey data on 19 European countries found differences across regional groupings (Young and Grundy, 2009):[2] in northern Europe (here comprising Sweden, Norway, Finland and Denmark) no association between living alone and low levels of well-being was identified. The authors conclude this may be due to the combination of older people's preferences for autonomy and independence, with the availability of relatively generous benefits and support from the state helping them to live independently (2009, p. 144). As Chapter 2 shows, the incidence of living alone is more established and widespread in northern Europe. There is strong evidence that in the United Kingdom elderly people often prefer to rely on state services than their adult children (Sixsmith, 1986; West, 1984; see also Crystal 1982 for the United States). A UK study (Arber and Ginn, 1992) demonstrates that those living alone are more likely than those living with others to receive support with domestic and personal tasks from formal services, and considerably more likely to be in receipt of support from friends and neighbours, support which Arber and Ginn contend may have resulted from reciprocal relationships and therefore have generated less of a sense of being a burden (1992, p. 103). Nevertheless, relatives still provided about half the sources of support with personal and domestic tasks for older people who lived alone.

The various interrelated factors impacting on the relationship between living arrangements and well-being, including partnership and parenting trajectories, confirm the need to consider individual routes into and duration spent living alone. Victor (2011), noting the distinct lack of a life course perspective in research on aging and loneliness, highlights the importance of this in understanding the impact of key life events (see also Davidson, 2004; Dykstra and Hagestad, 2007). People with experience of living alone over the long term may have developed capacities and resources which make them and their support systems more resilient, such as wider social networks. Thus they might be better equipped for the challenges of later years living alone than someone entering solo-living for the first time as the outcome of widowhood. Davidson's (2004) UK study on the social networks of older men notes that while research indicates that lone older men have an elevated risk of social isolation, there is little recognition of the way that marital histories lead to the growth or attenuation of family bonds. Her research, based on an analysis of the 1994 General Household Survey and qualitative interviews with 85 men aged 65 and over, distinguishes the experiences of older never-married men who are accustomed to living on their own and looking after their personal and domestic needs: unlike the widowed and particularly the divorced men, they were not discontented with their lifestyle. Davidson also observes that, as Cancian (1987) points out, we tend to measure the quantity and quality of social networks with a 'feminine ruler'. Many men in her study however held ambivalent attitudes towards central features of the 'female script' such as the need for intimacy based on mutual disclosure and social engagement.

It is also important to bear in mind that studies based on older men and women living alone at the turn of the century may be of limited relevance to those living alone at older ages in the future. Debate on ageing populations include discussion of the need to adjust dependency ratios given progress in important factors such as remaining life expectancies and disability rates (Sanderson and Scherbov, 2010). The extent of socio-demographic change of recent decades also means that the experiences of previous cohorts may be very different from those who will be living alone at older ages in years to come. Grundy and Murphy (2006), for example, note the possible cohort effect in their UK study on the 'oldest-old', for whom remaining unmarried was relatively unusual amongst men; they suggest never married men in very old age groups therefore may include a larger proportion of people with personal characteristics that reduced the chances of marriage and other close relationships. The pathways of future cohorts will include more varied partnership trajectories, and may include some who have lived alone at working age, an experience that might serve to equip them differently if undertaken in retirement. Does a spell of living alone during working age encourage the development of social relations with persons beyond the household? If so, are these persons kin, friends, neighbours? Are they envisaged as durable personal communities, likely to endure over the long term?

Socio-demographic changes in kinship and residential relations of recent decades have led to increasing acknowledgement across various disciplines of the need to consider relationships beyond the household (Buzar et al., 2005; Mulder, 2007). However, in comparison with the focus on living arrangements evident in the gerontological literature, there has been little attention to the social connectedness of those living alone at working age. There are a small number of country-specific studies based on large-scale survey data that compare the social networks of those living with others with those living alone, and these are considered below. However, indicators of social capital such as measurements of level of contact with others cannot address the meanings and motivations that actors place on their social relationships. We subsequently draw on our data to consider further the significance of personal networks to men and women living alone.

Living alone and social networks at working age

Studies of social networks based on secondary analysis of large datasets have shown that the more pessimistic accounts of the social connectedness of those living alone are over simplistic. Such connections often demonstrate more similarity to those living with others than difference. The analysis of Bien et al (1992) of survey data from 1988 of adults aged 18–55 in the Federal Republic of Germany found that those living alone under 55 have social networks that are similar in size, density and frequency of contact to their counterparts who live with others (1992, p. 172).[3] One difference observed was in the balance between friends and family in the social networks of those living alone, with the former predominating to a greater extent. A similar finding was identified in an analysis of survey data from 2001 of adults in Scotland (see Wasoff et al., 2005).[4] This research also indicates that gender differences may be more significant than living arrangements, with solo-living women reporting consistently higher levels of social involvement with family and community than men of the same age.

A slightly different picture is evident in an analysis of survey data from 2008 of adults aged 25–64 in Canada (Vézina, 2011).[5] This comparison of the personal networks of those living alone with those living in couples, with or without children, found that both groups have similar numbers of close friends. However, those living alone have fewer acquaintances and smaller family networks than people living in couples. These differences may be partly attributed to people living in couples having access to their partner's family and acquaintance network in addition to their own, hence more opportunities to broaden ties with family and extend their network of acquaintances. While both groups were almost equally likely to meet or speak with close relatives at least once a week, people living alone were in more frequent contact with their friends. They are also, however, more likely to experience a strong feeling of social loneliness than people living in a couple. The overwhelming majority, 85 per cent, expressed satisfaction with how frequently they were in contact with relatives, friends and acquaintances. However, a composite measure which combined network size, frequency of contact and feeling of social loneliness identified living alone as reducing the probability of having good quality personal networks, as did being male, being over 35 or having a lower income (Vézina, 2011, p. 69).

The combined effects of gender and cultural context were demonstrated in comparative analysis of the sociability and social support of those living alone and those living with others in the 30–59 age group across three regions within Europe, broadly matching the discrete regions Therborn (2004) identifies in his discussion of the legacy of the Christian-European family (Jamieson et al., 2009).[6] Levels of sociability and support were markedly lower in Eastern Europe, which has experienced considerable social and economic upheaval since the break-up of the Soviet Union. In each region, those living alone were more likely than those living with others to say that they 'meet socially with friends, relatives or colleagues' several times a week or everyday, though gender differences varied. In north-western Europe, the region with the most cultural support for living alone, working-age women were slightly more likely to frequently meet others socially than men, whether they lived alone or not, while the opposite was true in southern and eastern Europe. Sociability may remain more difficult for women living alone in countries where living alone remains exceptional for both men and women but particularly for women. Questions about whether people had anyone to discuss intimate and personal matters with, or found it easy to borrow money, again identified men living alone in eastern Europe as the group most likely to lack both these forms of support and to report much lower levels of access to someone to talk to than either women living alone or men living with others. In north-western Europe, solo-living men and women are not typically socially isolated or very different from their peers in terms of their access to social support.

Experiences of social connection: Men and women living alone at working age

Despite the diversity of the socio-economic circumstances and social networks of men and women living alone in our UK study, the majority described satisfying personal relationships and a sense of secure, meaningful social connections that were important dimensions of contentment with living alone. Some interviewees reported a pattern of social connections involving discrete geographically-dispersed relationships and others more integrated social worlds creating a sense of being embedded in local social relationships. Both patterns contributed to such contentment. However, a small group of respondents, mainly men, indicated a degree of social isolation and loneliness, and this group is looked at separately below. The personal relationships that the majority of interviewees identified as important routinely encompassed family and friends, and often also neighbours and colleagues. Exceptionally, others were listed instead of or as well as these categories, examples included a dog and health workers providing care. Variations in the extent and importance of relationships were apparent by gender, socio-economic circumstance, and age and stage in the life course. Mobility histories too played a role, imbricated with education and career trajectories.

Gender and social interaction

Gender was a key dimension shaping the social connectedness of UK research respondents, albeit operating in concert with social class and other aspects of biography. Classic research on the social networks of women and men in Europe and North America in the latter half of the twentieth century identified women's networks as more likely to be focused on kin and neighbours, and men's on non-kin, especially co-workers, a difference attributed to the different structural locations of women and men in the family and labour market (Fischer, 1982; Young and Willmott, 1957). The idea that women's relationships are more intimate than men's also surfaced over this period in the literature on friendship as well as in discussions about love (Allan, 1979, 1989; Cancian, 1986). Echoes of these themes recur in the twenty-first century despite ongoing transformation of gender relations, including the demise of the male-breadwinner family, and greater mobility and fluidity in personal life (Crompton, 2006; Spencer and Pahl, 2006; Swartz, 2009).

Various ways in which social networks are gendered surface amongst those living alone, despite there being no possibility of gendered division of labour within their home. As analysis of the Scottish Household Survey shows (Table A2.5a and A2.5b in Appendix 2), women living alone at working-age are much more likely to be in full-time employment than women of the same age living with others, a significant proportion of whom are living with and caring for children. Note solo women have higher rates of full-time employment than solo men, a difference even more marked among the 25–44 age group, reflecting men's higher rates of unemployment and influenced by women's higher educational qualifications (Table A2.4). Time spent in paid employment reduces time available for other things, including relationships with others. Nevertheless, survey data on the social interactions of those living alone at working-age suggests women are more likely to be attentive to kin relationships than men. The greater engagement of both men and women with female rather than male kin is another way in which the social networks of men and women living alone were gendered. Thus, where individual parents were identified as important people in the lives of respondents, mothers were far more likely to be designated than fathers.[7] Of those respondents with living fathers, around ten per cent (11/118) reported having little or no contact with them. Over a quarter of respondents who were fathers reported little or no contact with their children (6/21), while some respondents reported having no contact with nieces and nephews due to brothers' estrangement from their children. In terms of relationships with extended family, with the exception of one rural male whose parents were deceased and who designated his sister and an aunt, and one urban male designating his grandmother alongside mother and sister, only female respondents identified extended family members as 'key people', overwhelmingly grandmothers, aunts and nieces. Several respondents reported that their knowledge of or contact with extended family members was via their mothers: for example, Andrew (43, urban) commented 'I mainly keep in touch with them through my mum (laugh) who tells me all what's going on, she probably tells them what's going on with me'. In contrast with female respondents, male respondents rarely explicitly referred to proximity to family as important factors in shaping decisions about residential mobility, discussed further in the following chapter. The preference for friends of the same sex was another way in which social networks were gendered, with many respondents, both male and female, describing homosocial friendship networks.

Social suffusion of friends and family

Empirical research in the United Kingdom suggests that a 'social suffusion' between family and friendships is a more appropriate characterization of change in personal life than a 'decentering of the family' – the view that the significance of familial relationships has diminished. Our research also fails to confirm prominent stereotypes of people living alone as only maintaining relationships of choice or glibly associating choice with transience, 'elective affinities' in accordance with fickle personal inclination, 'liquid' relationships where an individual's engagements are overwhelmingly superficial and non-committal. Yet amongst our UK interviewees there was, for many, a clear prioritizing of family. Asked about people they felt were the most important in their lives, the overwhelming majority designated immediate kin, parents, siblings and/or own children. A small number named extended kin such as aunts or cousins.[8] In Chapter 3 we note the different degrees of commitment assigned to current partners amongst those in couple relationships; not all, indeed a minority, of those in such relationships identified their partners as a key person. While many respondents did identify friends as important, only a small number, more men than women, prioritized friends over kin.[9] In terms of who was identified as key, there was little evidence of a prioritizing of other relationships over family.

The primacy of immediate family might to some extent reflect normative expectations of their importance: for example, Sam (31, urban) commented 'Well, I suppose we'll do the family first, because I suppose in a way that always comes first'. Gregor (42, rural), when asked whether family ties would be a consideration in any future plans about where to live, replied: 'Yeah, of course they would, yeah. You've got to think of your family'.[10] However, several interviews indicated this prioritizing also reflected the centrality of family to the respondent themselves. Callum (44, urban), a gay man who designated his partner as key, responded when asked whether his family has been supportive 'God yes, my parents are the most important people'. Moira (33, urban), who designated parents, sister and a grandmother she visited twice weekly, responded when probed:

Interviewer: And any other key people in your life at the moment?

Em, I mean, I've got friends, but nobody particularly that I would say is important as my family, to be honest.

Nevertheless, friendships did feature as very important to the personal communities of several respondents, while for some they were prioritized as central. Scholars of friendship note the range of different types of relationship encompassed by the term (Adams and Allan, 1998; Allan, 2008; Killick and Desai, 2010; Spencer and Pahl, 2006). This was evident in the distinction made by some respondents between close friends who were akin to 'soul-mates', helpmates and confidantes performing different roles in their lives to those with whom it is pleasant to pass time in company. For example, Eve (43, rural) noted 'I've not got a lot of friends but I have a lot of acquaintances... my true friends I've known for sort of 20 years plus'. A few interviewees did place an emphasis on 'families of friends' rather than families of origin. Geraldine (45, urban), from a large family about which she noted 'we don't have a very close relationship', designated as key 'three or four close friends, and then I've got an older friend who I used to work with, she's retired now and she's like a mother figure to me'. Geraldine's friendship network also served as a more significant source of practical and emotional support to her than family. Asked whether family ties would influence future plans about where to live, Geraldine's response indicated both a sense of self-sufficiency as well as a reliance on friends: 'Not necessarily, no. I think I've always been my own person to a certain extent [...] And I think my friends are part of my family as well. So my close friends, so that might have a bit more effect... I think the support network to have there is good'. A few interviewees similarly used familial terminology to depict the closeness of non-biological kin. Thus Dawn (36, urban), when asked about how often she saw her brother's family, who lived in London, commented: 'I have nieces and nephews of friends, but not blood-related, that I see more often', and described friends' children staying with her on a regular basis. While some female respondents reported having children of relatives or friends to stay overnight, no men reported children except their own staying over, reflecting gendered possibilities in relationality with children for those living alone.

The narratives of several respondents suggested a 'blurring' of friend and family relationships. For example, Barry, a gay man had been living alone for six years in a central apartment in the city in which he was brought up, had family living locally, and was in a four year relationship in which he and his current partner were considering moving in together. The rich social network he depicts, encompassing family and friends who lived both locally and further afield, was also typical of many heterosexual interviewees. Asked about the important people in his life and level of contact, he responded:

> Well, first of all I would say my partner [who] lives close by. We see each other daily and speak on the phone, the usual kind of thing [...] My mum would be second. Again, she lives fairly close by. We speak to each other and see each other on a very regular basis. At least once a week that we see each other, but we speak on the phone every second day [...] Third would be my brothers.

> And how often are you in touch with them?

> Every couple of days and see them at least once a week. Then I would say my nieces and nephews. Sister-in-law. And then after that would be friends.

> So how often would you keep in touch with them?

> Daily. Phone, email, seeing each other, like visiting, or colleagues at work as well who are friends.
>
> (Barry, 26, urban)

Barry has no contact with his father or paternal grandparents. He holidays with his partner or friends, and spends Christmas at his mother's house. Family ties would be a factor in decisions about where he lives. He regularly (every two weeks) has friends staying at his home. Because Barry is gay, living alone and considering cohabiting in an openly gay relationship, his narrative fits with what Weeks et al. (1996, p. 5) call the 'pluralisation of domestic patterns and relationships' but in most respects there is little that is unusual or unconventional suggesting wider social change. There is some evidence of 'elective affinities' in the choice *not* to see certain family members. However, Barry is clearly embedded in relationships with specific family members as well as friends, both groups that he considers to be potential sources of support.

The frequency of contact Barry describes with key others is typical of many respondents; although the type of contact (whether in person or mediated) differed in relation to geographical distance from friends and family, the majority reported regular phone calls to immediate family, at least weekly and often more frequently. Several respondents also reported frequent contact with friends; for some, an important aspect involved 'checking in' to monitor each other's well-being. Thus Angela (44, rural) referred to a friend she speaks with regularly in addition to meeting weekly face to face: 'if she hadn't phoned me for about 3 days, I'd be phoning her to find out what's up'.

Receiving and providing support

How embedded interviewees were in relationships was demonstrated by exchanges of material and emotional assistance as well as levels of social interaction. The distinction between friends and family was often invoked as interviewees explained the types of support they had received, felt they could expect or would prefer. When asked about people with whom they could discuss personal matters or rely on for emotional support, the majority reported that they had this support, and the source varied from partners to family members to friends.

> I think I could discuss absolutely anything with my girlfriend ... I talk to her about absolutely anything at anytime.
>
> [Stephen, 41, urban]

> I'm close to my mum. I could tell my mum anything.
>
> [Ailsa, 28, urban]

> I've got a couple, well two close friends that I would [...] those people I tell loads of things [...] they know that if they wanted to phone me and say 'Alexandra, help' – they know I'd be here.
>
> (Alexandra, 41, rural)

Family, however, was the most prevalent provider of practical and/or financial support, reflecting a long-standing pattern found, for example, in Fischer's (1982) US and Willmott's (1987) British study, and more recent research on working-age adults (Spencer and Pahl, 2006) and older people (Wenger et al., 2007). People more often looked to non-kin for sociability and casual assistance, and relatives for more costly and critical help; the data in this study suggest this distinction maintains amongst men and women who live alone. Several referred to financial support from parents, though the amount and type of contribution differed considerably by parents' socio-economic situation: some respondents referred to help buying their property, for example, through loaning money for a deposit, an illustration of the multiplier effect of economic advantage. The practical support was also somewhat gendered, for example, male relatives were most often providers of 'DIY' activities around the house, while a few respondents referred to mothers cooking meals for them. A very small number of respondents with ongoing health issues reported receiving support via public services and from voluntary sector organizations: Murray (43, rural), for example, had regular visits from a Community Psychiatric Nurse, and participated in a voluntary sector support club.

Asked about whether they had someone whom they could call on for different levels of help requiring co-presence,[11] most respondents identified friends or neighbours who did or could provide occasional practical support. This varied by locality and residential history or time spent living in the area. Those in rural areas were more likely to identify neighbours as sources of practical support, whereas urban respondents, more likely to have moved to the area and less likely to know their neighbours, more often identified friends.[12] However, the majority expressed a preference that more personal or sustained support would be provided by partners or family, with a few giving instances where this was ongoing or had happened. Thus Catriona (37, urban) answered 'I did actually break my ankle last year... So, I was virtually housebound until the plaster come off... and my brother-in-law was great, he works (nearby) so he would pop in every day practically to see if I needed any shopping... he was great'. Cameron (39, rural) referred to moving in with a sister living nearby during a period of ill-health: 'when, like I went through that really bad period of depression... you know, I ended up, I had to stay at my sister's house for a while'. Stephen (41, urban), who had a degenerative spinal condition, described his teenage son helping with regular domestic tasks such as emptying bins. Some respondents without local family did identify friends as potential sources of sustained support, however others referred to the possibility of mothers moving in with them on a temporary basis to cope with accident, illness and short-term incapacity.

The support provided by respondents to others counters stereotypes about the selfishness of people living alone. Many had experience of providing practical or emotional support to others, although levels, type, and for whom varies[13]. Women were more likely than men to report providing care for other adults, consistent with conventional gendered scripts about care-giving, but some men were involved carers. Caring among men living alone was not confined to the hands-on fathers described in Chapter 3. For some, caring for another adult was a regular commitment. Ailsa (28, urban), for example, talked about taking her grandmother, who lived nearby 'for her shopping every Saturday, and drive her here and there if she's needing it'. Christine (43, urban) commented 'my mother is 85 so, you know, I go down and see her three times a week and take her out for her shopping...My brother's at home so he's really her main carer'. Hilary (37, urban) visited her elderly mother every weekend to do 'shopping, cleaning the house, kind of caring...like a carer sort of'. For others, this was more temporary or occasional: thus Ryan (25, rural) observed 'my mum's broken her foot so I'm helping her out at the minute if she needs it. I've cooked and just tidied up', while Kelvin (26, rural) did DIY jobs for his grandmother. Others described periods of more intensive care. Cameron (39, rural) had cared for his terminally ill father, 'helping him with like, you know, bathing him and changing him and stuff like that'. Cameron and his sisters currently provided help to his now widowed mother, along gendered lines: 'that's kind of my job, that's my duty, to do her gardening and help her with the garden and stuff. And then my sisters help her with her shopping and doing all that kind of stuff'. Frances (41, rural) described a period visiting her grandparents, who lived a couple of hours drive away which meant staying overnight at weekends, to 'pay their bills, get their messages [groceries] for them, make sure they were OK, check everything for them'.

For some who took on heavy caring responsibilities this lasted several years. Elspeth (43, urban) had lived with an uncle who had raised her and her siblings following her parents' death when she was very young, latterly taking care of him alongside her employment for about ten years until his death. Alison (42, urban) who now herself had health problems, described leaving school at 16 to look after her mother until her death when Alison was in her early thirties: 'I was a carer for my mother. My mother took a stroke and a brain haemorrhage'. High levels of support to kin, in some cases provided in conjunction with full-time employment, often involved a sense of duty and obligation. Moira (33, urban) described looking after her housebound grandmother along with her mother, who undertook the bulk of care. Moira visited three nights a week, cooking meals and on occasion staying over: 'sometimes after work, you know, the nights when it's bad weather and stuff, you think of 'God I could be doing something else', but you just...I'd feel too guilty coming home when she's either had no dinner or had nobody in to see her all day'.

Several respondents described helping out elderly neighbours, and this was reported frequently by men living in rural areas. For some, help was occasional, for example, Archie (39, rural) described cleaning gut-ters and changing car tyres for an elderly neighbour, while Catriona (37, urban) observed 'there's an elderly woman upstairs who a couple of times she's asked me to go up and move things about. Heavy lifting and I would, you know, if she needed any help like shopping and things I would do that'. For others, giving help involved regular arrangements. Harvey (38, rural) drove an elderly neighbour 'two or three times a week up the town to get his messages [groceries]'. Struan (44, rural) as well as providing practical support to others in his small island community, also talked about companionship to a now deceased neighbour: 'there was an old guy and he was pretty infirm. I used to go and play Crib [Cribbage] with him because he like playing Crib and he couldn't get out and that'. Some respondents referred to giving occasional help to friends, though the extent varied. For example, Dawn (36, urban) referred to visiting the home of nearby friends when they go on holiday: 'I water their plants, check the house, check the mail things like that'. Much less common was the more regular support provided to a friend described by Alistair (39, urban) who himself had health problems: 'one of my pals that I've met through the mental health system has got back problems, so I'll go to the supermarket for him once or twice a week...and I deal with his finances as well. I'll go to the Post Office to get his benefits for him and that sort of thing'.

Community service

Participation in local community groups is a form of civic involve-ment, but also an important means through which people can develop supportive social networks; depth of engagement in civic and volun-tary organizations and associations varied across our sample, sometimes reflecting different orientations to the locality discussed further in the next chapter. A wide range of experiences emerged but certainly no over-all picture of those living alone eschewing group activities. Some were involved in regular volunteer work, for example, Ryan (25, rural) was a crew member on a lifeboat. A few women reported active involve-ment with their Church, for example, Amy (25, urban) was involved in a Youth Fellowship group. Maggie (34, urban) noted 'I'm an elder within our church as well, so I have my parish group. And there's a few older people in that and if they need something when I'm in to see them they'll get me to do it. Or I'd maybe sort of see them during a Sunday anyway and they might say they need something done in which case I'll go and do it'. Many respondents, men and women, reported taking part in a range of leisure activities such as yoga groups, choirs, sports clubs and evening classes, and some, more men than women, described management or administrative contributions to organizations. The amount of time this required varied. Andrew (43, urban), for example, was an official in a sports club, currently vice-president and treasurer, and experienced some conflict between the time required to organise, and opportunity to take part in, competitions. Liam (44, rural) was a trustee of the local arts development trust which ran various classes in which he was 'heavily involved'. Benjamin (33, rural) described occasional voluntary weekend work 'just to get out of the house and meet people and that'. Neil (40, urban), engaged in various sporting activities, became involved in helping with Duke of Edinburgh[14] expeditions, in part as an opportunity to meet like-minded people; the level of commitment, however, was difficult to combine with self-employment and contract work that involved occasional travel. Several respondents reported lack of time as a factor in not being more involved in formal activities; high earners often had demanding jobs requiring long hours and low earners sometimes had more than one job. All had to balance the demands of achieving financial self-sufficiency, self-provisioning and domestic responsibilities, against time for other pursuits.

Partnership and parental status

Partnership and parental status, both their own and that of their friends and family were an important aspect of how 'age and stage' of the life course shaped friendships and social networks. Childlessness and being unmarried have been identified as factors associated with having more friendships, suggesting fewer restrictive commitments enabling one 'to tend one's garden of friendships' (Allan, 1996; Fischer, 1982, p. 115). Interviewees' accounts illustrate how partnership and parental status sometimes shaped how and with whom they socialized. Thus Brian (42, rural), who was about to move back to co-residence with the mother of his two children, described friendships centred on other couples with children: 'we're friends because our partner or our kids are friends with their kids [...] we kind of hang out, we kind of do dinner parties together, occasional cinema trips. It sometimes just revolves around the kids'. Chapter 3 illustrated how non-resident parents who were literally and figuratively keeping room for their children in their lives sometimes kept other relationships at a distance in order to enable this. Some mentioned the parenting responsibilities of others in their network impacting on sociability: thus Neil (40, urban) referred to now being more likely to visit the close friends with whom he previously went 'out and about', as 'they do now have three children and to get them to come out is a major operation'. Hugh (39, rural), described a social network now primarily centred on relatives: 'I don't really see much of [friends] anymore. They've all got families and kids and that, most of them these days, so I think that takes up most of their time'.

Accounts often highlight the importance that the 'route into' living alone plays in shaping the experience. For example, Eve (43, rural), now divorced after a lengthy marriage and with two adult children, talked about a biography of not having needed support from extended family as 'me and my husband and two kids have always been quite insular . . . and done everything just ourselves'. As other researchers have observed, a family life focused on the couple and parenting relationships often precludes much of the need or opportunity for outside social support, and the disruption of these relationships does not necessarily result in their rapid replacement with an alternative model of personal community. Eve designated her adult daughters whom she saw at least weekly as key in her social world, observing 'I do have friends and that but I wouldn't say they're vitally important, they're good friends but I can go weeks without seeing them'.

The extent to which exclusion from couple socializing was an issue for single respondents varied. For some, this had impacted on their friendship network. Moira (33, urban), currently single, commented 'as you get older, people just do pair off . . . you don't have the same circle of friends'. Clare (38, rural), was one of the small number of respondents who did want the amount of time she spent with others to change. She hoped to meet a partner with whom to live, and found living alone 'quite isolating . . . it's too quiet for me'. While she anticipated things would change over the longer term, meanwhile she felt relatively left out of her friends' lives: 'come retirement there'll be more people single because people having separated, kids left [. . .] at the moment other people are often involved with families or partners and therefore not making contact for doing things with single people'. Some younger respondents whose current social networks were an important dimension of contentment with solo-living may revise this if their networks similarly alter in this direction: Rachel (31, rural) jokingly commented that her friends are 'now sadly more couples than are not couples, and I'm getting left behind!'. As Clare's account suggests, being 'left behind' may not be experienced positively if this results in limited social interactions over time. Feminist critiques of a 'familist ideology' include the consequences for those outside the conventional family.[15] A few single respondents, more women than men, did suggest their partnership status impacted on their social possibilities, some experiencing exclusion from 'couple' activities. Nevertheless, this study, as with other studies considering the social connectedness of those living outside the conventional family (Klinenberg, 2012 and Trimberger, 2006 on the United States, Simpson, 2006 on the United Kingdom), suggests the ideology of familism has waned in the context of wider demographic and other social changes. Most men and women living alone portrayed contentment with their social network. While some respondents referred to occasional feelings of loneliness as a disadvantage of living alone, this was in most cases outweighed by other advantages; the small number for whom social isolation and loneliness did appear problematic are considered further below.

As discussed in Chapter 3, the majority of men and women living alone did not rule out the possibility of living with a partner at some point in the future. Only a few respondents depicted themselves as choosing to continue living alone, with the majority looking on the possibility of living alone into retirement with some trepidation. For respondents anticipating remaining alone, their social networks, in some cases also inflecting commitment to their specific locality, were evidently an important aspect of this ambition. Violet (40, rural) moved from England to a remote Scottish island with her then fiancée ten years previously, had been living alone for six years following the end of this relationship, and anticipated remaining in this locality. Asked about the important people in her life, Violet referred to good local friends, some of whom she knew through work. She also referred to a sexual relationship which she had deliberately kept casual and had just ended: 'he's out of the picture now, although he's still an important person'. Violet's full-time employment in a caring profession provides her with 'a lot of contact with people'. She described a range of leisure interests, as well as undertaking postgraduate study through distance learning, which in part she attributes to 'having a single household ... because if I was living with children and husband and stuff, I think it would not be feasible'. Violet's social networks and interests are an important aspect of planning to continue living alone into retirement: 'I will, if I'm fit and healthy, you know, still enjoy life and would very much see, even though I might not be in paid employment, I would still want to be active and contributing in either a voluntary capacity and that, so I would like to think that I still had an active social life'. In Wenger's terms, the network Violet anticipates in her older age is a 'wider community focused support network' found to be particularly common among older people in Australia.

Home alone and social isolation

A much smaller number of respondents offered accounts of their lives suggesting a degree of social isolation. While two-thirds (84/126) of those currently living alone felt their current level of contact with others was satisfactory, around a quarter (36/126), more men than women, expressed a desire for more. Not all of these respondents however demonstrated isolation in terms of the level of contact with others; rather, some expressed the desire for more time with particular others, constrained due to factors such as long working hours. A few others related their sense of isolation to working at home. In addition, limited social interaction was *not* necessarily associated with a negative emotional script. Previous researchers have noted that having many social contacts can nevertheless coincide with a desire for more, interpreting this as a preference for gregariousness (Fisher, 1982, p. 134). The converse of this is those with below average social engagements, with relatively limited social networks, who, nevertheless, express contentment with their levels of contact with others. While the difficulties of acknowledging 'loneliness' or 'isolation' must be borne in mind, a preference for solitude should not be treated with automatic scepticism. As noted in Chapter 4, home was sometimes seen as a place of refuge where the door was shut on the rest of the world. A desire for and enjoyment of occasional time alone was expressed by several respondents when discussing the nature and quality of their social relationships. For some, this was in the context of busy working and social lives, for example, in jobs that involved considerable engagement with other people, with 'me-time' presented as a welcome respite. In some circumstances, social contacts are experienced as burdensome, as if taking too much out of the self. A small number (6) of respondents, more women than men, reported wanting less contact with others. Thus Angela (44, rural) whose caring profession involved contact with others and who portrayed a busy social life with many friends as well as a partner living locally, commented on her level of contact 'for me it's just about right. Sometimes I feel it's too much because I'm a loner. There's days when I just think, 'I just want to be on my own. Want to knock the phone off'. But that's, again, through choice'.

Nevertheless, time spent alone when it is not experienced as a matter of choice sometimes feels very different; in other words, how people feel about spending time alone is bound up with their perception of their possibilities for spending time with others. For a small minority of respondents, predominantly male, the absence of a sustaining social network was evidently an element of a negative depiction of solo-living. This was often also combined with other factors, such as poor health and/or financial difficulties. A few men who were currently unemployed or reported financial difficulties depicted a pattern of social interaction based primarily around the local pub, a mode of sociability generally less available to women and rarely evident in the accounts of other respondents, male or female. For some men, questions about key others playing a part in their lives revealed none and little social life beyond that encountered in the pub.

The regulars in the pub basically. And that's about it'.

[William, 41, rural]

It's basically just sort of...it's like acquaintances like, sort of, you meet in the pub after work.

[Anthony, 34, urban]

If I'm in the pub by myself and I bump into someone I know I will stand there and speak to him for a while.

[Benjamin, 33, rural]

As we discuss in the following chapter, in a rural area the certainties of being known to others may provide opportunities for social interaction, opportunities not available to those who have moved to the city and for whom the anonymity may be a barrier to integration. However, in urban and rural contexts, a pub can become a site of social interaction for men, particularly among those who are regular customers. Anthony experienced a particular urban pub with a clientele of regulars sufficiently like himself to be a comfortable environment to share with his 'acquaintances'. The pub as an institution combines opportunities for a social life and alcohol as a means of self-medication when feeling low. The acceptability of this form of socializing, as well as a sense of comfort in any particular pubs, varies with social class, gender, sexuality and religion. Social class and sexuality mean that a local pub could not provide comfort to Harry (35, urban, gay), for example, as he expected a homophobic environment in which he would be at risk. Chapter 4 described how his feelings about his home were blighted by his negative view of his area of residence and its inhabitants, a working-class estate of social housing that he described his friends and family as being reluctant to visit. Harry had chronic depression and was currently not working. His mother was dead and he had limited contact with his father, who has remarried. Harry talked about two friends he met via the Internet who live elsewhere in Scotland, and occasional visits to his sister's family, who live in a nearby town. He expressed a desire for a social network very different from his current reality:

> The big thing for me would be...for friends to drop in or to go out and about, you know, meeting up with people, and things like that. Which I don't have. It's always, you're going around places on your own, you're coming home and it's empty. There's really not any inter-action when I am out, so I hardly go out. [...] I might not go out, I could be out once in ten days. I think there's a line in a song some-where about 'there's no one I know, there's nowhere I have to be, there's no one I know who's waiting for me', that's the one...I sup-pose you do become lazy, despondent – what's the point in going out? [...] I do feel isolated here...I mean I can go days without seeing anybody or talking to anybody. And that's hard.

The pub is one example of an institution structuring opportunities for meeting acquaintances that were important for people who had few social contacts; dog walking was another. Emily (34, urban) was alone in the parental home following the death of her parents and brother. She had left school at 16 with no qualifications and was working in low-paid shift work, currently working overtime due to having considerable debt. Her social network was limited and her main social contact was with a cousin's family that Emily visits fortnightly, and a friend whom she texted often yet saw infrequently as her friend also worked night shifts. Emily, however, did not depict herself as lonely. Although she had a three bedroomed house, she ruled out having a lodger as a poten-tial source of additional income, preferring the solitude that living alone afforded. She described how getting a dog had led to more social inter-action with others, as she met up with a group of fellow dog walkers every day in the local park. This routine place-and-activity structured socializing, like meeting acquaintances in a pub, provided a level of interaction that Emily depicted as satisfactory: 'if I didn't have the park I would be kind of on my own more...if I didn't take the dog to the park and meet people, well, I'd feel lonely I suppose'. Asked about potential sources of support, Emily included the people in her dog-walking group whom she felt could rely on to provide practical help; she referred to having someone from the group stay for a few weeks who was in need of temporary accommodation. Callum (44, urban) similarly reported becoming part of a 'community of dog walkers' who also provide practi-cal support: 'if somebody's working long hours they just take the house key and walk the dog at lunchtime or you come home and the dog's not there and you know it's in somebody else's house'. These examples illustrate the type of routine interactions through which acquaintance-ship is built, social relationships through which individuals may garner not just practical support but also sustain a sense of ontological security (Morgan, 2009).

For Anthony (34, urban), his socializing enabled by the institution, the pub, did not provide a sense of acquaintanceship sufficient to counter the negative impact of a limited social network. Anthony was amongst the small number regretfully stating that he 'does get lonely at times' and 'would like to have contact with people'. He too left school at 16 with no qualifications and was working in unskilled low-paid employment that provided little job satisfaction that had not kept him out of financial difficulties. Anthony had no contact with his son or ex-partner, and was estranged from his mother. Living in the area where he'd grown up, Anthony referred to being 'well known in the area', and yet he stated that he had few friends living locally: 'Well, Christ, I've sort of lost contact with a lot of people. Friends, like close friends, seem to have moved away from the area because they're in relationships'. Asked about his social network he replied 'it's sort of like people you see in sort of pubs and whatever, it's not people I'd see going out, like doing anything'. In contrast to Emily, Anthony's limited social interac-tion was accompanied by a sense of loneliness and dissatisfaction with living alone. For him, this was 'just something that I've become used to [...] I don't actually like being in the house myself. I don't like... I don't like it'.

Men describing a history of fractured family relationships and few friends often also had other disadvantages in their circumstances such as low paid employment or no employment, with little possibility of exit to a better situation because of low educational attainment, serious debts, mental illness or other health troubles, all of which might help to make 'being a loner' more possible than building social networks. Fractured family relationships can be both a cause and a consequence of other difficulties and mean the absence of women playing the role of 'kin keeper'. Robert (42, urban) left school at 16 with no qualifica-tions and has children from two previous partnerships; he is estranged from one child, though in occasional contact with his other, now adult, daughter, who visits him from England. He described himself as 'a bit of a loner', knowing lots of people but not considering them friends. Tommy (43, urban), unemployed for five years, also had no contact with his children. His mother lived in a care home in England and, while he keeps in touch with her by phone, the expense of travelling limits his visits: 'I've only seen her twice this year, because I can't afford it, it costs a fortune'. Probed about other people apart from his mother, Tommy answered 'No. My dog'. He has no contact with his large family of siblings: 'everybody has just, don't know where they are [...] don't really care'. While he stated he was living alone through choice, when asked about disadvantages of living alone, he answered 'Well, you're bored, you're depressed, stressed, everything, you get lonely'.

Social networks reflect individual preferences and personality, but are nevertheless also socially patterned. These accounts suggest patterns of circumstance that limit opportunities to form and maintain personal relationships. It is important not to exaggerate the disengagement of men given that most respondents, male and female, depicted active social networks. Nevertheless, for a few men, living alone was associated with a loss of contact with kin and others; a social isolation that was strongly associated with loneliness and possibly may become exacerbated in older age.

Concluding remarks

While much research suggests living alone in older age can be associated with negative outcomes in health and well-being, the picture is complex and the various contributory factors difficult to disentangle. Those living alone at any particular ages are a diverse group and it is important not to ignore sources of variation such as normative cultural expectations, socio-economic circumstances, gender and 'routes into' solo-living. Creating a sense of security and pleasure in a home is obviously more difficult when starting to live alone is an outcome of bereavement, or as a response to being made unwelcome in a shared home, than when living alone is through choice. Therborn's classification of family–sex–gender systems draws attention to regionally anchored socio-cultural variations framing how thinkable, socially acceptable and normal or deviant living alone is for men and women at different ages and stages of the life course. It is not surprising that Young and Grundy (2009) find no association between living alone and low levels of well-being in northern Europe, where living alone in older age is normatively accepted, statistically normal and well resourced. Research in Asia is more surprising, documenting living alone as a pragmatic compromise despite the cultural ideal stressing the co-residence of older people with their adult children and suggesting that living alone is preferable for well-being to living with others in tense and difficult circumstances.

In our UK study, the majority of men and women have rich social networks that are an important dimension of contentment with living alone, and provide a range of types of emotional and practical support. Despite considerable variation in a number of aspects of social networks, research respondents share an emphasis on the importance of family. Some commentators continue to ask whether 'chosen' relationships are ousting the genealogically 'given' relationships of family (Allan, 2008), but, as the earlier discussion of the suffusion of friends and family makes clear, prioritizing family relationships can be experienced as a choice and close family and very good friends can feel like similar types of relationships. The data presented indicate that men and women living alone are not typically supplanting kin relationships with alternative sources of solidarity. Rather, the social networks of many living alone express the importance of enduring friendships *and* relationships with family. The heterogeneity amongst those living alone, however, is reflected in the range and type of social networks, for example, some being very localized with others far more dispersed. This illustrates the multiplicity of factors underpinning the patterning of social networks. Here too factors such as gender and social class were to the fore, with a small number of respondents depicting a level of social isolation that they experienced as problematic; it was overwhelmingly men who experienced difficult circumstances such as low income and/or ill-health. The findings here suggest that those living alone are not so distinct; the patterning of their social networks parallels the findings of previous research across living situations, showing the shaping of social connectedness by histories of mobility and factors such as partnership status, age, class and gender. In terms of social connectedness then, living alone is not a definitive marker of difference from those who live with others.

It is tempting to only emphasize the social connectedness of the majority of those living alone in order to counteract the stereotype eliding isolation and loneliness but the smaller minorities who do not fit this pattern must also be acknowledged; they include those who enjoy solitary time to an exceptional extent and the few who are unintentionally and unhappily socially isolated and lonely. There is evidence of enjoyment of solitude among our interviewees, a state defined by Long and Averill (2003) as one of relative social disengagement. Living alone can facilitate desired time to oneself. There is considerable cultural variation across time and place in the extent to which time alone is considered to be socially desirable and normal; socio-economic circumstances also create different needs and possibilities. For some of our interviewees with working lives that involved services to others necessitating giving of the self, time alone was experienced as a relief. A preference for social disengagement, however, may be culturally inadmissible. Writing in the context of the Christian-European family tradition, Denise Riley (2002) refers to a 'compulsive sociability' and a long history of suspicion for anyone whose way of life exhibits solitude: 'as households of single people grow, the admission of even occasional loneliness remains taboo, while to be without visible social ties is inexcusable. Such common solitariness may be willed and preferred by its bearer, or may be barely tolerated, enforced: yet a taint of vice always clouds it' (2002, p. 8). Attention to the subjective meanings that social networks hold for individuals may discern a will to solitude; nevertheless, a prevailing discourse renders those living alone with limited social networks, even, and possibly especially, with contentment, somewhat suspect.

The majority of men and women expressed some consternation at the prospect of continuing to live alone into retirement, though a small number had considered this and a few referred to making provision to do so. This lack of planning may be related in part to the desire expressed by many for eventual cohabiting partnership, and the consternation reflects common stereotypes attached to living alone in older age. The review by Perissinotto et all (2012) of the literature on social isolation and the well-being of older people emphasizes the need to distinguish social isolation, depression and loneliness. They note that, while various studies demonstrate that measures of social isolation – the number of social contacts and the amount of social engagement – are associated with poor health outcomes, these quantitative measures of relationships may not adequately capture subjective distress. Our data suggest that small social networks and limited social engagements did not necessarily herald loneliness. The accounts of some individuals in such circumstances indicate that even relationships which only involve brief friendly acknowledgment can contribute to a sense of belonging, social competence and worth. Nevertheless, for some individuals living alone, more men than women, relative social isolation was associated with loneliness, lack of well-being and a desire for more contact with others. The intersections of gender, low income and ill-health indicate that living alone in itself is insufficient as an explanatory factor.

7
Place, Mobility and Migration

In this chapter, we consider the role that residential history and locality play in the embeddedness of men and women living alone in relationship to people and place. Urban and rural localities provide different opportunities to enjoy resources such as housing, employment and social spaces. How do these differences modify the experience of living alone? Some academic discussion of solo-living has particularly associated this trend with enhanced mobility and urban living (Buzar et al., 2005; Hall and Ogden, 2003). As was demonstrated in discussion of Japan (Chapter 2), solo-living has increased in both heavily and sparsely populated areas in some countries. The United Kingdom also demonstrates that solo-living can be a significant rural as well as an urban phenomenon.[1] We develop the discussion introduced in the previous chapter on the social connectedness of men and women living alone to consider sense of attachment to a particular locality, and how this might differ by factors such as gender and class. To what extent do people living alone see themselves as 'free agents', liberated from conventional ties to people or place? How far do they see living alone as significant in shaping a sense of belonging?

Living alone and residential histories

Research in North America and Europe maps how the choice of a certain residential location is closely related to different stages of the life course (Blaauboer, 2011; Feijten et al., 2008). Residential moves are often associated with household change and triggered by events in employment trajectories (Michielin and Mulder, 2008; South and Crowder, 1997). The relative importance attached to work and family life at different stages of the life course leads to preferences for a certain type of residential environment: studies have shown that a child-and-family-oriented lifestyle is associated with suburban living while a more work-oriented lifestyle is associated with a preference for living in urban areas (Bell, 1958; Bootsma, 1995; Brun and Fagnani, 1994). For many regions of the world, mobility is particularly associated with youth. For young people growing up in many rural areas across the globe, migration to an urban area is usually necessary for those with any ambitions of accessing higher education. The narrower employment opportunities of rural areas often makes return difficult if employment is to then match qualifications. Studies in rural areas of Australia and the United Kingdom document acceptance of the inevitability of rural youth out-migration, particularly among the middle class, expressed in the view that 'to get on you get out', which in turn devalues the choices of those who have never left (Gibson and Argent, 2008; Jamieson, 2000; Jones, 1999; Stockdale, 2004). At the same time, some young migrants often maintain lasting ties to their locality and the desire to return to a rural area similar to the place they grew up if not their actual place of origin (Jamieson, 2000). Jones (2001) has indicated that the structure of rural labour and housing markets make establishing an independent household particularly difficult for young women, while other authors suggest that more traditional conventions concerning appropriate gender roles in rural areas may limit women's choices. For example, research on the perceptions and experiences of women in an accessible rural area in England (Little and Austin, 1996) describes a pervasive stereotypical view of a 'rural idyll' which incorporates strong expectations that women will focus on a home-based mothering role. Is it more difficult for women living alone in rural areas to lead a life that does not follow a conventional gender script?

Although the UK household survey data support the view that people living alone are a more mobile population than those living with others, they also suggest that differences are modest and residential mobility is not the dominant pattern for either group. For example, the Scottish Household Survey data for 2011 (see Table A2.13, Appendix 2) indicates that among working age adults, less than 10 per cent living alone have lived at their current address for less than a year – twice the figure recorded for their peers living with others. However, it is also important to note that the residentially mobile are likely to be under-represented in household surveys, and data should be read as indicative rather than definitive. The Scottish Household data also show that a larger proportion of men than women living alone had lived in their current residence for less than two years: 30 per cent of men compared with 24 per cent of women and 19 per cent of men living with others. Reasons for residential mobility were explored in more in-depth follow-up interviews, including with nine of those living at their current address for less than a year. The pattern was more complex than moving to their current address for work reasons; most had prior experience of living in the area. Families and relationships were often implicated. Reasons included moving to be nearer a partner, exiting from living alone by moving to co-residence, moving home following partnership breakdown and moving to be closer to a parent who is ill.

The relatively modest proportion with higher levels of mobility are a warning not to assume that those who live alone are distinct from those living with others in attachment to their place of residence. The Scottish Household Survey suggests that the population living alone are also not very different in how they rate their area as a place to live. The majority of the population in the United Kingdom rate their locality as a good or very good place to live but with considerable variation by the level of deprivation of an area and its urban or rural characteristics. These differences are replicated among people living alone. Among men and women who live alone at working age, a higher proportion of those in rural areas classify the area as a very good place to live, and a smaller proportion find it fairly or very poor (see Table A2.14).

In the sample of 140 men and women living alone derived from the Scottish Household Survey of 2005/2006, about a quarter were migrants to Scotland (34), slightly more men (19) than women (15). Of these, the majority were born elsewhere in the United Kingdom, and had moved to Scotland for a variety of reasons, including moving for work, coming to Scotland to study and staying on, as well as having either moved with a partner or to be with a partner. These are also the main reasons given for internal mobility within Scotland. The international migrants reflect trends in migration and include persons from European countries, Asia and Africa. Scotland's near neighbour Ireland, and eastern Europe, are major sources of migrants to the United Kingdom. Amongst the sample in our qualitative study, several respondents had lived elsewhere, usually either within Scotland or in the United Kingdom, with a small number temporarily living abroad.

Table 7.1 illustrates mobility patterns by locality and gender, distinguishing whether people are living in the area where they were brought up, including those who returned after a period living elsewhere, from those who were 'incomers', having moved to their current locality from elsewhere. The first two rows of the table show men are more mobile than women, and this is consistent with the pattern in

Table 7.1   Place of residence by locality and gender (numbers)

Locality		Men	Women	Total
Urban	Living where brought up	11	22	33
	Incomer	25	13	38
Total		36	35	71
Rural	Living where brought up	23	13	36
	Incomer	16	17	33
Total		39	30	69
Total (N)		75	65	140

the total population in which urban dwellers predominate, but the pattern is different in rural areas. The small proportion of gay men in the sample are concentrated in urban areas. The majority of urban male respondents had moved there from elsewhere (25/36), whereas the majority of women in urban areas were living where they were brought up (22/35). In contrast, three fifths of rural men were living where they were brought up (23/39), whereas over half of women living alone in rural areas were in-migrants (17/30).[2] A sense of attachment to place is complex and cannot simply be identified through duration of residence but 'incomers' who had lived in their area for considerable periods of time typically felt settled there. Around half of the women who were incomers to a rural locality had moved there between 10 and 23 years previously. Some male incomers to both rural and urban localities described originally moving to the area as students nearly 20 years previously. In summary, about half of our sample of men and women living alone (69/140) were currently living in the locality where they had been brought up, although this differed by gender and type of locality.

The interview data indicated a range of motivations underpinning remaining in or returning to a place of origin and moving to a new locality; education and work opportunities are key factors for people moving to urban areas, which are generally characterized by educational facilities, leisure opportunities, and a broad range of low and high-skilled jobs. Limited employment opportunities in rural areas have been identified as a 'push' factor underpinning out-migration, especially for young people (Crow, 2010). Labour market restructuring in recent decades has drawn English managerial and professional migrants to Scottish cities (Findlay et al., 2002). For others, demographic transitions – both partnership formation and dissolution – underpinned mobility, with such moves often influenced by other factors such as housing or employment availability. A small number described decisions to move to or remain in a particular locality for 'quality of life' reasons: for example, a preference for the anonymity of the city, or rural locations providing opportunities for outdoor pursuits.

There were broad differences in the socio-economic situation of those living where brought up and those who had experienced mobility, with respondents from working-class backgrounds more likely to be amongst the former group and incomers from middle-class backgrounds the latter. Again, this is in line with research on who is most likely to experience mobility. However, several of those currently living in the area where they had been brought up recounted experiences of having moved elsewhere in the past due to limited local employment opportunities. The diverse motivations for moving (back) to or remaining in their current locality reflected the considerable heterogeneity amongst the sample in relation to gender, sexuality, partnership and socio-economic status, aspects of identity impacting on their experiences of place.

Living alone and embeddedness in place

Both urban and rural areas offer a range of social worlds, but the scale and diversity of social scenes more or less structured around social class, gender, sexuality, interest group and the like are much greater in urban contexts. These differences played out in the ways people spoke about where they lived. Amongst those living alone in rural locations, for example, a dominant theme was the depiction of a strong local community where people knew and were supportive of each other. This was evident both amongst those living where brought up, mainly men, as well as those who had moved to the rural area, mainly women. The local picture for those in urban locations, as might be expected, was far more variable. Nevertheless, for many respondents living where they were brought up, both rural and urban, the geographical proximity of wider family members was an important dimension of what Mulder (2007) refers to as 'location-specific capital', a major factor binding people to a place. For example, Jean (34, urban), a divorced secondary school teacher who lived minutes from her parents and her brother, responded when asked about her locality and future moves: 'I love where I live, otherwise I would have moved [...] I don't see me moving. It would need to be something amazing for me to move away from my family'. Several respondents also identified local friendships as important. Luke, 37, when asked about the rural area where he had always lived and intended to remain, commented: 'Grew up here and it's the area I like. All my family and friends are here'. For some respondents, a strong sense of belonging to and rootedness in a particular locality could encompass historical familial connections, confirming other research which found family roots important in return migration even in the absence of direct family networks (Maclean, 2003; Stockdale, 2002). Thus Brian, 42, a father living in a rural locality where his partner, children and wider family also lived, commented: 'I've lived here all the time [...] My great grandfather is in the war memorial for the first, the Great War [...] we're related to the fishermen going back to the 1700s from this town'. Cathy (26, rural) described moving in to her late grandmother's home, in part 'to keep it in the family'. Such strong senses of attachment to locality, whether expressed by those living where brought up or by incomers now 'settled' in their localities, counters stereotypes of those living alone as unbound to people and place.

Strong place attachment may underpin a sense of belonging that is an important dimension of ontological security. Nevertheless, assumptions of embeddedness in community as necessarily positive downplay the wider opportunities that mobility can provide. Studies of those living in deprived neighbourhoods in the United Kingdom (MacDonald, 2005; Rabe and Taylor, 2010) indicate that while social networks rooted in particular locales provide support to individuals in adverse circumstances, they simultaneously limit the possibilities of escaping conditions of social exclusion. A few respondents depicted encapsulation within very localized social worlds in conjunction with circumstances such as ill-health or unemployment; for several, proximity to family was an important factor in their remaining in the locality, and we consider the extent to which residential stability here may serve to sustain or compound disadvantage.

In contrast, some respondents depicted little attachment to a particular locality. This was evident mainly amongst those who had both moved there from elsewhere, and whose social networks, employment and or leisure activities were far more dispersed. Not surprisingly, lack of attachment was particularly acute when a career likely to require further mobility was the reason for being there. Detachment was not, however, the case for all respondents who had experienced mobility; several women who had moved to rural areas, some working in professional employment, described strong attachments to the area in which they lived. Their social networks were an important dimension of their 'spatial rootedness' (Gilbert, 1998). For some, decisions about potential moves from the locality in relation to career progression or to live with their partner were in tension with their attachment to the place where they lived. We explore these divergent attitudes further below.

Locality, belonging and community

A strong sense of local community was evident in the accounts of many living alone in rural locations, both amongst those living where brought up and those who had moved there. This, as well as good relationships with neighbours, was an important dimension of a contentment with where they lived. Thus Angus (35, rural, living where brought up) stated: 'it's just a fine, peaceful place to bide and everybody kens [knows] everybody, everybody gets on fine, very neighbourly'. Several women who had moved to their rural locality depicted a sense of community as a factor in the decision to do so: for example, Melissa (33, rural) listed 'fantastic neighbours, great community – that really makes it for me. Quiet, easy access to beach, have a dog as well so it's great'. Some, however, noted the consequent lack of privacy: 'the other side of the coin of that sense of community is the fact that everybody knows your business' (Paula, 36, rural). Urban residents were not only less likely to depict a strong locally-based sense of community but also unlikely to know their neighbours. Ernest's (38, urban) observation that 'the neighbours don't have anything to do with each other really, you know', was typical, as was Mark's (33, urban) description of his area as 'centre-of-the-town flats, so you just don't really see anybody'. There were exceptions: a few urban respondents described neighbours as friends, and as providers of companionship or practical support, most often those living in the area where they were brought up. For example, Elspeth (43, urban), who travelled a great deal for work, described neighbours staying in her home to look after her cat, bringing her soup when she broke her leg, as well as coming to her to ask for financial advice: 'because I've lived here all my life, and it's older neighbours, they knew my parents and they knew me growing up'.

The importance of being known in a locality to a sense of belonging was particularly evident in the narratives of men living in the rural localities where they were brought up. Hugh, 39, who had spent a couple of years working in Edinburgh in his twenties before returning to the area where he'd been brought up, contrasted experiences of anonymous city living with being 'hailed' by known others: 'The difference between a city and here is, basically nobody really looked at you in the town you know, whereas everybody goes past here and gives you a wave or talks to you, you know, it's more friendly'. Some depicted very localized social networks, with their most frequent social interactions arising from chance encounters. Mitch, 39, a fisherman, when asked whether he had friends in the area whom he saw more or less weekly responded:

> Who I see every day. Because I talk to everybody every day.
>
> What sort of things do you do together? Do you do stuff together?
>
> Not really, no. We just moan about fish prices [laughs] and the weather.

Some of these rural residents did not distinguish friendships with particular others from such circumstantial interchanges. Angus, 35, who had 'lived within about five minutes of where I am now all me life', described a very localized social network with both local family and neighbours he had always known. Asked whether he would like to spend more time with others, Angus indicated that interactions through his employment were sufficient: 'I'm in contact with folk every day, I'm working on building sites every day…I'm seeing folk the whole time'. In the context of his rural locality, the 'folk' are not an endless churn of different people but known named others. For Angus, this interaction equated with the quality of social contact provided by living with others: 'It's no different from biding [living] on my own or with somebody because I'm working in folk's houses, customer's houses…doesn't make that much difference'. Morgan (2009) describes acquaintanceship, the space between intimates and strangers, as encompassing mutual recognition and knowledge of or by the other. In the previous chapter, we noted that in urban as well as rural areas, places of institutionalized activity, such as the pub and sites of dog walking, can be sites of acquaintanceship. In a rural area with residential stability and small populations, opportunities for acquaintanceship are multiplied and diffused across the locality. The routine interactions and familiarity with others described by several rural men suggests that their residential stability and particular local knowledge enabled the possibility of 'little fragments of intimacy' (2009, p. 4) that were an important dimension of both a satisfaction with living alone and a sense of belonging.

The importance of close-knit communities was also evident amongst 'incomers' to rural areas. This might be in terms of the social activities it afforded, as well as a supportive environment in times of trouble. Both were evident in Struan's account of the small island community that he had relocated to and where he intended to remain. 'It's got a good social life, you know, it's got a good community spirit. There's always events, you know, dances and Burns suppers and the poker league in the restaurant. Most days I'll go for a few pints after work, you know, all the boys'. Struan (44, rural), a self-employed builder, described how living where he did enabled him to continue working after losing his driving licence:

> Because people know my predicament, that I'm banned, so when they employ me they come and get me and take me back, you know. I'm quite fortunate really, if that had been anywhere else I'd be knackered wouldn't I, you know what I mean, working as a builder but people up here seem to accept it and they like me work, so....

A community in which most inhabitants were known to each other was also identified as 'safe', an observation made mainly by women living alone. Several living in rural localities also reported how people would offer help if required. Chapter 6 discussed the reliance on family for practical support; for those who had moved to areas some distance from their families, a sense of potential help on hand was important. Sophie, 38, said of the rural area to which she had moved: 'People are very friendly and very supportive of each other ... what is lovely about being in a place like [village], and I suppose it is particularly the case if you live on your own ... simply the fact that you are somebody who lives in the village, people would always help you out'.

The extent to which this sense of a local supportive community shaped a sense of attachment, however, varied considerably. For some it was part of an enjoyment of living there at that time rather than long-term commitment. Thus Sophie, who had moved to the area initially to undertake postgraduate study and was now working in a management position, described a dispersed social network, with most friends and family living elsewhere in the United Kingdom. While she did socialize with friends living locally, she also travelled regularly to meet up with friends and family, and enjoyed leisure activities such as attending cultural events in nearby cities on her own. Sophie had previously lived abroad for several years, and described herself as 'quite self-sufficient'. She was currently considering moving elsewhere to get a larger house, and keeping open the possibility of leaving Scotland in the future. Sophie's account suggests an 'elective belonging' more common amongst but not exclusive to urban-based mobile professionals.

Employment mobility, social class and 'elective belonging'

Jobs and education are the key reasons for people moving location within Britain, with those in middle-class professional occupations almost twice as likely to move as those in working-class unskilled jobs (Donovan et al., 2002). Employment was the main driver for respondents moving to a new area, especially amongst the more educated, some of whom had experienced considerable residential mobility. While some rural respondents described previous experiences of moving away temporarily due to lack of local employment options, most employment-related mobility was portrayed in terms of the 'pull' of career progression. This was particularly evident amongst urban professional men; several respondents in this group depicted a lack of connectedness to their locality. Jake, 28, a professional originally from a rural area elsewhere in Britain, had moved to Edinburgh two years previously, after studying and working in London for several years. He described deciding initially to spend a year in Edinburgh to see how it went, 'and if I didn't like it I would go somewhere else'. He bought a flat after a period living in shared accommodation as he wanted to get on the property ladder; however, living there was envisaged as temporary: 'I mean it's one of these areas like a lot of places they say it's up and coming, but up and coming places never arrive. They are just somewhere that people move to for a while before they go somewhere else'. As Chapter 4 has noted, seeing a home as a stage on the property ladder suggests willingness to be geographically and socially mobile. A home's location is then considered as temporary until employment related relocation, or as a stepping stone to the next property in a more 'desirable' location.

Jake did not feel 'at all' involved in his local area, and described relationships with his neighbours as 'pretty anonymous'. He was currently in a relationship of a few months' duration, 'a potential rather than a serious partner'. Living alone was clearly one factor in a sense of himself as a 'free agent', along with his sense of 'home' not being bound to the locality. He is described in Chapter 4 as using his home to host visits from long standing friends across his dispersed social network as well as a means of entertaining and developing relationships with new Edinburgh friends, a process he will repeat if he moves elsewhere. When asked about the possibility of moving, Jake answered: 'Yes. Absolutely yes. I have moved around quite a lot as it is so I wouldn't rule out another move [...] I think living on my own and not being married or anything at the moment, that helps me keep an open mind towards something like that'. He perceived this as a common experience shared by his cohort reflecting social change since his parent's generation and his description is consistent with academic characterizations of the fluidity of contemporary modernity: 'I think people are much more independent and more nomadic and move around a lot more, as I have done'. His main leisure activity was not adversely affected by moving around as it involved an interest-based community rather than a place-based one. His account, as with several other respondents who had experienced and anticipated future career-related mobility, is suggestive of 'elective belonging'.

The experience of career-related mobility also compounded a sense of the relative unimportance of geographical proximity to wider family. Albert (38, urban), who was a manager, had moved from England for work. He liked his current locality: gay, he felt 'living in an inner city that's very sort of accepting, cosmopolitan...is important'. Asked about key people, he spoke first about his parents, who lived 180 miles away. However, asked whether family ties would be a factor in any future plans to move, he replied: 'I would say no, because I've always sort of moved around and go with the job and I've always been able to keep in touch with family, in contact anyway, so there hasn't been a problem, so I would say they wouldn't be a big factor'. Fiona (31, urban) who had returned to the city where she had been brought up after several years living in London, was open to the idea of future mobility, which she related both to her previous experience and being 'quite driven in terms of career'. Asked about family ties, Fiona responded these 'would definitely be an influence...but I wouldn't, it wouldn't stop me from changing location because we can always work round these things...I'm considering potentially moving overseas and I wouldn't go to Australia...for a long period because that is just too far but somewhere in Europe you know, I think that's quite manageable'.

For some respondents, employment mobility was presented more as a necessity than a choice. Laura (31, urban), a public service professional, was living a considerable distance from her parents and sibling in England: asked whether this was something she expected or would like to change in the future, Laura replied, 'I suppose I've just kind of got used to it...I kind of have to detach myself from those kind of ideas because I have to be where the work is'. Craig (43, urban) had moved to Edinburgh more than 20 years previously; he was currently commuting to his professional work in another city and had bought a flat to live there during the week, returning home at weekends. His attachments to Edinburgh outweighed the option of relocating permanently. He described several colleagues who also commuted, some living in bedsits or caravans during the week: 'a lot of the people I work alongside are in exactly the same circumstance as me in that they only work in [city – removed for anonymity] and then they disappear at the weekends'. Craig had a partner living in yet another city, with whom he spent most weekends. They have not considered cohabiting as 'she doesn't want to give up her job and I don't want to give up my job'. Asked whether he expected that he might continue living alone, Craig answered: 'I think probably yes, actually [...] I would for the immediate future in so far as my work circumstances kind of dictate that that is how I have ended up'. Craig's account might seem to illustrate mobility resulting in a purely instrumental approach to place. Nevertheless, the pattern of commuting he describes encompasses sustained commitments elsewhere, alongside this disengagement in the locality of his employment.

Putnam argues that frequent movers have weaker community ties (2000, p. 204–205, see also Coleman, 1988). The experience of residential mobility, however, may play a role in a subsequent opting for residential stability and community involvement. Catriona (37, urban), for example, had recently returned to live in the urban area where she had been brought up, a town on the edge of Glasgow. This followed several years living in 'loads of different places' in various cities in the United Kingdom and abroad, for education and employment. Catriona's parents fell ill when she was in her early thirties, whereupon she transferred her employment to Glasgow, and subsequently moved back to her home town. Her social network included distance relationships with friends she had met while living elsewhere, long-standing local friendships and nearby family. Catriona's account depicted efforts to establish a sense of 'spatial rootedness'. She was active in a local history group as well as various other organizations, and indicates that her previous mobility was a factor shaping involvement in her local area: 'when I moved into the area I consciously made an effort to join the neighbourhood watch group and the tenancy group and things as well'. Catriona contrasted her current neighbourhood with the anonymity she had experienced living elsewhere:

> It's community living rather than, you know, living in a street with people that don't know you, and you know, you know your neighbours, whereas in some other places, people like yourself that you don't see until, you know, maybe you pass them on the stairs on a Sunday or something.

Catriona's narrative demonstrates the influence of various factors underpinning a residential strategy of return migration. This included her experience of considerable employment-related mobility: it is in part *because of* previous mobility that Catriona is now working to establish a sense of embeddedness in her local area through community activities.

The accounts of respondents with school-level qualifications in low-paid employment are more often of abandoned desires for mobility, and illustrate how the difficulties of finding housing on a low income act as barriers. While some young adults remain in or return to rural and small town localities because of place-based commitments to friends, family or local community, others confess to being trapped by the difficulties of moving and sustaining life elsewhere. Benjamin (33, rural, living where brought up), at first interview an unskilled worker with the only local industrial employer and subsequently unemployed, wanted to move to the nearest city. He was currently on the waiting list for social housing and past experience of living in low standard accommodation meant he would wait as long as it took: 'I'm on a waiting list for a council house, and the list is as long as the A9![3] So that will take me ages, it will take me two years yet to get a house like [...] I'm not wanting to go back and stay in digs, I've done that before, I've been in some dodgy places like, you know. I've been in some right doss houses before so I want to get my house first and then start looking for a job. No way am I going back to temporary digs again, no way'. Alice (36, rural, living where brought up) moved to a nearby city for work in her late teens; however, she returned to her parents' home after six years having been made redundant and in part because of the difficulty in finding suitable accommodation: 'I just ended up in terrible lodgings and kept moving... I was on the council waiting list but obviously with [city] there were so much more a need [demand outstrips supply] that I would have been like bottom of the pile'.

At interview Alice worked as a cook in the public sector and had a second part-time job to help make ends meet. She lived in a local council house after waiting a long nine years: 'I didn't live with my parents through choice, it was through necessity [...] I found it really hard [...] I couldn't rent privately because I mean I don't earn a great [wage], you're lucky if you make it month to month really'. Ford et al (1997) note the limited availability of social housing in rural areas, while increased housing costs also affect the housing transitions of young people in rural areas (Leyshon and DiGiovanna, 2005). Interviewees' accounts indicate the difficulties in accessing social housing in both rural and urban environments, and the limits this poses on potential working-class mobility, reaffirming the importance of establishing the subjective experience of apparent rootedness as well as mobility.

Relating at a distance

Geographically spread-out social networks were characteristic of the particularly mobile, relatively affluent and predominantly middle-class professionals living alone. Their narratives indicate the importance of 'network capital', the capacity to engender, sustain and reap emotional, financial and practical benefit from an array of relationships with people not physically proximate, generated through the proliferation of mobilities facilitated by communication and transport technologies (Raine and Wellman, 2012; Urry, 2007). The majority of respondents reported using email, social networking sites and mobile phones. All users deploy communication technologies in a range of ways. Relationships that were initiated in such mediated forms of communication and remained beyond face-to-face were very rare, but, as the discussion of Internet-dating in Chapter 3 illustrated, and is discussed further below, a minority proportion of interviewees had initiated relationships through the Internet and moved them to face-to-face relationships. The most common use of such technologies was to maintain contact with friends and family living locally, including those seen face-to-face frequently, but they are also the mainstay of mediated relationships with those living elsewhere and met infrequently. Those with higher education tend to live further from their place of origin and can have friends located at a very significant distance (Donovan et al., 2002). Chapter 4 notes the importance of visits to and from friends and family in the lives of many respondents with dispersed social networks. Mobility was routinely coupled with the maintenance of social relationships that were once face-to-face over distance, with mediated communication sustaining a sense of connection between direct personal visits.

Respondents with considerable experience of mobility typically described accumulations of friends from across the life course. Thus Sophie (38, rural) observed: 'I do actually have a very large pool of friends, but they're very dispersed and they've been collected over a very long time, in a whole lot of different contexts, and what I find is I tend to hang on to two or three people from most phases of my life'. Harriet (35, rural), who has lived in several places and changed career, noted 'you collect different friends at different stages of your life [...] I've got one that lives 400 miles away, I've known her it must be 15 years now [...] another bundle from when I taught [...] some from where I am now, and some from childhood as well'. More uncommon was Ray's (44, urban, gay) account depicting place-specific and hence transitory friendships left behind mentally as well as physically with every city-hopping job change: 'I think friends come and go with me to be honest [...]

I probably don't keep friends because with my job I've moved around quite a lot, but although I've been in Edinburgh for six years it's the longest I've stayed in any one place so probably I don't have any friends that go back longer than six years'.

The importance of communication technologies in facilitating new mobilities was especially evident in the accounts of migrants who had moved to the United Kingdom from overseas. For example, Janek (27, urban, gay) had moved to Edinburgh two years previously from Eastern Europe to live with his then-partner. He speaks to his parents and grandparents, as well as his sisters in North America, regularly: 'My family's scattered all over the globe [...] I call them every month, maybe twice a month. But we talk for two hours (laugh), one hour is the minimum'. Sunil (38, urban), had initially moved to Glasgow, where his then-wife lived, a couple of years previously, staying on following his divorce. Also with siblings living 'all around the world', Sunil phones them and other family living in his country of origin in Africa weekly, as well as keeping in touch via email. He also maintains contact with childhood friends, some also migrants, via the Internet. Sunil returns annually for a holiday, although cost constraints means he cannot make desired visits to siblings living elsewhere in Europe, North America, Australia and the Middle East. Like several respondents, a sense of emotional closeness with transnational kin relationships is maintained through digital technologies.

A few respondents described having formed relationships on the Internet with people they subsequently travelled to meet up with, or who visited them. Angela (44, rural), for example, included 'my internet friends', two women she met online nine years previously, amongst the people important to her. They now visited each other regularly and spoke on the phone as well as chatting online. Angela considered these friends to be intimates who provided emotional support to each other in times of difficulty:

We chat on the internet I'd say at least twice a week [...] I know they're the type of friends that if I really, really was sort of down or stuck or something, I wouldn't go online, I'd pick the phone up and they'd be the ones that I'd...I'd spill everything to.

Online relationships between initial strangers that are sustained over long periods of time often start to approximate to friendship developed 'offline' (Chan and Cheng, 2004; Jamieson 2013), yet such convergence often involves adopting additional means of communication beyond the digital context (Baym, 2010). The ability to form and sustain relationships at a distance may be particularly important for those living alone, and digital technologies and travel enabled the maintenance of relationships at a distance for many. Nevertheless, the accounts of some respondents demonstrated the limits of long-distance relationships, and this was particularly so for those relating a desire to move in with partners living elsewhere. Co-presence remains important to the development of intimacy in the sense of feeling close to and in a special relationship with another (Jamieson, 2013). This desire, however, could be in tension with commitments in and to their current locality. The accounts of some women who had moved to rural locations and had lived there for some time depicted strong place attachment; despite their previous mobility, the building of local social networks over time had led to a sense of 'spatial rootedness' for many. As noted in Chapter 3, the limited 'partnership pool' was mentioned by several respondents living alone in rural areas, although the extent to which this was presented as problematic varied. Some described using the Internet to meet partners; for those living alone in rural areas, this was particularly likely to mean forming relationships with people living some distance away. However, their attachment to place was difficult to reconcile with a desire to partner since it created resistance potentially to moving to cohabit with partners.

Alexandra (41, rural) had moved to Scotland as a student more than 20 years previously. Since then she had always lived in the same area, moving to her current locality when an opportunity came up to purchase a house there: 'I just love it [...] it's a wee village that I really, I've always liked but never thought I could actually afford'. Alexandra had retrained as a teacher a few years previously; while she 'really liked' the school where she worked, she was conscious that promotion would require moving to a new school. Alexandra had met her current partner who lived 50 miles away six months previously via the Internet. Her narrative indicated a sense of anxiety about reconciling a desire to live with her partner, ambitions to progress in her career, and practical considerations about deciding where to live: 'I'd like to maybe look at being a principal teacher, so that would mean having to move out of the school, but it also depends on how this relationship goes in the next year as to where that's going to be'.

Paula, 36, originally moved to Scotland as a postgraduate student, then to a rural village in the mid-1990s. Living in social housing, she was working in employment she described as 'alright for where I live ... but by no stretch of the imagination is it a fantastic job'. Paula described where she lived in very positive terms: 'I do love where I live... the beauty of the area... I've got great, fantastic friendships here, I love the sense of community here'. The 'biggest drawback' had been 'not meeting somebody', a factor in Paula previously considering moving to a town or city, where 'you've got a bigger pool to fish from'. However, Paula then met her current partner using Internet dating 18 months previously. Paula's partner lived in an English city 400 miles away, and they travelled regularly to meet via a budget airline. They were discussing the possibility that he moved to live with her, getting employment locally. Yet, as well as difficulties associated with cohabiting after a period living alone, Paula was conscious that available employment, alongside the higher costs of living in the area, made this unfeasible: wanting to start a family, this would only be possible if her partner worked in the nearest city as lack of local childcare meant she would give up her job. While Paula had ruled out moving to live in his city, they had discussed the possibility of moving to be near her widowed mother who 'is not getting any younger and would love me to move back'. This, however, was presented as quite a daunting prospect due to low housing availability in her current locality, which limited the prospects of returning if the relationship ended:

> I do have doubts sometimes... it's quite a scary prospect... possibly I could be happier but what if I'm not as happy and then there's no stepping back... if I give up here it would be very difficult to ever come back.

These accounts indicate a complex interrelationship between attachment to place, housing and employment possibilities, and prospective co-residential partnership. Chapter 4 notes the importance of property as an investment and security for many. Yet owning property complicates things and is likely to prolong negotiation of co-residential arrangements: property has to be sold to start afresh together, while divestment of such a significant asset heightens a sense of risk. The limited supply of social housing for people living alone means that tenancies are also long awaited and highly valued by those who cannot afford to buy. A very high sense of risk is attached to giving them up. Lewis' research (2006) on the extent to which individuals regard partnership and childbearing as risks situates this in a context of the erosion of a taken-for-granted traditional family model alongside an increasing expectation of individual responsibility for economic security across the life-course. Greater fluidity in intimate relationships, which has given more choice to individuals in partnering, has also transformed the economic dependence on men that women have traditionally experienced as a possible source of protection into a much more straightforward risk-risk that is exacerbated on the arrival of children. In addition to material considerations, some accounts suggest the significance of *other* dimensions in deliberations about moving to cohabit. As these excerpts demonstrate, and the discussion in Chapter 3 about those who may be less likely to partner also illustrates, various considerations had to be weighed in decision-making about cohabitation, including an attachment to place that may also be perceived as at risk. Such attachment is a locational tie that complicates decision-making about future cohabitation.

Qualified belonging?

Factors such as sexuality, gender and partnership status worked alongside living alone in particular residential settings to shape an individual's experience of 'place'. The extent to which such status distinctions were problematic for respondents in this study varied; their experiences suggest ways in which localities are open or closed to people of particular status who live alone. Researchers have noted the importance of sexuality to processes of migration, belonging and identity: large cities are associated with greater tolerance of sexual diversity, and many lesbian and gay people move to urban environments in search of a more visible queer community (Binnie, 2004; Weston, 1997). The small number of gay and lesbian respondents living in rural areas did not foreground their sexuality as a factor shaping their place of residence, though Cameron (39, gay, rural) noted: 'I think it's easier if you're gay to live in a city because it's...you know, you're less...it's less obvious I think'. Richard (31, gay, urban) noted 'I wouldn't live in a place where I couldn't date anyone'. A few respondents depicted their rural localities as intolerant of gay and lesbians, for example, Benjamin (33, rural) commented 'being a small town if they find out you're that way you tend to get blokes picking on you, picking fights', citing an uncle's experience as an example. A few respondents living in urban housing estates where they had been brought up expressed a sense that their area may not be welcoming to those seen as in some way 'different'. Asked whether they would recommend their area to someone in similar circumstances to themselves, Aileen (27, urban) observed her neighbourhood would not be open to ethnic minorities. Annabel (30, urban) replied: 'No I wouldn't actually. I think it is different if you're brought up in an area and you're sort of known about and people know your face but I think a single young female coming in to it, no, even like a single young man coming into the scheme'. In Chapter 4 we noted that Harry (35, gay, urban) living in a deprived neighbourhood whose rough reputation meant family and friends wouldn't visit felt his own class background marked him as out of place and ruled out his neighbours as possible companions.

Ray (44, gay, urban) described preferring the anonymity of the city; his employment had led him to live in several small towns, where he found cohabiting in a same-sex relationship difficult. Now single, he was living in an area of the city which was convenient for his work, however, where he spent little time and felt little sense of attachment: 'I don't dislike it, but I keep myself very much to myself, I live here, I go to work in the morning, I come home at night and if I'm socialising I'm socialising in the centre of Edinburgh. I only live here because it's convenient for work'. He observed that 'it would be probably quite difficult to be an open and out gay man or gay woman in this area that I live in...it's mainly families'. Yet this wasn't depicted as a matter of particular concern for Ray, whose experience of residential mobility suggested limited attachment to particular locality, while living in the city provided a preferred option of 'separating out' his social and home life.

Some respondents noted that living alone in itself distinguished them from their neighbours in certain localities. This was the experience of two fathers, who had moved to their current neighbourhoods following divorce. Mike (33, urban) had chosen a place near his child and 'because it had a garden'. However, he described some self-consciousness at being 'the only single guy in the street'. Bruce (34, rural) who had his children to stay frequently and was in a relationship, nevertheless, commented: 'I think there's probably certainly a couple of ladies around the village that have viewed me with a certain suspicion'. Lauren (37, urban) felt similarly out of place as a single woman when she moved to a middle-class neighbourhood of Glasgow in her mid-thirties:

> It doesn't really have much of a transient population and, therefore, you are still a little abnormal...you know, being single and not having any family here, whereas previously when I worked in [other UK cities] I didn't feel the same, but I think they've got larger transient populations, they're much more cosmopolitan...everybody I worked with already had relationships or close family and lived and worked in Glasgow all their lives, so it was much harder.

The extent to which experience of difference mattered to individuals' sense of attachment to an area varied. Those whose residential histories related to career mobility and who depicted little place attachment seemed more sanguine. For some fathers whose route into living alone was the outcome of a disrupted partnership, being distinguished on the basis of living alone was experienced with discomfort.

A few research respondents went further to suggest, like Annabel quoted above, that any incomer who was not intrinsically of their locality was not likely to be made welcome. Harvey (38, rural), when asked whether he'd recommend the remote rural village where he'd lived all his life, observed:

> There's a lot of people that are 70 plus that knew my parents, that knew my grandparents and through that they know me. But I would think if I was to move in myself with no connection, I think a lot of them would have probably blanked me [...] There's a saying up here called 'interloper', meaning someone from outside, and that could even be somebody from five miles away. How close-minded can you get?
>
> (Harvey, 38, rural)

However, as a number of researchers of UK rural communities have noted, the cultural boundaries between 'insiders' and 'outsiders' are often flexible and their construction a contested process (Crow and Maclean, 2006; Crow et al., 2001; Maclean, 2003). Writing about a parish in the north of Scotland, Catherine Maclean notes that 'attributes such as valued skills or personal characteristics that led to an individual being well liked and respected could over-ride or mitigate what otherwise might be seen as "incomer" or "white settler" characteristics' (2003, p. 170–221).

Previous research on a rural area in England demonstrated strong conventional expectations about women's roles (Little and Austin, 1996). For the majority of women in rural areas participating in our study, living alone did not inhibit a sense of their being part of the community. Solo-living per se was not sufficient as a marker of difference and departure from the conventional role of wife and mother was not automatically problematic. Nevertheless, women were often mindful of their visibility as women living alone and conventions concerning female respectability. Those who were incomers typically had professional positions that involved engagement in community activities. Most indicated a strong sense of being embedded and settled in their locality. Rhona (40, rural) had moved to a remote island location for employment in her 20s. Asked about her area she replied: 'I love it...the community, everybody's extremely friendly, welcoming and supportive'. Her work and interests had provided her with an active social network: 'I've met a lot of friends usually through work or through the Church... I see friends most days here, if you don't see them at work you see them in the shop and have a gossip'. At the same time she observed this did also incorporate a lack of privacy: 'you can't do anything without everybody knowing about it, that's the one disadvantage. Your private life isn't really'. Rhona described an incident where a local man turned up at her door drunk one night, after which she was reassured by others that they would make sure this would never happen again. Angela (44, rural), who similarly depicted the close-knit community she had moved to very positively, described her and her partner choosing to regularly spend a weekend together elsewhere rather than stay over at each others' houses, as the 'gossips are just terrible'. Angela depicted this as of little import: 'I'm not bothered, if they talk about me in the Co-op then they're leaving somebody else alone'. Both she and Rhona were settled in their localities with no plans to move. Nevertheless, fear of gossip had impacted on Angela's behaviour. Without the reassurance of others, the experiences of Rhona, having been targeted as a woman living alone, might have heighten a sense of difference that works against a sense of belonging. Visibility in the community was experienced as both protective and supportive inclusion and censoring surveillance.

Attachment to people in place

For those currently living where they had been brought up (more often working-class respondents) proximity to family and friends was an important dimension of a sense of belonging to a particular locality. The centrality of family was particularly evident amongst women in urban areas and men in rural areas, many of whom had left school at 16, the minimum school leaving age. Ailsa, 28, was living in the post-industrial town where she had grown up and to which she had returned following the dissolution of a two year marriage spent in a town nearby. She worked full-time in the same role she had been working in since leaving school at 16, albeit in different companies. Living alone for six years, she described close relationships with family, eating at the parental home several nights a week, joined by siblings also living locally. Asked about her local area, Ailsa commented:

It's just what we're used to. I mean it's not the most exciting place but it's nice but that could just be because friends and family are close by.

I like the security of knowing that they're there. As a town it's not got that much to offer.

Both family ties and local friendships were clearly central to Ailsa's commitment to her locality. Asked whether her approach to relationships had any bearing on her feelings about where she lived, Ailsa responded:

It would have to be with somebody that will be willing to live in the same area. I don't want to move away from friends and family.

For many of these interviewees, ties to people bound them strongly to their place of residence. Christie, 42 and living in the rural area where he was brought up, described how family ties led to his deciding against emigration with a then-partner, who subsequently ended their relationship: 'having no siblings of her own, she didn't understand that'. Annabel (30, urban) described moving from Glasgow to an English city in her early twenties with a then-partner who had moved for employment. However, she returned due to missing her family, subsequently ending the relationship:

We'd obviously discussed like children and stuff like that as well, getting married, and we thought it would be really good for us as a couple to actually go down, because...we'd have our own house [...] I found it really hard...I have a really good close relationship with my sister and her kids...and I just thought 'no, I can't do this, I want to come home' [...] I never realized I was such a homebody.

Annabel continued living in the area, where her family also lived, despite observing it had 'definitely deteriorated', and acknowledged that family ties would always be a factor in any future considerations about moving away.

For some respondents, the importance of local family was bound up with other factors such as poor health and/or unemployment. Kylie, 36, living in social housing on a peripheral housing estate of Glasgow, had not worked since her early 20s due to ill-health. She described her local area as having 'quietened down a lot now, it used to be quite a bad place [...] a lot of shootings and stabbings and things'. Kylie's parents live very nearby, as do some siblings and extended kin, most of whom she speaks to daily and who visit her regularly and take her shopping. Asked if she would consider moving in the future, Kylie answered that she had put in a request for another house to the housing authority due to problems with drug dealers in her building, but that this would have to be local: 'if it was maybe 15 minutes away then yeah I'd still take it ... I just couldn't be too far away from my mum'.

An attachment to family that acts as a drag on mobility in the context of deprivation and inequality may perpetuate disadvantage. Nevertheless, some accounts indicate that social networks with family and friends may sustain individuals in, or help them resolve, adverse circumstances. Isobel's (29, urban) narrative depicts her local social networks as important in coping with and potentially overcoming difficult conditions. Isobel had not worked since leaving university to care for her parents, then subsequently experiencing ill health herself. Her parents died when Isobel was in her early twenties, and she remained living in the parental home, social housing on a peripheral housing estate in Glasgow. Her brother lived nearby with his girlfriend and her extended kin also lived in the same city. Isobel described a rich social life with both friends and family, centred mainly in her immediate neighbourhood and especially in her home: 'there's constantly people in this house ... I don't think I am alone'. As well as frequent visitors, her cousin's children stay with her at weekends. Isobel is hopeful her health will improve enough to return to university. While she doesn't rule out moving in the future, she commented:

> Most people when they're going away they're kind of leaving something or they don't have anything to stay for, but I don't feel like that at all. I feel like I'm really happy with the people, my friends and my family especially, and therefore I don't feel that need to kind of 'go and explore new pastures', because I need those people. Not in a whole desperate needy way ... just purely because to me that's what makes your life, it's not all the other crap, it's the important people in it.

Parents and place

A very specific instance of the importance of family ties was demonstrated in the narratives of some non-resident parents whose residential choices centred on their desires to remain involved in their children's lives. Arthur (43, rural) had been living alone following divorce. Nevertheless, his residential arrangements remained tied to his children. When his ex-wife and children moved back to the rural community that they were originally from, he consequently only saw his children every two weeks and subsequently also returned to this locality. By the time of interview, he had two of his four children living with him: 'I moved because of the family... I'm actually just a few doors down from my elderly parents'.

Connor, 42, had moved with his wife and children five years previously to the rural locality where her parents lived. Following his divorce, his own parents had subsequently also moved to the area: 'They actually moved up here when we split up... [to be] not just local to me, but local to my kids'. Connor's 'moorings' to the locality are his own children and, now, his parents. Asked about his local area, Connor replied:

> I like the countryside and I've got family up here now. That's basically the main reason I stay in the area [...] if I didn't have the family here, I think I would clear off to Spain or something [laughs].... I don't have a lot keeping me here now apart from the kids [...] If my folks cleared off, I wouldn't have to stay in this area really.

These excerpts demonstrate life course transitions such as divorce triggering moves not just for non-residential parents, but also grandparents. Here, 'belonging' was to particular others rather than a particular locality. Yet, as Connor's excerpt suggests, decisions about residential location choice made in relation to particular events, such as divorce, or stages in the life course, having dependent children, remain open to revision.

Concluding remarks

In this chapter, we analyse the data from our UK study to consider the extent to which locality shapes the experience of living alone, and what impact it plays in attachment to people and to place. Living alone at working-age is often identified with an urban lifestyle; however, while solo-living is prevalent in urban areas, it is not exclusively so, and the trend of increase is also evident in rural areas. The data demonstrate the importance of residential history, with the length of time spent in a locality often associated with a sense of 'belonging'. The patterning of residential location indicated again the importance of gender and social class. In accordance with mobility patterns generally, those with tertiary education and professional employment were the most likely to have experienced mobility: in our sample, more men than women had experienced career mobility drawing them to urban localities. Moving to rural locations was more common amongst women, again mainly working in professional employment. Those with school-level qualifications were more likely to be living in the locality where they had been brought up, more men than women in rural areas, and more women than men in urban areas.

Mobility is often assumed to mean rootlessness, transitory lifestyles and resultant fleeting attachments. Only a minority group of predominantly urban men in our sample approximate to this characterization. For mobile professionals with dispersed social networks and anticipating future mobility, residence did not express belonging to a 'place' as an aspect of their identity. Some mobile professionals did demonstrate a sense of 'elective belonging', with their current locality depicted more as a stepping stone in a trajectory of geographic and social mobility. Yet this was not universally the case. Several who had experienced previous mobility depicted themselves as 'settled' in their locality, with some consciously working to establish 'spatial rootedness' through community involvement as a reaction to previous residential mobility. Others whose employment required mobility worked to maintain attachments to people and places where they had existing commitments. Several who had experienced mobility described dispersed social networks, and here digital communications were important in enabling the maintenance of a community of 'affect' over time and distance.

Yet strong 'moorings' to locality were also evident amongst respondents living alone, with the people in that place an important dimension of their 'place attachment'. Very localized social networks occurred amongst those living alone in the locality where they were brought up. For some, networks were centred on neighbours rather than close family or friends and dependent on being 'known' in the locality: as David Morgan (2009) suggests, this recognition and routine interaction was an important aspect of a sense of belonging and attachment to place. The extent to which place attachment might be considered as sustaining or constraining relates to the circumstances in which it is experienced. For some respondents the difficulty of accessing social housing as a person living alone also acted as a constraint on potential mobility. In a context of deprivation, attachment to place may act to limit flexibility that might otherwise enhance opportunities.

Localities differ in the extent to which they enable or inhibit the social inclusion and moral acceptance of those living alone. As anticipated, a sense of 'community' was more typical of rural than urban areas and this was identified as important by many rural residents. Rural localities more readily afford a sense of being embedded in relationships with people and place; the sense that 'everybody knows everybody', being known and knowing others in a network of acquaintances, underpins belonging and inclusion. This was cited as a factor in feeling 'safe' by some women and seemed to provide 'ontological security' for men who had few, if any, close ties. It cannot be presumed, however, that rural places are always experienced as welcoming to strangers, although most in-migrant rural residents were enthusiastic about the local community, stressing the safety and friendliness of their locality. On the other hand, several men who had grown up in their place of rural residence described their locality as unwelcoming of gay or lesbians. In both rural and urban areas, some people living alone feel 'out of place' due to factors that they felt distinguished them from the 'community', being the only gay or the only single person in an area of family households, or apparently single with visiting children, for example. It is important to note that living alone per se was not typically a key marker of difference that distinguished individuals.

8
The Future of Living Alone

Future trends

The number of people living alone is likely to continue to increase globally, both among the elderly and the working-age population, although it remains much more unthinkable and practically impossible in some regions of the world. In some parts of Europe and the United States, recession may cause pause and reversal, but, in general, where the trend has more recently started, it is more likely to continue towards higher levels, albeit not necessarily achieving the current levels in northern Europe. Gradations in the levels of living alone will continue more or less mapping onto the family–sex–gender systems outlined by Göran Therborn. It will remain very low for working-age adults in regions where family–sex–gender systems are more securely patriarchal, exercising tighter control over women and young people. It has long been anticipated that the growing opportunities for waged work of global capitalism and the more rapid global flows of discourse, including the celebration of gender equality and intimacy, will weaken patriarchal arrangements. However, such predictions have often underestimated their resilience. There are still many contexts in which young people have limited or no access to a period of independence beyond parental control and prior to marriage. For women, living alone is neither practical nor desirable when the normative order requires their supervision and the majority lack routes to secure economic independence, denying them easy exit from marriage and ensuring divorce or widowhood are economic catastrophes without the support of kin. In countries experiencing rapid economic growth and individualization, living alone is a rapidly growing trend, but persisting gender inequalities and differences will continue to mean that working-age women are less likely to live alone than men and, as long as women continue to live longer, older women are more likely to do so than men.

The global trend of living alone should not be caricatured as all bad or all good. It is not the culmination of trends signifying social disintegration and the end of durable caring relationships. Treating the trend as symptomatic of current problems, as if it represents the ultimate outcome of selfish individualism, feeds into the negative stereotypes of people living alone as either turning their backs on others or as left behind, abandoned, bereft of others. These stereotypes do considerable violence to the variation of circumstances and routes leading people to live alone at different states and ages, and underestimate the range of their social networks and commitments to family, friends, places and, for some, communities. Older people can, of course, live alone without being sad and lonely and the typical young person living alone is not self-absorbed, lacking ties to others. While such stereotyping wanes as the proportion of people living alone increases, its continued circulation gives rise to self-doubt and the burdensome anticipation of prejudice or pity among those living alone.

Diversity in population characteristics and outcomes

Throughout this book we have emphasized the heterogeneity of the solo-living population, a heterogeneity that should not be reduced to simplistic generalizations about those living alone. The proportion of one-person households should never be used as an indicator of social isolation or anomie. Even within one cultural tradition or national context there are variations among those living alone by gender, health, sexuality, socio-economic status and in rural versus urban localities. The significant presence of a sector that is both multiply disadvantaged and relatively affluent challenges an understanding of solo-living as the preserve only of the financially secure. Those who live alone can also be partners and/or parents and/or sustain caring relationships for older people across households and those who are not or do not may, nevertheless, be embedded in caring personal relationships. Representations that construct living alone as a social problem typically ignore the variability of experiences and exaggerate the problematic. For example, public campaigns that seek to address the issue of loneliness among the elderly undermine their own pro-elderly aims if they simplistically equate the rate of loneliness with the prevalence of living alone in older age.[1] As we note in Chapter 6, comparative research on the relationship between living alone and well-being in older age shows it is wrong to presume a negative impact on well-being for those living alone in north-western Europe, the region with the most cultural support for living alone, including support from the state enabling independent living. Across many national contexts, the possible negative issues associated with living alone shape public discourses; such discourses are the stock material individuals use to make sense of their own experiences. Lack of attention to the diversity of experience potentially downplays the positive dimensions of living alone in ways that are unhelpful to people who live alone.

At the same time, simply celebrating the trend to living alone, as if there were no associated issues, also does disservice to the range of evidence. Our research adds to the bodies of knowledge seeking to combat negative stereotypes but without tending to the opposite extreme of overcompensating by stressing only the positive headlines. At an individual level, there are losses and gains from living alone, even if it is unhelpful to talk in terms of losers and winners. In circumstances in which women live alone as a political choice, standing up for their own independence against the odds, as it is for unmarried women in their thirties in South Korea, the stakes are high and comfort is always elusive since the wider context remains hostile. In regions where living alone is already established, men and women fall into living alone by a variety of routes, often without intending either any political stance or lifestyle statement. Most working-age adults begin living alone believing it is a temporary stage, and remain open to co-resident partnership arrangements. Research in the United States suggests that some become radicalized by their experiences of prejudices, and more militant about being single and living solo as a life style. In our UK study, there was little evidence of this militancy but, as in the United States, most people living alone over time describe themselves as living happily alone and are conscious of the benefits of their residential arrangement. Nevertheless, there is a minority who do indeed feel sad and lonely and most people living alone can itemize negatives as well as positives. Parents sometimes regret the reduced contact with children and the difficulties of parenting across households or distance. Many people living alone find it difficult to enjoy eating alone, particularly those who do so daily without any interrupting rhythm of routine arrangements with family or friends. The pleasures and freedoms of living alone can sometimes feel like unshared burdens of responsibilities and risk. While most people living alone are embedded in support networks of friends, family and organizations that can deliver assistance in times of need, this is not true for all. Nor are all who are living alone in mid-adulthood able to make or think in terms of making financial provision for living alone in older age. There are reasonable policy concerns about growing burdens of care for older people who have neither partners nor children to assist them. The possibility that the trend will also add to the planet's burden of carbon footprint is a very real threat. However, the potential also exists for people living alone to be part of the solution rather than an added element of the problem.

Globalization, individualization and resilience of patriarchy

The late twentieth and early twenty-first century witnessed a speeding-up of developments with a global reach. For theorists seeking to draw broad brush pictures of global social change, globalization is linked to the social process of individualization, although the mechanisms remain sketchy. Processes of individualization are, in turn, linked to the trend of living alone; indeed, living alone is a form of individualization, if the term means social processes in which the individual is distinguished from rather than subsumed within wider collectivities. Capitalism has long been seen as fostering individualization by drawing more of the global population into patterns of production and consumption in ways which are claimed to encourage people to see themselves as mobile individual earners and consumers. As knowledge-based economies develop, more people are drawn into extended education as a form of individual self-development of their 'human capital'. The Internet is seen as further accelerating trends of global access to alternative sources of knowledge, extending awareness of different possible lives in ways which undermine certainties of tradition and render people more self-aware and self-reflexive. Current commentators in East Asia (Chang, 2010; Yan, 2010, 2009, 2003) argue that individualization need not spell an end to collective values or go hand in hand with individualism. However, individualization and individualism have often been elided in 'Western' contexts, and the prospect of their long-term separation ignores theoretical expectations of some alignment between practice and values.

The stereotyping of people choosing to live alone in order to look after no one but themselves plays to a fictitious history (and projected future) promulgated by American functionalist theorists who hold that Europeans and Americans have recently turned away from extended kin in order to focus on their nuclear families, as mobile units that fit with capitalist systems of production (Goode, 1970). This fictitious history makes it seem more plausible that people are now turning from their nearest and dearest to care only about themselves. A more sophisticated picture is needed than reading off individualization and individualism from the development of capitalism, and that acknowledges different cultural arrangements for organizing family, gender and sexuality. In terms of creating the necessary and sufficient conditions for living alone, family–sex–gender systems have to allow men and women to see this as a possible and desirable living arrangement and social and economic conditions need to make it achievable. Access to individual financial independence across a life course requires access to and the valuing of autonomy and control, not just the opportunity to earn a living wage. Therborn's (2004, 2011) commentary on family–sex–gender systems and Castell's (1996) commentary on 'network societies', anticipate the slow demise of women's subordination to men everywhere. Feminism has succeeded to the extent that the demise of gender subordination at the core of traditional arrangements is no longer openly lamented and commitment to gender equality is official in many regions of the world.

Some demographers continue to anticipate the global spread of 'the second demographic transition' (Lesthaeghe, 2010), a pattern of demographic changes associated with the demise of traditional arrangements, gender equality and living alone. Trends of delayed partnership, reduced fertility and childlessness need not be interpreted as 'spread' implying the same underlying causes. Such modifications of traditional arrangements may not reflect 'choice biographies', personalized projects involving strategic, individualized life planning (Beck, 2000; Giddens, 1991, p. 58). These demographic trends are only associated with greater possibilities of living alone for women and men if both have access to financial independence and affordable housing. Similarly, high rates of couple dissolution only feed into living alone if combined with the possibility of women and men subsequently having the means of maintaining their own households rather than returning to live with kin. Longevity, combined with the decline in extended and three generational families in some parts of Asia where this is the traditional family form, extends the probabilities of living alone in later adulthood to new regions only when older people have access to a means of economic support.

The association of the increasing trend of living alone with widening access to economic independence and economic growth also ties in with growing consumption and environmental pressure. Unless the 'work-to-spend' cycle (Schor, 2010) is broken, higher incomes tend to be associated with higher consumption. However, living alone is not the driver of the connections between economic growth, consumption and environmental damage. Environmental damage would not be averted simply by people desisting from living alone, although this fact does not reduce the desirability of considering how the carbon impact of the trend might be reduced.

Everyday lives effecting social change

The trend to living alone is both an outcome and progenitor of social change: increasing numbers living alone at different stages across the life course contribute to the widening possibilities of living in this arrangement at different ages. Changing visibility of the trend, in historical time, modifies cultural understandings and representations of an appropriate life course which in turn act as a resource for building an individual identity. The experience of living alone, over biographical time, changes practical knowledge, meanings and competences, shifting perceptions and potentially feeding wider cultural change. Research in Europe and North America finds participants who are contentedly living alone in their thirties or forties, who did not imagine that satisfaction in such a situation would be possible when they began living alone as a temporary arrangement in their twenties. Thus the self-identity of contentment with living alone potentially feeds into a shift in the public identity associated with this living arrangement.[2] In the language of current theorists of everyday life and how it changes (Shove et al., 2012), living alone is a 'process of doing' that forges and reproduces social practices.

Those living alone are effecting social change and yet their own accounts of changing practices are often absorbed into narratives that present their actions as normal or conventional. In the context of the United Kingdom, this is more often because living alone continues to require identity work, resisting being stigmatized as 'different', than because it has become fully normalized. For example, accounts of leaving the parental home to live alone draw on the convention of being 'too old' to live with parents or make reference to validated aspirations of establishing oneself on the property ladder; living alone and being single are explained in terms of 'natural progression' or 'fate', not having yet met the desired partner with whom to set up home; explanations of LAT relationships draw on the importance of financial autonomy and avoidance of risk; one participant described currently living apart from his partner and children as embarked on 'for the good of the children', and was now considering re-cohabiting for the same reason. Certainly, no participants in our study presented themselves as pioneering and the majority did not account for decisions to live alone as the outcome of deliberative choice. Nevertheless, as we note in Chapter 3, and as Elizabeth Shove and her co-authors remind us (Shove et al., 2012), consciously setting out to be pioneering is not the only way of effecting social change; those who live alone are contributing, through doing, to changes in the structuring of the adult life course.

For most, the pleasures of living alone grow with time. Getting on with developing the pleasures of living alone while hoping for a partner is completely consistent with popular wisdom in Euro-American culture concerning how to be an independent adult and find a partner. The longer that people live alone, the more likely it is that the experience starts to generate forms of resistance to living with others. Setting up home alone, even when embarked upon as a temporary phase, complicates aspirations to partnership and parenthood. For those in relationships, complex practicalities such as the difficulties of shifting jobs or housing, and the trials of moving accumulations of stuff weighed against decision-making about co-residence. For some, factors such as the loss of proximity to people engendered by geographical moves or other commitments, such as children from previous relationships, militated against co-residential partnership. We note that deliberately-chosen 'living apart together' relationships were applicable only to a minority of our participants in couple relationships. Yet, while the majority were either planning or keeping open the possibility of eventual co-residence, the ambivalence expressed by some suggests that shifting into a more settled LAT relationship remains a possibility. The term 'LAT' and concept of this type of relationship is not yet widely recognized; however, if it becomes so, then the redefining of co-resident relationships as LAT may become more frequent, escalating the social acceptance of LAT and solo-living.

Living alone is both reflective and generative of changing gender scripts, even when women themselves are not aware of making the kind of difficult choices faced by pioneering women choosing to live alone in parts of the world where they are viciously stigmatized and discriminated against. Women living alone represent financial autonomy and a level of self-sufficiency that challenges conventions of complementarity in masculinity and femininity. Some women are very conscious of not having to 'look after' a co-resident partner and it seems that, for some, the desire for a partner may wane once age means childbearing is no longer an expectation. The separation of co-residence and partnership in unambiguous LAT relationships challenges normative assumptions of 'natural progression' of stages in hetero-relationality.

The separation of co-residence and parenting gives rise to non-resident fathers experiencing sole responsibility for childcare, at least some of the time. Men living alone too are undertaking sole responsibility for domestic roles such as cooking and cleaning traditionally scripted as feminine. While gender differences are evident in the varied stories of men and women living alone in this book, there are also indications of practices that not only challenge conventional gender identities but also counter the more pessimistic interpretations of the trend to living alone. Anxieties that this trend signifies a turning away from family or an increase in social isolation are not supported by the evidence we present in this book: the majority of women and men in our study depicted social networks rich in both friends and family. A minority of men, those living alone in circumstances of ill-health and financial constraint, did depict limited social interaction. Research on the well-being of men living alone in older age demonstrates it is divorced/widowed older lone men who experience most strongly the loss of the 'protective effect' of marriage. The interview data suggest that, while patterns of social interaction remain gendered, most men of working age living alone maintain both 'kin-keeping' and friendship practices: the increase in experience of living alone at younger age suggests the opportunity for the development of capacities that challenge conventional gender scripts and anticipate very different experiences of living alone at older age for future cohorts.

Identity, individualism, consumption and 'plenitude'

It should not be assumed that people living alone are hyper-individualist, self-absorbed consumers or likely to become so. One of the most oft-cited benefits of living alone articulated by UK research participants aged 25–44 was being able to 'please myself'. Their home was their site of pleasing the self, but not necessarily through consumption or through the exclusion of others. The part played by consumption of mass produced goods and services in the personal lives of people living alone was very varied, appropriate to a range of gendered social class positions involving diverse performances, self-presentations and senses of distinction (Bourdieu, 1984; Goffman, 1959; Slater et al, 1997; Southerton, 2009). Individualized meanings of home (a place of being one's self, privacy, refuge, sanctity, security, ownership and control) did not obliterate social and collective meanings (home as a place of family, love, intimacy, belonging, origin/roots, community and nation). Many homes of people living alone display, express and facilitate family and friendship relationships. For some, the location of their dwelling, near family and friends, in a friendly neighbourhood, community or a particular landscape, was more important than its contents. Homes are sites of personal consumption but for people living alone it seems they only exceptionally become shrines to the self. Even those who expressed love of their highly personalized home typically sought to maintain homely and friendly homes that were hospitable to others. We have suggested that the inappropriateness of stereotyping those who live alone as self-absorbed, self-pleasing consumers is further illustrated by the difficulties those without regularly visiting partners or children report in finding pleasure in meals and holidays. Most people living alone see eating and taking holidays as ideally sociable activities to be enjoyed with others.

Among our UK sample of working-age adults living alone, very few were explicitly focused on the environmental impacts of being a one-person household, but awareness of the higher costs of living as one person, and the difficulties in avoiding waste when purchasing food, were recurrent themes. The carbon footprints created by people living alone will vary with their levels of income and spending, reinforcing the importance of understanding the diversity of the population. Jo Williams has constructed a comparative estimate of per-capita carbon footprint for those living alone and those living with others focusing on use of domestic energy, land and domestic goods (Williams, 2005, 2007). However, total carbon footprint contains many more elements. Among the current working-age population in the United Kingdom, we suggest that the lower levels of car ownership and the propensity of urban dwellers to live in high-density areas, walking and using public transport to access services, offsets their tendency to purchase readymade meals and possible higher use of domestic energy, an argument also made by Klinenberg (2012) on behalf of those living alone in the high-density inner cities of the United States. We note the risk that at the level of the nation-state or region, an increase in the proportion of the population living alone will mean an increase in material infrastructure and domestic consumption per head of population, but also the contribution of the trend to lower fertility and hence reduced pressure on resources. In terms of the future, in those places where the trend is increasing, modification may be required of housing and transport to avert the potential loss in energy savings or increase in energy use per household as a consequence.

Juliet Schor, an economist, is one of a number of social scientists writing about the future and seeking an appropriate response to the building ecological catastrophes facing the planet. In her book (Schor, 2010) and

Plenitude blog Schor advocates an end to the work-to-spend cycle and a shift toward self-provisioning outside of the market, including growing food and generating energy using small-scale high-productivity technologies, a much higher use of second-hand (rebranded as 'new to you') products, car-sharing and restricting purchases to long-lasting goods. There is no evidence of people living alone becoming early adopters of such possibilities. Their freedom to 'please myself', may afford room for manoeuvre to think differently, albeit assuming fears about 'becoming set in my ways' do not narrow the window of opportunity. The vulnerability of the less affluent to rising costs at a time of recession, given their dependence on one income, may also create opportunities. In combination there are some grounds for hope about the willingness of a perhaps significant proportion of people living alone to engage with such approaches, but it remains important to remember the diversity of the population.

Disembedding and networked individualism

In contrast to the pessimistic views of a world in which all people are increasingly dislocated from family and kin groups or place and people of origin, the idea of 'networked individuals' suggests a shift to individualized arrays of ties, constantly connecting people wherever they may be, facilitated by technologies that make proximity and co-residence increasingly irrelevant (Castells, 1996; Raine and Wellman, 2012). This is a theme given some support by Klinenberg (2012) when he argues that the attractions and pleasures of living alone opened up with the mobile telephone and Internet. In the United Kingdom, the diverse population of people living alone is reflected in the diversity of their social networks, which include those whose friends and family are geographically dispersed and those who are embedded in a densely knit web of local social ties. The former remain more typical of mobile middle-class professionals and the latter of residents occupying working-class urban and rural areas where they were brought up. The fit between the ideal-typical mobile 'networked individual' able to transcend local and proximate ties and the lives of the working-age people living alone is sufficiently imperfect to reject this depiction as capturing the overall direction of change.

In a sample of 140, only about half have a history of mobility. The majority of women in urban areas and men in rural areas were living where they had grown up. Gender, urban/rural residence, social class, socio-economic circumstances, health and sexuality complicate patterns of mobility and residence. Housing tied some to their place of residence, an experience in the United Kingdom that is particularly acute for those on low incomes who are reliant on social housing. Not all those living alone are networked in the sense of being Internet-connected. Working-age people living alone have the same gradient of increased likelihood of Internet access with affluence as among the population as a whole. In the United Kingdom, the overall take up of home Internet connections has increased significantly but rates remain lower among those living alone. The Scottish Household Survey shows the 2011 take-up in the working population to be around 90 per cent of family households but 30 per cent less among men living alone (Tables A2.16a, A2.16b). The composition of dominant patterns of social networking are not reconfigured by the affordance of technologies enabling constant connectedness. Key relationships retain their significance and do not fade into the wider diffuse networks of contacts. Conventional family ties most often loom large as the important others in both dispersed and local networks, and across class, demonstrating the resilience of 'family' beyond both co-residence and proximity. The very common practice of continuing to honour the festival of Christmas as a time to be spent with family or kin was testimony to this.

Place continues to matter in a range of ways to people living alone. Local, face-to-face interactions with acquaintances can play an important part in the identities of people living alone, particularly when their social network contains few or no intimate relationships. As David Morgan has noted, emotional support can be derived from routine interactions with acquaintances offering the possibility of 'little fragments of intimacy' (Morgan, 2009, p. 4). The possibility of this form of support was richer for those who lived in rural communities. A sense of mutual acknowledgement, 'knowing' and 'being known' by everybody, enhances satisfaction with living alone in the context of a feeling of belonging and being at home in the rural community. On the other hand, some solo-living men, including some gay men in both suburban and rural contexts, felt they were living somewhere where they were 'different' and 'out of place'. For them, awareness of the possibilities of surveillance, judgement and social exclusion within their local neighbourhood encouraged separation between their social life and their place of residence.

One of the ironies revealed in our research is the mismatch in class-background, education, mobility and occupation between men and women living alone and wishing to find partners; for those in rural areas, Internet dating is only a partial solution to transcending the limits of place.

From living alone to living-alone-together?

Particular combinations of circumstances are needed if the global trend of living alone is not only to avoid damage to social ties and increasing carbon footprints per capita but also to perhaps go further and contribute to the kind of step changes advocated by Schor (2010) and others. Research in Europe and North America shows that the problem of impoverished social contact afflicts only a minority proportion of those living alone, typically the most economically as well as socially disadvantaged. The issues of the trend fuelling carbon footprints is contested (Klinenberg, 2012), but cannot be fully repudiated, given that high carbon footprints are undoubtedly a problem, and known to be associated with the economically and socially rich, who are also a proportion of the population living alone. Reflection on how to minimize these potential harms points towards forms of social development that work against social segregation of rich and poor, combining environmentally friendly one-person dwellings with forms of social life that could be described as living-alone-together. Is it possible that as a set of social practices, living-alone-together might be a particularly fruitful environment for fostering lower carbon futures? We conclude with a brief discussion of the most frequently-suggested options for potentially reducing the carbon footprint of the trend in the richer parts of the world, while also addressing the frequently-voiced difficulties of provisioning for one and eating alone.

'Intentional communities', cohousing or cooperative housing have each been advocated as more community oriented and sustainable alternative forms of residence to conventional housing developments. Each brings together forms of housing that may incorporate environmentally-conscious planning and technologies with social institutions for collective management that may facilitate environmentally conscious practices. Their combination of physical and social elements enable 'careers and trajectories of practices' (Shove et al., 2012) that are more than conventionally collective, supportive and environmentally friendly. This provides fertile ground for growing a virtuous 'circuit of reproduction' recursively supporting practices outside 'the work-to-spend' cycle. Of these housing options, intentional communities are the most demanding of participants' time and energies, often organized around collectivist beliefs, sustaining close interaction with each other, eating communal meals and taking part in joint activities, as well as creating individual homes and collectively managing a housing project. However, the number of people living in such arrangements remains very small and the levels of commitment involved may mean such arrangements are likely to remain marginal. Lucy Sargisson (2010) contrasts this form of intentional community with cohousing first emerging in Nordic countries in the 1970s, then expanding from the late 1980s in North America, where developments are beginning to be supported by mainstream funders and planners.

Cohousing involves clusters of individual homes with shared common space and facilities which are controlled by the residents, in what Helen Jarvis describes as consensus-based collective self-governance (Jarvis, 2011). Often the housing has been planned and built to the specification of the residents who have worked together, sometimes for years, to bring their communities to fruition. Sargisson (2010) notes differences in tenure that distinguish and make a difference to the cultures of first and second wave cohousing. Those of first wave continental Europe almost always seek a social mix by combining rented and privately-owned homes, or view cohousing as a solution to social housing and tend towards entirely rented housing in communities that are state owned. In North America, most communities are privately owned by residents and do not contain any rented homes. As originally conceived, the idea of cohousing was deliberately to foster an 'inclusive community' which typically means bringing together different types of households including people living in families and on their own across ages, as well as a range of socio-economic circumstances. Yet the cohousing idea is now advocated as a form of housing for elderly people and includes the construction of communities which are exclusively of elderly people rather than deliberately mixing generations (Brenton, 2013). Cohousing now encompasses a range of arrangements. Most include mutual acceptance of some collective responsibilities for property management and good neighbourliness building a 'community' element. However, the 'community' may be narrowly homogenous rather than reflective of the wider population and anti-radical rather than promoting justice or seeking social change. Nevertheless, the lack of any vision of social change may coincide with growing practical knowledge of making changes which in turn may ultimately help to shift meanings as well as competences contributing to changes in practice.

The potential environmental benefits of cohousing for people living alone are advocated by Williams (2007, 2005). Participants in cohousing movements are not always focused on environmental concerns or advocacy of lower-carbon lives. Nevertheless, Sargisson's (2010) review of the self-presentation of 50 member organizations of the Co-Housing Association of the United States found 'conservation', 'sustainability' and 'sound use of resources' to be recurrent themes. It is generally agreed that, as a form of social innovation, cohousing opens up the possibilities of collective technical innovation using sustainable technologies such as pooling 'resources for the use of small-scale renewable energy technologies, rainwater harvesting, grey water recycling, and more sustainable construction materials and designs unavailable to individual households' (Seyfang and Smith, 2007).

Cooperative housing associations are another model of housing that potentially offers advantages of living alone, independence and control of domestic space in combination with collective property management, which fosters opportunities for building companionship and support, for reducing energy use and consumption through the way homes are constructed, and for the sourcing, sharing and pooling of resources. Historically, the organization and building of such housing is associated with socialist cooperative movements and their contribution to current housing stock varies with the historical legacy of such movements. In Europe, contemporary cooperative housing associations range from tenant-owned and managed housing developments to organizationally-owned (usually local authority or charitable body) and tenant-managed housing. A common feature of their organization is that tenants share collective management and responsibility and a framework exists for collective decision-making, enabling development and management of shared activities and facilities. Maja Bruun's (2009, 2011) anthropological research on cooperative housing associations in Denmark, which make up a third of the housing market in inner city Copenhagen (Kirstensen, 2007), suggests that sharing facilities such as common backyards and laundry rooms creates spaces 'in-between' the private and public that are valued for the experience of community (*fællesskab*) and good neighbourliness (*godt naboskab*) that they enable (2009, p. 8). However, this is in the context of an ethos of shared responsibility and effective institutions for reaching decisions and agreements.

Housing policies and investments can seek to generate clusters of energy-efficient, one-person housing units with carbon footprint savings through shared facilities such as heating systems, bookable guest spaces,[3] shared domestic appliances, such as washing machines, and shared services such as cleaning, gardening or on-call emergency care, even in the absence of the collective forms of management of co-housing and cooperative housing. Privately-funded models of such housing are exclusive and involve high maintenance fees for the management and delivery of collective services. The sharing of facilities and services by individual users has a different character if it also creates and draws on social solidarity; pooled facilities without paid management services or naturally-occurring supervision or sanctions can involve tensions over disputed use and abuse, particularly when cultural norms create sharp distinctions between private and public spaces. Lack of success in sharing is likely to reinforce adherence to conventional privatized arrangements and successfully sharing facilities may be inhibited by current practices, such as the model of the 'good neighbour' current in the United Kingdom, which means remaining a friendly but distant acquaintance, taking care not to intrude or interfere (Crow, 2002b).

Historical shifts in circumstances can create new opportunities for changes in practice, just as biographical disruptions such as the transition to living alone are known to create such opportunities. The financial crisis that started in the United States in 2007 and became recession in many parts of Europe and North America put many young people's aspiration of independent living and home ownership on hold (for example, see Heath, 2008 for the United Kingdom) and resulted in record rates of home repossessions by financial institutions, with associated increases in hidden and visible homelessness. Growth in cohousing or cooperative housing associations might have particular success in this climate offering investment-efficient routes of opening up affordable homes and home ownership for those whose experiences lead them to resist non-familial co-resident sharing. Many of the people living alone that we interviewed in the United Kingdom describe previous experiences of sharing unfavourably or as something that they have outlived. Not surprisingly, interviewees did not talk of cohousing or cooperative housing options, since neither was widely available. Previous careers of practice also well equip some people living alone to participation in such housing developments. The previous chapters have shown that it is not unusual for people living alone to be involved in voluntary associations. It is plausible that some would be prepared to make the effort and commitment involved in taking part in the tenant meetings that are the institutional framework of cooperative housing associations, even if they would not undertake the more demanding long-term project of creating a cohousing community. Many interviewees also had competences that would be highly valued in cohousing or cooperative groups including DIY, building-trade, cooking and organizational skills. Forms of collective living-alone-together have the potential to provide social benefits and develop outside-of-the-market self-provisioning (Schor, 2010). Time-sharing and skill-sharing schemes among those living-alone-together could provide a range of services enhancing living alone without reliance on the State or the market. For example, the incorporation of a reasonable cost, good food cooperative café into a housing development, offering the possibility of always being able to eat with friendly acquaintances and eating alone without feeling socially awkward, would have obvious social benefits to many people living alone. Vegetable growing allotments and composting facilities could work alongside the café to deliver additional environmental benefits. The State and the market may remain the key suppliers of labour-intensive, skilled services that are critical to quality of life, such as the provision of high-quality care in infirmity of older age, but elements of self-delivery by those living-alone-together could come to play a significant part.

As a set of social practices, living-alone-together involves collectively attending to proximate social ties with those sharing facilities and services built around cohousing or cooperative housing, as well as managing the facilities and services themselves. These practices require sustained attention, whether or not people are occasionally or frequently residentially mobile and regardless of whether they are embedded in virtual, transnational and non-local networks. Such a shift in practices is a much bigger departure from the model of living alone occupied by some sectors of this diverse population than it is for others and this makes its success likely to be uneven. It is difficult to anticipate the extent to which the growth of the cohousing or housing cooperative movements may provide a viable option for environmentally aware 'living-alone-together', and whether this would be considered as an attractive or 'least worst' option to many of the potential residents. Either way, the practical knowledge gained – assuming the experiences of living and participating in cohousing or cooperative housing is positive and fosters collective social and environmental benefits – will contribute to change. The process of doing transforms practical knowledge, meanings and competences which shift careers of practice in ways which then potentially contribute to the circuits of reproduction of practices (Shove et al., 2010). However, for this to be even at the starting line, appropriate housing elements have to be in place. There seems little likelihood of many Western governments expanding provision of affordable housing with shared facilities or services in the short term, given the economic climate and widespread cuts in welfare provision. Nevertheless, this is a matter of public and political priority which may shift over time under increasing pressure to reduce environmental impact, given the increasing acceptability and desirability of living alone in a growing number of countries across the globe.

Appendix 1: The Rural and Urban Solo Living: Social Integration, Quality of Life and Future Orientations Study[1]

The research methodology for this study, funded by the Economic and Social Research Council, involved various stages. First, secondary analysis of the Scottish Household Survey (SHS), a large-scale annual omnibus survey that collects information on the composition, characteristics, attitudes and behaviour of households and individuals in Scotland, was carried out to provide representative data on the socio-economic characteristics of men and women living alone at working age (18–59/64).[2] This statistical profile also provides comparisons with working-age men and women living with others, and information on those aged 25–44 (see Appendix 2).[3] Second, semi-structured telephone interviews were conducted with men and women aged between 25 and 44 who had lived alone for at least six months in the previous five years: 140 individuals living in a range of urban and rural localities across Scotland participated in this stage. Finally, 35 in-depth interviews were conducted with a subset of these participants, selected to allow the follow-up of particular themes of interest, with the majority conducted in participants' homes. Telephone interviews allowed a wide range of information to be collected while the follow-up interviews allowed even more detailed exploration of the subjective understandings and meanings that people themselves ascribe to their experiences.

Sampling strategy

The SHS (2005/2006) was used as a sampling frame to identify men and women aged 25–44 living alone in selected types of urban and rural locations.[4] SHS consent procedures allow re-contact of individuals who have given the relevant permission (about 60% of the total sample). In total, the contact details of 485 individuals from the 2005/2006 sample who seemed to match the criteria, that included having given consent and a telephone number, were provided by the SHS.[5] Telephone interviews were conducted with 140 men and women, mainly in late 2007. We invited men and women who no longer lived alone but had lived alone for at least six months in the preceding five years to take part, as their reasons for and experience of changing living arrangements were considered of interest to the study. Our sample included 14 men and women now living with either partners (10), a parent (mother), flatmates or children. Thirty-five respondents subsequently participated in in-depth face-to-face interviews, mainly in late 2008. Criteria for selection of these respondents included a spread across localities by gender, as well as those who experienced particular circumstances or issues identified as important in the first stage of the project. More men (75) than women (65) were interviewed in the main sample. The ratio was not as skewed towards men as in the actual population in the age group (closer to 2 to 1).

Data collection

The semi-structured telephone interviews were carried out using a mix of closed and open questions, and varied in length from just over 30 minutes to nearly 2 hours. These questions established the respondent's history of and route into solo-living, their partnership history, residence history, socio-economic circumstances (employment, education, health, housing, income), sense of well-being, 'work-life balance' and quality of life. These interviews also explored relationships with family, friends and neighbours, and asked about locality, leisure and caring and volunteering activities. The research explored gender differences in narratives of being or becoming a person living alone and orientations to partnering and parenting. Questions about future orientation included plans for migration, career orientations and expectations concerning future employment, partnerships and children. Answers were recorded by interviewers using an online survey tool (Bristol Online Survey, http://www.survey.bris.ac.uk) and the data exported to Excel and SPSS in order to conduct cross-tabulations of the more structured answers. The telephone interviews were also digitally recorded and subsequently transcribed, as were the follow-up in-depth interviews. All interviews were coded and thematically analysed using the qualitative data analysis software package NVivo.

The follow-up interviews with selected respondents took place mainly in respondents' own homes.[6] These interviews lasted between 40 and

90 minutes. They investigated the meaning of 'home' to respondents, who else had access, how they used their home for socializing or entertainment, and the management of domestic tasks such as cleaning and cooking. Respondents were asked about their sense of financial security, and where they felt they could turn if in financial need. These interviews also provided an opportunity to ask more about potentially sensitive topics (such as whether they had considered/drawn up a will, how their last birthday/holiday was spent), and to deepen our knowledge of respondents' motivations and understandings of their various 'trajectories', such as education and employment as well as partnership and parenthood.

After each telephone and in-depth interview, interviewers wrote up brief fieldnotes capturing immediate thoughts and observations, including about respondents' homes and neighbourhoods: these notes were also drawn on in the analysis. Analysis of the data combined a more 'quantitative' distinguishing of patterns, similarities and differences in relation to axes such as gender and locality, with an interpretive analysis aimed at identifying common themes in relation to topics identified as important in the relevant literatures.

Sample characteristics

In terms of age and socio-economic characteristics, the distribution of the telephone interviewee sample broadly matches that of the wider population living alone at age 25–44. Those living in rural localities were over-represented in both the telephone and in-depth sub-sample in order to be able to make comparisons with those living alone in urban areas. The telephone sample included men and women with a range of socio-economic characteristics. Table A1.1 summarizes some of the key characteristics of the men and women interviewed for our study.[7] The circumstances of some who were interviewed twice had changed between interviews.

Table A1.1 provides information on the age, gender and employment status of our participants, as well as information on their partnership and parenthood status, annual income (banded), tenure and residential history (whether they were living in the area where they had been brought up, or that they had moved to as an adult).

Table A1.1 Characteristics of interviewees[8]

Name	Sex (M/F)	Age	Whether currently living alone	Whether current relationship	Whether parent	Housing tenure	Locality	Employment status	Annual income	Residential mobility
Abigail	F	44	Yes	Yes	Child(ren) living elsewhere	Buying	Large urban	Self-employed	>£40,000	Incomer
Adam	M	44	Yes	No	Child(ren) living elsewhere	Renting (social)	Large urban	Full time	£16,000–20,000	Living where brought up
Adrian	M	34	Yes	No	No	Buying	Large urban	Full time	£26,000–30,000	Incomer
Aileen	F	27	Yes	Yes	No	Renting (social)	Large urban	Full time	£10,000–15,000	Living where brought up
Ailsa	F	28	Yes	Yes	No	Buying	Large urban	Full time	£16,000–20,000	Living where brought up
Albert	M	38	Yes	No	No	Buying	Large urban	Full time	>£40,000	Incomer
Alexandra	F	41	Yes	Yes	No	Buying (ex-social)	Accessible rural	Full time	£21,000–25,000	Incomer
Alfie	M	41	Yes	No	No	Buying (ex-social)	Remote small town	Full time	£26,000–30,000	Incomer

Alice	F	36	Yes	No	No	Renting (social)	Accessible rural	Full time	£10,000–15,000	Living where brought up
Alison	F	42	Yes	Yes	Child(ren) living elsewhere	Renting (social)	Large urban	Permanently sick/disabled	<£10,000	Living where brought up
Alistair	M	39	Yes	No	No	Renting (social)	Large urban	Permanently sick/disabled	<£10,000	Incomer
Amy	F	25	No (living with flatmate)	No	No	Renting (private)	Large urban	Full time	£10,000–15,000	Incomer
Andrea	F	26	Yes	Yes	No	Buying	Large urban	Full time	£21,000–25,000	Incomer
Andrew	M	43	Yes	No	No	Buying (ex-social)	Large urban	Full time	£21,000–25,000	Incomer
Angela	F	44	Yes	Yes	No	Buying	Remote small town	Full time	£26,000–30,000	Incomer
Angus	M	35	Yes	Yes	Child(ren) living elsewhere	Buying	Remote rural	Full time	£26,000–30,000	Living where brought up
Annabel	F	30	Yes	No	No	Renting (social)	Large urban	Full time	£21,000–25,000	Living where brought up

Table A1.1 (Continued)

Name	Sex (M/F)	Age	Whether currently living alone	Whether current relationship	Whether parent	Housing tenure	Locality	Employment status	Annual income	Residential mobility
Anthony	M	34	Yes	No	Child(ren) living elsewhere	Buying (ex-social)	Large urban	Full time	£16,000–20,000	Living where brought up
Archie	M	39	Yes	No	No	Buying	Remote rural	Self-employed	<£10,000	Incomer
Arthur	M	43	No	Yes	Living with Child(ren)	Buying	Remote rural	Self-employed	£26,000–30,000	Living where brought up
Ava	F	30	Yes	Yes	No	Renting (private)	Remote rural	Full time	£10,000–15,000	Incomer
Barbara	F	36	Yes	Yes	No	Buying	Remote rural	Full time	£26,000–30,000	Living where brought up
Barry	M	26	Yes	Yes	No	Buying	Large urban	Full time	£26,000–30,000	Living where brought up
Benjamin	M	33	Yes	No	No	Renting (social)	Remote small town	Full time	<£10,000	Living where brought up
Brenda	F	33	Living with partner, newborn child			Own outright	Remote small town	Self-employed	<£10,000	Incomer

Brian	M	42	Yes	Yes	Child(ren) living elsewhere	Own outright	Remote small town	Self-employed	Not known	Living where brought up
Bruce	M	34	Yes	Yes	Child(ren) living elsewhere	Buying	Accessible rural	Full time	£31,000–40,000	Incomer
Callum	M	44	Yes	Yes	No	Buying	Large urban	Full time	£31,000–40,000	Living where brought up
Cameron	M	39	Yes	Yes	No	Buying	Accessible rural	Permanently sick/disabled	<£10,000	Living where brought up
Campbell	M	34	Yes	Yes	No	Buying	Accessible rural	Full time	£31,000–40,000	Incomer
Cathy	F	26	Yes	Yes	No	Buying	Remote rural	Full time	£21,000–25,000	Living where brought up
Catriona	F	37	Yes	No	No	Buying	Large urban	Full time	£26,000–30,000	Living where brought up
Charles	M	35	Yes	No	No	Buying (ex-social)	Remote small town	Full time	£10,000–15,000	Living where brought up

Table A1.1 (Continued)

Name	Sex (M/F)	Age	Whether currently living alone	Whether current relationship	Whether parent	Housing tenure	Locality	Employment status	Annual income	Residential mobility
Charlotte	F	31	Yes (partner on temporary work sabbatical)	No	No	Buying	Large Urban	Full time	>£40,000	Incomer
Christie	M	42	Yes	No	Child(ren) living elsewhere	Buying	Accessible rural	Full time	Not known	Living where brought up
Christine	F	43	Yes	Yes	No	Buying	Large urban	Full time	£26,000–30,000	Living where brought up
Claire	F	38	Yes	No	No	Own outright	Accessible rural	Part time	£21,000–25,000	Incomer
Colin	M	39	Yes	Yes	No	Buying	Accessible rural	Full time	£26,000–30,000	Incomer
Connor	M	42	Yes	No	Child(ren) living elsewhere	Buying	Accessible rural	Full time	>£40,000	Incomer
Craig	M	43	Yes	Yes	No	Buying	Large urban	Full time	>£40,000	Incomer

Daisy	F	30	Yes	No	No	Buying	Large urban	Full time	£26,000–30,000	Living where brought up
Danny	M	35	Yes	No	No	Renting (social)	Accessible rural	Full time	£10,000–15,000	Incomer
David	M	33	Yes	No	No	Tied to job	Accessible rural	Full time	£16,000–20,000	Living where brought up
Dawn	F	36	Yes	No	No	Buying	Large urban	Full time	£26,000–30,000	Living where brought up
Denise	F	34	Yes	No	No	Buying	Remote small town	Full time	£16,000–20,000	Living where brought up
Donald	M	28	Yes	No	No	Buying	Accessible rural	Self-employed	Not known	Incomer
Donna	F	31	Yes	No	No	Social shared ownership scheme	Remote small town	Full time	£31,000–40,000	Living where brought up
Eleanor	F	29	Yes	No	No	Buying	Large urban	Full time	£21,000–25,000	Living where brought up
Elspeth	F	43	Yes	No	No	Buying	Large urban	Full time	£26,000–30,000	Living where brought up

Table A1.1 (Continued)

Name	Sex (M/F)	Age	Whether currently living alone	Whether current relationship	Whether parent	Housing tenure	Locality	Employment status	Annual income	Residential mobility
Emily	F	34	Yes	No	No	Renting (social)	Large urban	Full time	£10,000–15,000	Living where brought up
Ernest	M	38	Yes	No	Child(ren) living elsewhere	Renting (private)	Large urban	Self-employed	>£40,000	Incomer
Euan	M	42	Yes	Yes	Child(ren) living elsewhere	Buying	Accessible rural	Full time	£31,000–40,000	Incomer
Eve	F	43	Yes	No	Child(ren) living elsewhere	Buying	Accessible rural	Fulltime	£10,000–15,000	Incomer
Fergus	M	40	Yes	No	No	Buying	Remote rural	Full time	£31,000–40,000	Living where brought up
Fiona	F	31	Yes	Yes	No	Buying	Large urban	Full time	>£40,000	Living where brought up
Frances	F	41	Yes	Yes	No	Own outright	Remote rural	Full time	>£40,000	Incomer
Frank	M	36	(Living with partner)		No	Buying	Large urban	Full time	>£40,000	Incomer

Name	Sex	Age				Tenure	Location	Employment	Income	Status
Geraldine	F	43	Yes	Yes	No	Buying	Large urban	Full time	£10,000–15,000	Incomer
Grace	F	29	Yes	No	No	Buying	Large urban	Self-employed	£20,000–25,000	Incomer
Graham	M	37	Yes	Yes	No	Buying	Large urban	Full time	>£40,000	Incomer
Gregor	M	42	Yes	No	No	Buying (ex-social)	Remote rural	Full time	£10,000–15,000	Living where brought up
Hannah	F	44	Yes	No	No	Own outright	Large urban	Unemployed	Not known	Incomer
Harriet	F	35	No (living with mother)	No	No	Rent relative or friend	Remote rural	In education	<£10,000	Incomer
Harry	M	35	Yes	Yes	No	Renting (social)	Large urban	Unemployed	<£10,000	Incomer
Harvey	M	38	Yes	No	No	Renting (social)	Remote rural	Permanently sick/disabled	<£10,000	Living where brought up
Helmut	M	42	Yes	No	No	Buying	Remote rural	Full time	£16,000–20,000	Incomer
Henry	M	40	Yes	Yes	No	Buying	Accessible rural	Self-employed	>£40,000	Incomer
Hilary	F	37	Yes	No	No	Buying	Large urban	Full time	£26,000–30,000	Living where brought up

Table A1.1 (Continued)

Name	Sex (M/F)	Age	Whether currently living alone	Whether current relationship	Whether parent	Housing tenure	Locality	Employment status	Annual income	Residential mobility
Hugh	M	39	Yes	No	No	Renting (social)	Accessible rural	Full time	£10,000–15,000	Living where brought up
Isobel	F	29	Yes	No	No	Renting (social)	Large urban	Unemployed	<£10,000	Living where brought up
Jack	M	38	Yes	No	No	Renting (private)	Large urban	Full time	£31,000–40,000	Incomer
Jake	M	28	Yes	Yes	No	Buying	Large urban	Full time	>£40,000	Incomer
Janek	M	27	Yes	No	No	Renting (private)	Large urban	In education	Not known	Incomer
Jean	F	34	Yes	No	No	Buying	Large urban	Full time	£31,000–40,000	Living where brought up
Jessica	F	31	Yes	No	No	Buying	Large urban	Full time	£21,000–25,000	Incomer
Julie	F	33	Yes	Yes	No	Buying	Large urban	Full time	£16,000–20,000	Living where brought up
Kapoor	M	29	(Living with partner)		No	Renting (private)	Large urban	Full time	£26,000–30,000	Incomer

Name	Sex	Age								
Kathryn	F	44	Yes	No	No	Buying	Accessible rural	Full time	£16,000–20,000	Incomer
Katie	F	28	Yes	Yes	No	Buying	Large urban	Full time	£21,000–25,000	Incomer
Keith	M	36	Yes	No	Child(ren) living elsewhere	Renting (social)	Remote rural	Full time	£31,000–40,000	Living where brought up
Kelvin	M	26	No (unofficial lodger)	No	No	Rent relative or friend	Accessible rural	Full time	£26,000–30,000	Living where brought up
Kevin	M	25	Yes	No	No	Renting (private)	Remote rural	Full time	£21,000–25,000	Living where brought up
Kylie	F	36	Yes	Yes	No	Renting (social)	Large urban	Permanently sick/disabled	<£10,000	Living where brought up
Laura	F	31	Yes	No	No	Buying	Large urban	Full time	£26,000–30,000	Incomer
Lauren	F	37	Yes	Yes	No	Buying	Large urban	Full time	>£40,000	Incomer
Lawrence	M	43	Yes	No	No	Buying	Accessible rural	Full time	£26,000–30,000	Living where brought up

Table A1.1 (Continued)

Name	Sex (M/F)	Age	Whether currently living alone	Whether current relationship	Whether parent	Housing tenure	Locality	Employment status	Annual income	Residential mobility
Leo	M	36	Yes	No	Child(ren) living elsewhere	Buying	Accessible rural	Part time	£10,000–15,000	Incomer
Lewis	M	39	(Living with partner)		Child (decreased)	Own outright	Remote small town	Full time	£31,000–40,000	Living where brought up
Liam	M	44	Yes	No	No	Renting (social)	Remote small town	Full time	£26,000–30,000	Living where brought up
Louise	F	29	Yes	No	No	Buying	Remote small town	Full time	£16,000–20,000	Living where brought up
Lucy	F	30	Yes	No	No	Buying	Large urban	Full time	£26,000–30,000	Incomer
Luke	M	37	Yes	Yes	No	Buying	Accessible rural	Full time	£21,000–25,000	Living where brought up
Madeleine	F	36	Yes	Yes	No	Own outright	Accessible rural	Full time	£31,000–40,000	Living where brought up

Maggie	F	34	Yes	Yes	No	Buying	Large urban	Full time	£26,000–30,000	Living where brought up
Mark	M	33	Yes	Yes	No	Buying	Large urban	Full time	£31,000–40,000	Living where brought up
Martin	M	31	Yes	Yes	No	Renting (private)	Large urban	Full time	£31,000–40,000	Incomer
Matthew	M	41	Yes	Yes	No	Buying	Accessible rural	Full time	£26,000–30,000	Incomer
Megan	F	25	Yes	Yes	No	Buying	Large urban	Full time	£31,000–40,000	Incomer
Melissa	F	33	Yes	Yes	No	Buying	Accessible rural	Full time	>£40,000	Incomer
Mike	M	36	Yes	Yes	Child(ren) living elsewhere	Buying	Large urban	Full time	>£40,000	Living where brought up
Mitch	M	39	Yes	No	No	Renting (social)	Remote rural	Self-employed	>£40,000	Living where brought up
Moira	F	33	Yes	No	No	Buying	Large urban	Full time	£26,000–30,000	Living where brought up

Table A1.1 (Continued)

Name	Sex (M/F)	Age	Whether currently living alone	Whether current relationship	Whether parent	Housing tenure	Locality	Employment status	Annual income	Residential mobility
Morgan	M	40	Yes	No	No	Renting (private)	Remote small town	Full time	£21,000–25,000	Living where brought up
Morris	M	25	Yes	Yes	Child (deceased)	Buying	Remote small town	Full time	£21,000–25,000	Living where brought up
Murray	M	43	Yes	No	Child (deceased)	Renting (social)	Remote small town	Permanently sick/disabled	<£10,000	Incomer
Nathan	M	40	Yes	No	Child(ren) living elsewhere	Buying	Large urban	Full time	£16,000–20,000	Living where brought up
Nazeen	M	40	Yes	No	No	Buying	Large urban	Part time	<£10,000	Incomer
Neil	M	40	Yes	No	No	Own outright	Large urban	Self-employed	£31,000–40,000	Incomer
Nicole	F	36	(Living with partner)		Child(ren) living elsewhere	Renting (social)	Accessible rural	Full time	£16,000–20,000	Living where brought up
Paula	F	36	Yes	Yes	No	Renting (social)	Remote rural	Full time	£16,000–20,000	Incomer

Name	Sex	Age				Housing	Location	Employment	Income	Status
Paul	M	43	Yes	No	No	Renting (private)	Large urban	Self-employed	£16,000–20,000	Incomer
Rachel	F	31	Yes	No	No	Buying	Accessible rural	Full time	>£40,000	Incomer
Ray	M	44	Yes	No	No	Buying	Large urban	Full time	£31,000–40,000	Incomer
Richard	M	31	Yes	Yes	No	Buying	Large urban	Full time	>£40,000	Incomer
Robert	M	42	Yes	No	Child(ren) living elsewhere	Renting (social)	Large urban	Full time	£16,000–20,000	Incomer
Rona	F	40	Yes	Yes	No	Buying	Remote rural	Full time	£21,000–25,000	Incomer
Ryan	M	25	Yes	Yes	No	Buying	Remote small town	Full time	£26,000–30,000	Living where brought up
Samir	M	26	Yes	No	No	Renting (social)	Large urban	Unemployed	<£10,000	Living where brought up
Sam	M	31	Yes	No	No	Buying	Large urban	Full time	£31,000–40,000	Incomer

Table A1.1 (Continued)

Name	Sex (M/F)	Age	Whether currently living alone	Whether current relationship	Whether parent	Housing tenure	Locality	Employment status	Annual income	Residential mobility
Sandra	F	31	Yes	No	No	Buying		Full time	£26,000–30,000	Living where brought up
Sarah	F	27	Yes	Yes	No	Buying	Large urban	Full time	£21,000–25,000	Living where brought up
Sebastian	M	35	Yes	No	No	Buying	Large urban Large urban	Full time	£26,000–30,000	Living where brought up
Shona	F	37	Yes	Yes	No	Own outright	Remote small town	Full time	£16,000–20,000	Living where brought up
Simon	M	31	Yes	Yes	No	Buying	Large urban	Full time	£21,000–25,000	Living where brought up
Sophie	F	38	Yes	No	No	Buying	Accessible rural	Full time	£31,000–40,000	Incomer
Stephen	M	41	Yes	Yes	Child(ren) living elsewhere	Renting (private)	Large urban	Permanently sick/disabled	<£10,000	Living where brought up

Name	Sex	Age								
Struan	M	44	Yes	Yes	Child(ren) living elsewhere	Renting (social)	Remote rural	Self-employed	£10,000–15,000	Incomer
Sue	F	34	Yes	No	No	Buying	Remote small town	Full time	£26,000–30,000	Living where brought up
Sunil	M	38	Yes	No	No	Renting (private)	Large urban	Full time	£16,000–20,000	Incomer
Sylvia	F	34	(Living with partner)		No	Buying	Large urban	Full time	£21,000–25,000	Living where brought up
Theresa	F	35	(Living with partner)		No	Buying	Remote small town	Full time	£16,000–20,000	Incomer
Thomas	M	28	(Living with partner)		No	Buying	Large urban	Self-employed	>£40,000	Incomer
Tommy	M	43	Yes	No	Child(ren) living elsewhere	Renting (private)	Large urban	Unemployed	<£10,000	Incomer

Table A1.1 (Continued)

Name	Sex (M/F)	Age	Whether currently living alone	Whether current relationship	Whether parent	Housing tenure	Locality	Employment status	Annual income	Residential mobility
Tracy	F	25	Yes	Yes	No	Buying	Remote small town	Full time	£26,000–30,000	Incomer
Veronica	F	37	Yes	Yes	No	Home owned by relative, rent free	Remote rural	Full time	£16,000–20,000	Living where brought up
Violet	F	40	Yes	No	No	Buying	Remote rural	Full time	£31,000–40,000	Incomer
Vivien	F	39	Yes	No	No	Renting (private)	Remote small town	Full time	£16,000–20,000	Living where brought up
Walt	M	32	(Living with partner)		Child(ren) living elsewhere	Buying	Large urban	Full time	>£40,000	Incomer
Wendy	F	28	(Living with partner)		No	Buying	Large urban	Full time	£16,000–20,000	Living where brought up
William	M	41	Yes	No	Child(ren) living elsewhere	Renting (social)	Remote small town	Unemployed	<£10,000	Incomer

Appendix 2: Characteristics and Circumstances of Working-Age Men and Women Living Alone in Scotland

We provide below a detailed overview of the characteristics and circumstances of working-age (16–59/64) men and women living alone in Scotland, based on analysis of the 2011 Scottish Household Survey.[1] We compare rural and urban men and women living alone, and also include specific information on those aged 25–44, the age group of interest in our study.[2]

Section 1: Housing

Tables A2.1a and A2.1b provide a breakdown of housing tenure. Table A2.1a shows two-fifths of working-age men and just under a third of working-age women are housed by local authorities in urban areas, with the proportions about 10% less in rural areas.

Table A2.1a   Housing tenure: Locality, gender, solo, working-age adults (%)

	Urban		Rural	
	Solo men	Solo women	Solo men	Solo women
Owned outright[3]	12	14	26	18
Buying with loan/mortgage	27	36	27	36
Rent – public/social sector	40	31	27	23
Rent – private sector	21	19	17	19
Other	1	1	3	5
Total (100%)	1111	799	219	129

Source: Scottish Household Survey (2011)

Table A2.1b   Housing tenure: Gender, solo, age 25–44 (%)

Tenure	Men	Women
Own outright	5	4
Buying with loan/mortgage	32	47
Rent – public/social sector	38	23
Rent – private sector	24	24
Other	1	1
Total	543	336

Source: Scottish Household Survey (2011)

Among the 25–44-year-old age group the numbers are not large enough to sensibly pursue a further break down by location but it again shows men as more likely to be in the public/social renting sector than women (38% versus 23%) and markedly less likely to be owner occupiers than women (37% versus 51%).

The Scottish Household Survey shows that people living alone are much more likely to be in a flat or part of a larger property than in a terraced, semi-detached or detached house. Men and women living on their own are also more than twice as likely to be living in a flat than men and women living with others.

In the 25–44 years age group, women living alone are more likely to be living in a house than men living alone (34% compared with 26%).

Those living alone are far more likely than those living with others to live in a one bedroom home. Nevertheless, the majority have more than one bedroom and by some average measures of access to space, people living on their own as a group would be more advantaged than people living with others. Women living alone are more likely to have two or more bedrooms than men living alone.

Table A2.2a   Accommodation type: Gender, solo or not,[4] working-age adults (%)

Accommodation type	Solo men	Solo women	Men not solo	Women not solo
Flat/maisonette	65	58	26	28
House or bungalow	34	41	74	72
Other	1	1	0	0
Total (100%)	1330	928	2762	3579

Source: Scottish Household Survey (2011)

Table A2.2b Accommodation type: Gender, solo, age 25–44 (%)

Accommodation type	Men	Women
Flat/maisonette	73	66
House or bungalow	26	34
Total	543	336

Source: Scottish Household Survey (2011)

Table A2.3a Number of bedrooms: Gender, solo or not, working-age adults (%)

Number of bedrooms	Solo men	Solo women	Men not solo	Women not solo
One	36	28	5	3
Two	44	45	30	34
Three or more	20	26	65	63
Total	1330	928	2762	3579

Source: Scottish Household Survey (2011)

Table A2.3b Number of bedrooms: Gender, solo, age 25–44 (%)

Number of bedrooms	Men	Women
One	37	33
Two	49	48
Three or more	14	20
Total	543	336

Source: Scottish Household Survey (2011)

In the age group 25–44, 37% of men and 33% of women living on their own were in one-bedroom properties. This is a slightly higher proportion that the average across all working ages and in comparison with all ages they were less likely to be in large properties with three or more bedrooms.

Section 2: Socio-economic and demographic characteristics

The proportions of people living in public/social housing typically reflect patterns of socio-economic disadvantage. This section uses education, employment, income, and health to show the distribution of advantage and disadvantage comparing working-age men and women

Table A2.4 Educational qualification: Gender, solo or not, working-age adults (%)

	Solo men	Solo women	Men not solo	Women not solo
Degree/professional qualification or higher	26	35	29	31
HNC/HND or equivalent	13	12	14	13
School-level qualifications	37	36	42	42
Other qualifications	2	2	3	2
No qualifications	22	15	13	12
Total (100%)	1319	925	2750	3562

Source: Scottish Household Survey (2011)

living alone and with working-age men and women living in family homes, and in some cases looking specifically at the 25–44-year-old age group. It also provides tables by marital status and showing caring responsibilities for others.

Table A2.4 shows that the distribution of educational qualifications among working-age women living alone in Scotland in 2011 involves a larger proportion with degrees or professional qualifications (35%) than all men and among women who are not living alone. Working-age men living alone are more likely that all women or men living with others to have no qualifications, over a fifth (22%).

Table A2.5a shows that among those living alone a larger minority proportion are not in employment because of sickness or disability. Moreover, among men living alone, a larger minority proportion (15%) are unemployed than among women living alone and men and women living with others.

Differences between men and women are more marked in the 25–44-year-old age group which shows three-quarters of women (75%) in some form of employment (64% full-time, 8% part-time, 3% self-employed) compared to only 64% of men. Men living alone in this age group are also more than twice as likely to be unemployed (16%, compared to 6% women living alone).

Although there are more men in higher managerial and professional occupations regardless of living situation, when lower and higher managerial and professional occupations are combined, women living on their own are more likely to be in managerial and professional occupations (48%) than either men living on their own (33%) or men and women living with others (37%) (Table A2.6).

Table A2.5a Employment status: Gender, solo or not, working-age adults (%)

Employment status	Solo men	Solo women	Men not solo	Women not solo
Full-time employment	44	49	59	39
Part-time employment	4	11	4	24
Unemployed	15	8	6	5
Self-employed	8	4	11	4
Looking after home/family	1	2	1	16
Permanently sick or disabled	16	14	4	3
Permanently retired	5	2	6	1
Short-term ill health	3	2	1	1
Higher/further education	5	9	6	5
Other*	1	1	3	2
Total (100%)	1330	928	2762	3579

*Government work/training scheme, at school.
Source: Scottish Household Survey (2011)

Table A2.5b Employment status: Gender, solo, age 25–44 (%)

Employment status	men	women
Full-time employment	52	64
Part-time employment	4	8
Self-employed	8	3
Unemployed	16	6
Permanently sick or disabled	12	9
Higher/further education	3	5
Other*	4	5
Total (Ns)	543	336

*Includes the following categories: Government work/training scheme, unable to work due to short-term illness, looking after home/family, permanently retired from work.
Source: Scottish Household Survey (2011)

There are differences in employment patterns between people living alone in urban and rural areas: a smaller proportion are jobless in rural areas, with women in rural areas most likely to have more than one job (Table A2.7).

Table A2.8a uses net household income which is all income (after taxation and other deductions) from employment, benefits and other sources that is brought into the household by the highest income householder and/or their spouse or partner and it includes any contribution to household finances made by other household members (e.g. dig

Table A2.6 Socio-economic classification of occupation: Gender, solo or not, working-age adults (%)

NS-SEC*	Solo men	Solo women	Men not solo	Women not solo
Higher managerial and professional occupations	13	13	14	9
Lower managerial and professional occupations	20	35	23	28
Intermediate occupations	8	17	8	21
Small employers and own account workers	9	3	10	5
Lower supervisory and technical occupations	16	4	15	6
Semi-routine occupations	15	20	13	23
Routine occupations	20	9	17	10
Total (100%)	978	709	2379	2857

*The National Statistics-Socio Economic Classification is a system of classifying all occupations.
Source: Scottish Household Survey (2011)

Table A2.7 Number of jobs: Gender, locality, working-age adults (%)

Number of jobs	Urban		Rural	
	Solo men	Solo women	Solo Men	Solo Women
None	44	37	36	19
One	54	59	60	72
Two or more	2	4	4	9
Total (100%)	1111	798	219	129

Source: Scottish Household Survey (2011)

money, a contribution towards living costs). This procedure of counting income makes it inevitable that two or more adult households (here note that these households do not include lone parent households) will have a higher income than one person households. However, note that nearly a third (31%) of working-age men and women living alone are in the lowest income group of under £10,000, compared with less than 10% of two or more adult households. Over half of men and women living alone have a household income of less than £15,000, compared with less than a fifth of households with two or more adults, hence a larger proportion of those living alone experience living on a low income.

Table A2.8a Annual household income: Gender, solo or not, working-age adults (%)

Annual income band	Solo men	Solo women	Men not solo	Women not solo
£0–10000	31	31	8	8
£10001–£15000	24	25	10	10
£15001–£20000	18	19	14	11
£20001+	27	25	68	71
Total	1262	878	2655	2828

Source: Scottish Household Survey (2011)

Table A2.8b Household income: Gender, solo, age 25–44 (%)

Annual income band	Men	Women
£0–£10,000	28	22
£10,001–£15,000	21	24
£15,001–£20,000	21	21
£20,001+	30	33
Total (Ns)	522	323

Source: Scottish Household Survey (2011)

In the age group 25–44, over a quarter of men living alone (28%) and fifth of women (22%) have an income of less than £10,000. A slightly higher proportion of women than men (33% and 30%) have incomes over £20,000.

Analysis of the SHS (not shown) indicates that a higher proportion of people living alone are in receipt of state benefits than people living with others, and this is particularly marked for men. For example, three times as many men living alone are in receipt of Income Support compared with men living with others (11% and 3%, respectively), compared with 11% of women living alone and 8% of women living with others. Men and women living alone are also more likely to be in receipt of Housing Benefit (30% and 22%), compared with men and women living with others (8% and 16%)

A higher proportion of people living alone have serious health problems; almost four times as many are classified as permanently sick or disabled than the equivalent gender living with others, 16% and 14% of men and women living alone respectively, compared with 4% and 3% of men and women living with others.

Table A2.9   Partnership status, gender, locality, solo working-age adults (%)

Partnership status	Urban		Rural	
	Solo men	Solo women	Solo men	Solo women
Married/Cohabiting	2	2	3	14
Single Never–Married	69	64	60	48
Ever–married	29	34	37	38
Total (100%)	1111	799	219	129

Source: Scottish Household Survey (2011)

Table A2.9 shows the legal marital status of those living alone in rural and urban areas. Nearly one in seven (14%) rural solo women are married and/or have a co-resident partner who is living elsewhere at the time of the survey. In rural areas a larger proportion of the solo-living population are ex-married (widowed, divorced or separated). Those who are single (never married) are a slightly larger proportion of men living alone in urban areas (69%) than of urban women living alone (64%) or those living alone in rural areas (60% of men and 48% of women).

Women living alone were as likely to be providing regular help or care to somebody who was classified as sick, disabled or elderly as women living in couples or family households. In both cases a slightly higher proportion of women provided care than men.

Table A2.10   Caring for others, gender, solo or not, working-age adults (%)

Providing regular help/care for sick/disabled/elderly person not living with you?	Solo men	Solo women	Men not solo	Women not solo
Yes	8	11	8	11
No	92	89	92	89
Totals (100%)	1328	928	2760	3576

Source: Scottish Household Survey (2011)

Section 3: Type of locality, transport, Internet access

The majority of the Scottish population live in urban areas but, among working-age adults, people living alone are slightly more concentrated

Table A2.11   Locality: Gender, solo or not, working-age adults (%)

Locality	Solo men	Solo women	Men not solo	Women not solo
Urban	88	89	82	83
Rural	12	11	18	17
Total (100%)	1330	928	2762	3578

Source: Scottish Household Survey (2011)

Table A2.12   Working-age men and women, by living arrangement and locality[5] (%)

	Large urban areas	Other urban	Small accessible towns	Small remote towns	Accessible rural	Remote rural	All areas
Men in one-person households	26	19	19	26	14	18	21
Multi-person households	74	81	81	74	86	82	79
Total (Ns)	2297	2041	580	355	771	617	6662
Women in one-person households	17	12	10	11	8	11	13
Multi-person household	83	88	90	89	92	89	87
Total (Ns)	2457	2180	605	339	791	598	6971

Source: Scottish Household Survey (2011)

in urban areas: slightly more than 1 in 10 of working-age people living alone are in rural areas.

Another way of looking at the geographical distribution of living alone among working-age adults is to consider the proportion of one-person households in different types of areas. Across all type of areas men living alone outnumber women. In large urban areas and remote small towns men living alone are 26% of all households with working-age men, compared to 18% in remote rural areas. Rural areas close to towns and cities have the lowest proportion of one-person households among working-age adults.

The Scottish Household Survey collects information on how people liked their local area, the length of time they had spent at their current address, and how they rate it as a place to live.[6] In terms of length of

Table A2.13   Length of residence: Gender, solo or not, working-age adults (%)

Length of residence	Solo men	Solo women	Men not solo	Women not solo
Less than 1 year	9	8	4	5
1–2 years	21	16	15	16
3–4 years	14	14	13	15
5–10 years	26	29	25	29
11–15 years	12	13	12	14
More than 15 years	20	20	30	22
Total (100%)	1227	866	2641	3399

Source: Scottish Household Survey (2011)

Table A2.14   How rates area: Gender, locality, solo working-age adults (%)

How rates area as a place to live	Urban		Rural	
	Solo men	Solo women	Solo Men	Solo Women
Very good	43	46	62	64
Fairly good	46	46	34	36
Fairly poor	8	6	4	1
Very poor	3	2	––	––
Total (100%)	1107	793	217	129

Source: Scottish Household Survey (2011)

residence, a larger minority proportion of solo men and women have lived in their current address for less than two years than their peers living with others, a difference more marked for men than women.

In terms of rating the area as a place to live, the majority of all working-age adults rate their area as either very or fairly good, and there is little difference by gender. There are clear differences by locality, with rural solos far more likely to classify the area as a very good place to live, and less likely to find it fairly or very poor.

As Table A2.15a illustrates, people who live alone are far more likely to have no car than people living with others. This is consistent with the type of housing and neighbourhoods occupied by people living alone as well as the economies of scale which make it easier for couples to afford to run at least one car. Analysis of the SHS (not shown) indicates that working-age men and women living on their own are also less likely on

Table A2.15a Household vehicles: Gender, solo or not, working-age adults (%)

Household vehicles	Solo men	Solo women	Men not solo	Women not solo
None	50	46	15	21
One	47	51	42	43
Two or more	3	3	44	36
Totals (100%)	1330	928	2762	3579

Source: Scottish Household Survey (2011)

average to have a full driving licence (67% and 63%) than those living with others (79% and 66%). Note the difference is more marked among men than women, but the size of this difference is very reduced in rural areas for men and slightly reversed for women. Solo men are the most likely to be disqualified from driving or to have their licence suspended for health reasons, 3% of urban and 4% of rural solo men compared to 2% of rural solo women and less than 1% of others.

Car ownership and access to a household car varies significantly between urban and rural areas, being widely regarded as an absolute necessity in the latter context. Men and women living alone in rural areas are far more likely to have a car than men and women living alone in urban areas, although they are still less likely to do so than men and women in rural areas who live with others.

In the age group 25–44, the difference between the proportion of men and women living alone with no car is more marked.

Table A2.15b Household vehicles: Gender, locality, solo or not, working-age adults (%)

Household vehicles	Urban				Rural			
	Solo men	Solo women	Men not solo	Women not solo	Solo men	Solo women	Men not solo	Women not solo
None	53	50	17	24	29	15	6	7
One	45	49	43	44	60	70	34	37
Two or more	3	1	40	32	10	15	61	56
Totals (100%)	1111	799	2167	2866	219	129	595	712

Source: Scottish Household Survey (2011)

Table A2.15c   Household vehicles: Gender, solo or not, age 25–44 (%)

Household vehicles	Solo men	Solo women	Men not solo	Women not solo
None	52	40	15	22
One	45	57	44	46
Two or more	3	3	41	32
Totals (100%)	543	336	1063	1854

Source: Scottish Household Survey (2011)

Just as people living alone are more likely to be without a household car, so also are they less likely to have the Internet at home. Comparison with analysis conducted on a previous wave of the SHS (2005/2006) shows a dramatic increase in the proportions of all working-age adults with Internet access at home, nevertheless this remains lower amongst men and women living alone.

The proportion of people living alone with intenet access at home is higher in the age group 25–44 than it is for all of working age.

Comparisons by locality (not shown) indicate levels of Internet access at home are slightly higher in rural than urban areas: for example, 64% of rural compared with 60% of urban men living alone. Levels

Table A2.16a   Home Internet access: Gender, solo or not, working-age adults (%)

	Solo men	Solo women	Men not solo	Women not solo
Yes	61	70	91	89
No	39	30	9	11
Totals (100%)	996	685	2101	2674

Source: Scottish Household Survey (2011)

Table A2.16b   Home Internet access: Gender, solo or not, age 25–44 (%)

	Solo men	Solo women	Men not solo	Women not solo
Yes	68	79	93	90
No	32	22	7	10
Total (100%)	410	241	785	1392

Source: Scottish Household Survey (2011)

of Internet access also varies radically by socio-economic indicators of deprivation or advantage. For example, 45% of men living alone in the most deprived areas and 79% in the least deprived areas have Internet access (bottom and top quintiles using the Scottish Indicator of Multiple Deprivation). A set of questions about whether the Internet has ever been used for a range of goods, services and information suggests that patterns of use are not markedly different between urban and rural areas.

Notes

1 Introduction

1. For example, the US Census defines a household as all the people who occupy a 'housing unit', which is in turn defined as 'a house, an apartment or other group of rooms, or a single room...when it is occupied or intended for occupancy as separate living quarters; that is, when the occupants do not live and eat with any other persons in the structure and there is direct access from the outside or through a common hall'. The 2001 British Census defined a household as one person living alone or a group of people (not necessarily related) living at the same address with common housekeeping – sharing either a living room or a sitting room, or at least one meal a day.
2. We sampled from respondents aged 25–44 at the time of the survey. However, there was a lag of about one year between the survey date and our interview, hence some respondents are of age 45 and few are of age 25.
3. England's ten times greater population determines the United Kingdom's place in the world league of living alone, near the bottom of the top-ranked group, as shown in Chapter 2. One-person households were 33 per cent of all households in Scotland in 2011 compared to 29 per cent in the United Kingdom.

Part I Living Alone, Life Course and Life Transitions

1. The phrase 'first demographic transition' refers to a fall in fertility and mortality across Europe peaking in the nineteenth century and associated assumptions made by demographers about the stages of change.
2. For example, an annual National Singles Week; see also de Paulo (2011) and the website 'Unmarried America' at www.unmarriedamerica.org/main. html, accessed 15 August 2012. Eric Klinenberg discusses the US-initiated websites Quirkyalone.net, SingularCity.com and the Brooklyn-based organization, the Alternative to Marriages Project, which advocates for people living in arrangements outside the institution of marriage (Klinenberg, 2012).

2 Geographies and Biographies of Living Alone

1. People living alone may be disproportionately undercounted in census data particularly in parts of the 'global south'. Many poor countries have circumstances that work against accurate census data, including transitory and large populations living in undocumented self-constructed dwellings with no legal tenure. Such settlements are certainly not predominantly people living alone but they may, nevertheless, create opportunities for doing so (Kellett, 2000). Undercounting is unlikely to transform the overall picture.

2. As De Vaus and Richardson (2009) emphasize, it is important to distinguish between the percentage of one-person *households* and the percentage of *individuals* that live alone. These statistics may be conflated in commentary on living alone (for example, Furedi, 2002). The percentage of one-person households will always be greater than the percentage of individuals living alone. Imagine a village of ten houses. If in two of them somebody lives alone they are a fifth or 20 per cent of the households. However, if two people live in each of six houses and three people live in each of two houses then the total population is 20. So the two people who live alone are only a tenth, or 10 per cent of the population.

3. A range of countries are shown in Table 2.1, but not all regions of the world are equally represented; this reflects reliance on summary sources and levels of difficulty in accessing national statistics over time for different parts of the globe, particularly comparative data for countries of the 'global south'. The parts of the world where the trend of living alone is most developed, however, are well covered.

4. The OECD International Futures Programme projects growth from mid to early 2000s to 2025/2030: as these projections are based on certain assumptions about behaviour patterns, they cannot be certain; hence are projections rather than predictions (OECD, 2011a).

5. This distinguishes liberal, corporatist and social democratic, and subsequently a Mediterranean regime type, in accordance with a specified set of criteria such as the degree of decommodification, freedom from the market, in relation to level and type of welfare-state provision. It is a schema that was modified by feminist critique noting that women's equality has been restricted as much by economic dependency on familial relationships as the market (Cunningham-Burley and Jamieson, 2003; Lister, 1997).

6. It would take further analysis by age to help explain the exception of Italy that has one of the 'oldest' populations in Europe, with 20 per cent of Italians older than 65. The percentage of people aged 65 and over rose from 10.8 in 1970 to 18.2 in 2002. Rapid increases in the proportion of the population aged 65 and over reflect dramatic reductions in fertility (Di Santo and Ceruzzi, 2010).

7. This research shows partnership occurring earlier than home-leaving in the case of Slovakia and Poland, indicating it is common for young adults to remain living with parents while they also live with a partner: these are countries with very low proportions of young people living alone (Iacovou and Skew, 2010, pp. 89–90). Iacovou and Skew also note considerable heterogeneity between counties in eastern Europe: thus Slovakia, Slovenia and Poland are more similar to southern European countries, whereas the Czech Republic and Hungary have more in common with north-western countries. The Baltic countries are more divergent.

8. There are many historical examples of young people living away from parents but remaining closely supervised (Anderson, 1998; Hareven, 2000; Wall, 1989), and contemporary examples of migrant children working for their family rather than pursuing an independent trajectory (for example, Magazine and Sanchez, 2007), as well as young migrants or young people left behind by migrant parents (Dreby, 2010; Parreñas, 2005) finding new freedoms in their situation.

9. There has been a dramatic decline in fertility rates, with the average TFR (total fertility rate) among OECD countries below replacement level since 1982 (OECD, 2011b: 20). Fertility replacement level is defined as a TFR of 2.1, which would ensure the replacement of the previous generation and therefore population stability, assuming no net migration and no change in mortality rates. Demographers distinguish between three levels: (i) low fertility, below replacement but at least 1.5 children per woman; (ii) very low fertility, less than 1.5 but at least 1.31; and (iii) lowest low fertility, that is, less than 1.31 children per woman. The TFR is the most common measure of comparison; however, it is sensitive to changes in the number and timing of births.
10. The number of young people living with parents in owner-occupied accommodation is projected to increase from 2008 by approximately 550,000 to 3.7 million in 2020, those living with parents in private rented accommodation will increase by approximately 170,000 to 400,000 and those living with parents in social rented accommodation are predicted to increase by approximately 170,000 to 870,000 (Clapham et al., 2012, p. 4).

3   Solo-living with and without Partnering and Parenting

1. Eighteen of the 55 were interviewed a second time to gain additional depth. The sample is not a convenience sample but recruited through a sampling frame based on a random sample across the population of people living alone. The sample differs from the populations surveyed in other LAT studies because the participants were living alone and in the age group 25–44 years. Quantitative studies of LAT typically include all living situations (for example, shared accommodation, living with children) across all age of adult life.
2. As is discussed in Chapter 4, encouraging home ownership was government policy in the 1980s and was boosted by legislation giving local authority tenants the right to buy their home. Home owning became much more difficult for young adults following the recession of 2007, causing the British press to adopt the phrase 'generation rent'.
3. Twenty-one of the 75 men had a child or children and a further three were fathers of children who had died. Four of the 65 women had a child or children but in two cases they were adult and had left home; another participant was now living with her partner and baby, however, was interviewed about her experience of living alone prior to becoming a mother. Of the 21 fathers, over half (12) were involved fathers of dependent children in regular contact with them, three had some contact and six little or no contact.
4. The Waltons was an American television series about a family with seven children. The CSA is the UK agency that at this time collected a father's contribution to his child's upkeep using the money to reduce the cost to the UK state of benefits paid to the mother.

Part II Home, Consumption and Identity

1. Examples include overviews from particular disciplinary perspectives such as that of the geographers Blunt and Dowling (2006); a number of edited

collections bringing together anthropological or sociological studies such as Allen and Crow (1989), Cieraad (1999) and Miller (2001); and a brave attempt at interdisciplinary overview by Mallet (2004) as well as more specialist text looking at the impact of technology on the home such as Silva (2010).

5   Living Alone, Consuming Alone?

1. The package includes an international flight to a tourist-destination country with local transport to and accommodation in a tourist resort.
2. In the Scottish cities of the 1970s, it would have been possible to find hotels serving food and drink to the public on Christmas day but not on New Year's day, and everything shut early on Hogmanay to allow people to travel home in time to be with family. No such allowance was made on Christmas Eve. Hogmanay retained an aspect of community festival. In twenty-first-century Scotland, there is no public holiday in which everything is closed and Christmas is the dominant festival.

Part III Networks, Community and Place

1. For example, see 'Singleton Society', Furedi (11 October 2002) www.spiked-online.com/Articles/00000002D3A&.htm, accessed 15 August 2012, 'No Country for Old Men', *The Guardian* (11 June 2008), www.guardian.co.uk/society/2008/jun/11/longtermcare.socialcare1, accessed 15 August 2012.
2. In the United Kingdom, the coalition government established the Office for Civil Society in 2010 to promote the agenda of the 'Big Society', including fostering community engagement and a culture of voluntarism, philanthropy, and social action (see speech by Prime Minister David Cameron on the Big Society, 19 July 2010, www.number10.gov.uk/news/big-society-speech/, accessed 27 June 2012). President Obama launched the 'United we Serve' scheme in 2009, highlighting the importance of expanding the size and impact of volunteer efforts in the context of the economic downturn: 'Economic recovery is as much about what you're doing in your communities as what we're doing in Washington – and it's going to take all of us, working together', 16 June 2009, www.serve.gov/remarks.asp, accessed 2 August 2012.
3. The literature that could be cited here is extensive but examples of the former view include Bellah et.al. (1985), Popenoe (1993) and Cherlin (2009) and of the later include Skolnick (1991), Giddens (1992), Weston (1997 [1991]), Weeks et al. (2001), Budgeon and Roseneil (2004) and Stacey (2011).

6   Solo-living and Connectedness

1. See Young and Grundy (2009, p. 128–130) for a review.
2. These were constructed on the basis of established typologies of predominant family cultures, welfare regimes and geographic location, comparing countries of northern, eastern and southern Europe.

3. Data from the survey of the adult population of the FGR conducted as part of the 'Change and Development of Family Life Patterns' project (Bertram et al., 1986, cited in Bien et al., 1992).
4. Data from the Scottish Household Survey social capital module 2000/2001.
5. Data from Canada's General Social Survey 2008.
6. This compared north-western European countries (Sweden, Norway, Finland, Denmark, the Netherlands, Belgium, Switzerland, France, the United Kingdom, Austria, Germany), with southern (Spain, Portugal, Italy, Greece) and eastern European (Czech Republic, Hungary, Poland, Slovenia).
7. One or both parents of 24 respondents had died, more fathers (22) than mothers (12); nevertheless, the gender difference remained.
8. Some of those prioritizing siblings or extended kin no longer had any living parent.
9. Other relationships amongst extended social networks also identified as important included godchildren, friends from work, Internet friends, art class members, bowling colleagues and spiritual community.
10. Questions specifically referring to family ties or designated family members may have missed other people also considered important, however the interviews as a whole did have many opportunities for consideration of relationships with non-kin.
11. The questions included the hypothetical examples of being on holiday and wanting someone to water plants, and breaking an arm and needing some level of help around the home.
12. Relationships with others in one's local community are considered further in the following chapter.
13. When recruiting the sample, a few potential participants stated they could not afford the time to take part because of their caring responsibilities for ill siblings or grandchildren.
14. A youth charity organizing various outdoor activities for young people.
15. Barrett and McIntosh's (1991[1982]) 'The Anti-Social Family', for example, argues that an ideology of familism delegitimizes the value of non-familial relationships: 'in privileging the intimacy of close kin it has made the outside world cold and friendless, and made it harder to sustain relations of security and trust except with close kin' (1991, p. 80).

7   Place, Mobility and Migration

1. Survey data show around 1 in 7 men and women living alone at working age in Scotland are located in small remote towns or rural localities (see Appendix 2 A2.12).
2. Employment in rural Scotland has traditionally involved a wider range of opportunities in agriculture, forestry, fishing and service industries for men than women and there is a long history of higher rates of out-migration by young women than men. The higher number of in-migrant women in rural areas seems to reflect a higher level of take up of the small number of professional positions advertised in rural areas by women than by men.
3. The A9 is a 432.9 kilometre route from central Scotland to the north coast.

8 The Future of Living Alone

1. See 'Campaign to End Loneliness', www.campaigntoendloneliness.org.uk/, accessed 12 August 2012.
2. Klinenberg's (2012) enthusiastic representation of the experiences of living alone is one example of the emergence of alternative discourses on solo-living.
3. However, such guest space would not satisfy those seeking to maintain a 'home from home' for a regularly visiting child, partner or other friend or family.

Appendix 1: The Rural and Urban Solo Living: Social Integration, Quality of Life and Future Orientations Study

1. This ESRC-funded study, 'Rural and Urban Solo Living: Social Integration, Quality of Life and Future Orientations', was conducted between 2007 and 2009 (Grant RES-062-23-0172).
2. The respective state pension ages for women and men, respectively, at time of interview.
3. The information reported in Appendix 2 is from the latest available SHS data (2010/2011).
4. The SHS uses a sixfold urban–rural classification based on settlement size and accessibility in drive-time to a larger settlement: 'large urban areas' (settlements of over 125,000 people), 'other urban' (settlements of 10,000 to 125,000 people), 'small accessible towns' (settlements of between 3000 and 10,000 people and within 30 minutes drive of a settlement of 10,000 or more), 'remote small towns' (settlements of between 3000 and 10,000 people and with a drive time of over 30 minutes to a settlement of 10,000 or more), 'accessible rural' (settlements of less than 3000 people and within 30 minutes drive of a settlement of 10,000 or more) and 'remote' rural areas (settlements of less than 3000 people and with a drive time of over 30 minutes drive of a settlement of 10,000 or more). In order to maximize urban–rural comparison and enhance our chances of appropriate-sized matched samples, we selected interview respondents living in large urban areas, remote small towns and accessible and remote rural areas. Given size and distance to larger settlements, we categorized remote small towns as rural, and our analysis compares 'urban' (large urban areas) with 'rural' (remote small towns, accessible rural, remote rural).
5. Around two-fifths (113), however, were either not eligible, having lived alone for a period of less than six months or now living outside Scotland, or non-contactable due to incorrect or out-of-date telephone numbers.
6. One took place at the University of Edinburgh, another in a public library and a third at the respondent's workplace.
7. Note all names are pseudonyms.
8. Status on first interview: several had changed status (for example, moving in with a partner or ending previous relationship so now single) by the second interview.

Appendix 2: Characteristics and Circumstances of Working-Age Men and Women Living Alone in Scotland

1. This analysis is based on data collected from randomly selected adults, designed to be representative of the Scottish adult population. It does not compare households, but the household experiences of random adults either living alone ('solo') or with others in private households. Adults of working age are 16–64 for men, and 16–59 for women.
2. This breakdown does mean some of the confidence intervals where sample sizes are below 300 will be quite large (for example, for solo women in rural areas the effective sample size means confidence intervals of ±9.5% on an estimate of 50%).
3. The larger proportion of people owning their homes outright in rural areas requires further investigation but age distributions and patterns of migration are important. Rural areas have fewer people living alone at younger ages. Older working-age owner occupiers are both more likely to have paid off mortgages and to have inherited homes than younger owner occupiers. Inheritance may be an important route of access to housing in some rural areas. For in-migrants arriving in rural areas with relatively inexpensive housing from more expensive urban housing markets, outright purchase of a home can be achieved relatively quickly. However, rural areas vary significantly in the cost of housing.
4. This category collapses all private households of working-age adults involving more than one person. These are predominantly classified as 'family households' comprising couples without children, parents and children, lone mothers or fathers with children.
5. See footnote 3 above.
6. In questions about the local area, the SHS questionnaire uses prompts for urban of 'the street you live in and the streets nearby', and for rural of 'the local area' (SHS 2006).

Bibliography

Aassve, A., Iacovou, M. and Mencarini, L. (2006) 'Youth poverty and transition to adulthood in Europe', *Demographic Research*, 15, 21–50.

About Families (2012) *Extended Adolescence: What UK and International Research Exists on Extended Adolescence?*, Evidence Report prepared by About Families for Parenting Across Scotland, April 2012 www.aboutfamilies.files.wordpress.com/2012/07/erb-evidence-response_extended-adolescence1.pdf, accessed 21 July 2012.

Adams, R. and Allan, G. eds. (1998) *Placing Friendship in Context* (Cambridge: Cambridge University Press).

Adkins, L. (2004) 'Reflexivity: Freedom or habit of gender?', *The Sociological Review*, 52, 191–210.

Administration on Ageing (2011) *A Profile of Older American 2011*, U.S. Department of Health and Human Services, www.aoa.gov/aoaroot/aging_statistics/Profile/2011/docs/2011profile.pdf, accessed 3 August 2012.

Agrawal, S. (2012) 'Effect of living arrangement on the health status of elderly in India', *Asian Population Studies*, 8, 87–101.

Alders, M.P.C. and Manting, D. (2003) 'Household scenarios for the European Union, 1995–2025', *Genus LVII*, 2, 17–47.

Allan, G. (1979) *A Sociology of Friendship and Kinship* (London and Boston: Allen and Unwin).

Allan, G. (1989) *Friendship* (London: Harvester).

Allan, G. (1996) *Kinship and Friendship in Modern Britain* (Oxford: Oxford University Press).

Allan, G. (2008) 'Flexibility, friendship, and family', *Personal Relationships*, 15, 1–16.

Allan, G. and Crow, G. (1989) 'Home and family: Creating the domestic sphere', in Allan, G. and Crow, G. eds. *Home and Family: Creating the Domestic Sphere* (London: Macmillan).

Allan, G. and Phillipson, C. (2008) 'Community studies today: Urban perspectives', *International Journal of Social Research Methodology*, 11(2), 163–173.

Allerton, C. (2007) 'What does it mean to be alone?' in Astuti, R., Parry, J. and Stafford, C. eds. *Questions of Anthropology* (Oxford: Berg).

Amato, R., Booth, A., Johnson, D. and Rogers, S. (2007) *Alone Together: How Marriage in America Is Changing* (Cambridge, MA: Harvard University Press).

Anderson, M. (1985) *Approaches to the History of the Western Family, 1500–1914* (London: Macmillan Studies in Economic and Social History).

Anderson, M. (1980) 'The relevance of family history', in Anderson, M. ed. *Sociology of the Family* (Harmondsworth: Penguin).

Andersson, L. (1998) 'Loneliness research and interventions: A review of the literature', *Aging and Mental Health*, 2(4), 264–274.

Andrew, M., Eggerling-Boeck, J., Sandefur, G.D. and Smith, B. (2007) 'The "inner side" of the transition to adulthood: How young adults see the process of becoming an adult', in MacMillan, R. ed. *Constructing Adulthood: Agency and Subjectivity in Adolescence and Adulthood* (Amsterdam: Elsevier).

Andrews, A., Clark, K. and Whittaker, W. (2010) 'The determinants of regional migration in Great Britain: A duration approach', *Journal of the Royal Statistical Society: Series A: Statistics in Society* Article first published online: 14 September 2010. doi: 10.1111/j.1467-985X.2010.00656.x.

Arber, S. and Ginn, J. (1992) 'In sickness and in health': Care-giving, gender and the independence of elderly people', in Marsh, C. and Arber, S. eds. *Families and Households: Divisions and Change* (London: Macmillan).

Archer, M.S. (2007) *Making our Way through the World: Human Reflexivity and Social Mobility* (Cambridge: Cambridge University Press).

Arnett, J.J. (1997) 'Young people's conceptions of the transition to adulthood', *Youth & Society*, 29(1), 3–23, doi: 10.1177/0044118X97029001001, accessed 8 October 2012.

Arnett, J.J. (2000) 'High hopes in a grim world: Emerging adults', views of their futures and 'Generation X', *Youth and Society*, 31(3), 267–286.

Arnett, J.J. (2001) 'Conceptions of the transition to adulthood: Perspectives from adolescence through midlife', *Journal of Adult Development*, 8(2), 133–143.

Arnett, J.J. (2004) *Emerging Adulthood. The Winding Road from the Late Teens through the Twenties* (New York: Oxford University Press).

Aronson, P. (2008) 'The Markers and meanings of growing up: Contemporary young women's transition from adolescence to adulthood', *Gender and Society*, 22, 56–82.

Baldassar, L. (2007) 'Transnational families and aged care: The mobility of care and the migrancy of ageing', *Journal of Ethnic and Migration Studies*, 33, 275–297.

Baldassar, L., Baldock, C. and Wilding, R. (2007) *Families Caring Across Borders: Migration, Aging and Transnational Caregiving* (Palgrave Macmillan: London).

Barnett, J. (1954) *The American Christmas: A Study of National Culture* (New York: Macmillan).

Barrett, M. and McIntosh, M. (1991 [1982]) *The Anti-Social Family* 2nd edn (London: Verso).

Bauman, Z. (2001) *The Individualized Society* (Cambridge: Polity Press).

Bauman, Z. (2003) *Liquid Love: On the Frailty of Human Bonds* (Cambridge: Polity Press).

Bauman, Z. (2005). *Liquid Life* (Cambridge: Polity Press).

Bauman, Z. (2007) *Liquid Times: Living in an Age of Uncertainty* (Cambridge: Polity Press).

Baym, N.K. (2010) *Personal Connections in the Digital Age* (Cambridge: Polity Press).

Beaujouan, E., Regnier-Loilier, A. and Villeneueve-Gokalp, C. (2009) 'Neither single, nor in a couple: A study of living apart together in France', *Demographic Research*, 21, 75–108.

Beck, U. (1992) *Risk Society: Towards a New Modernity* (New Delhi: Sage).

Beck, U. (2000) *The Brave New World of Work* (Cambridge: Cambridge University Press).

Beck, U. and Beck-Gernsheim, E. (1995) *Normal Chaos of Love* (Cambridge: Polity Press).

Beck, U. and Beck-Gernsheim, E. (2001) *Individualization: Institutionalized Individualism and its Social and Political Consequences* (London: Sage).

Bell, C. and Newby, H. (1976) 'Communion, communalism, class and community action: The sources of new urban politics', in Herbert, D. and Johnston, R. eds. *Social Areas in Cities, Volume 2* (Chichester: Wiley).

Bell, S. and Coleman, S. (1999) 'The anthropology of friendship: Enduring themes and future possibilities', in Bell, S. and Coleman, S. eds. *The Anthropology of Friendship* (Oxford: Berg), 1–19.

Bell, W. (1958) 'Social choice, life styles, and suburban residence', in Dobriner, W.M. ed. *The Suburban Community* (New York: Putnam's Sons).

Bellah, R.N., Madsen, R., Sullivan, W.M., Swidler, A. and Tipton, S.M. (1985) *Habits of the Heart: Individualism and Commitment in American Life* (Berkeley: University of California Press).

Bengston, V., Biblarz, T. and Roberts, R. (2002) *How Families Still Matter: A Longitudinal Study Of Youth In Two Generation* (Cambridge: Cambridge University Press).

Bennett, J. and Dixon, M. (2006) *Single Person Households and Social Policy: Looking Forwards* (York: Joseph Rowntree Foundation).

Benson, J. and Furstenberg, F.F., Jr. (2007) 'Entry into adulthood: Are adult role transitions meaningful markers of adult identity?', in MacMillan, R. ed. *Constructing Adulthood: Agency and Subjectivity in Adolescence and Adulthood* (Amsterdam: Elsevier).

Berger, P. and Kellner, H. (1964) 'Marriage and the construction of reality: An exercise in the microsociology of knowledge', *Diogenes*, 12, 1–24, doi:10.1177/039219216401204601.

Berger, P. and Luckman, T. (1971 [1966]) *The Social Construction of Reality: A Treatise in the Sociology of Knowledge* (Harmondsworth: Penguin Books).

Bianchi, S.M., Robinson, J.P., Milkie, M.A. (2006) *Changing Rhythms of American Family Life* (New York: Russell Sage Found).

Bien, W., Marbach, J. and Templeton, R. (1992) 'Social networks of single-person households', in Marsh, C. and Arber, S. eds. *Families and Households: Divisions and Change* (London: Macmillan).

Billari, F.C. (2004) 'Becoming an adult in Europe: A macro (/micro)-demographic perspective', *Demographic Research, Special Collection*, 3(2): 15–44, www.demographic-research.org/special/3/2/ doi: 10.4054/DemRes. 2004.S3.2.

Billari, F.C. and Liefbroer, A.C. (2010) 'Towards a new pattern of transition to adulthood?', *Advances in Life Course Research*, 15, 2–3, 59–75.

Binnie, J. (2004) *The Globalization of Sexuality* (London: Sage).

Bittman, M. and Pixley, J. (1997) *The Double Life of the Family: Myth Hope and Experience* (Sydney: Allen and Unwin).

Blaauboer, M. (2011) 'The impact of childhood experiences and family members outside the household on resident environment choices' *Urban Studies*, 48(8), 1635–1650.

Blaauboer, M., Mulder, C.H. and Zorlu, A. (2011) 'Distances between couples and the man's and woman's parents', *Population, Space and Place*, 17, 597–610. doi: 10.1002/psp.648.

Blunt, A. and Dowling, R. (2006) *Home* (London: Routledge).

Bone, J. and O'Reilly, K. (2010) 'No place called home: The causes and social consequences of the UK housing "bubble"', *British Journal of Sociology*, 61, 231–255.

Bootsma, H.G. (1995) 'The influence of a work-oriented life style on residential location choice of couples', *Netherlands Journal of Housing and the Built Environment*, 10, 45–63.

Bourdieu, P. (1984[1979]) *Distinction: A Social Critique of the Judgement of Taste* (New York: Routledge & Kegan Paul).

Bourdieu, P. (1997) 'The forms of capital', in Halsey, A., Lauder, H., Brown, P. and Stuart Wells, A. eds. *Education: Culture, Economy and Society* (Oxford: Oxford University Press).

Boyle, P., Halfacree, K. and Robinson, V. (1998) *Exploring Contemporary Migration*. (Longman: Harlow).

Brannen, J. (2006) 'Cultures of intergenerational transmission in four-generation families', *Sociological Review*, 54:134–154.

Brownlie, J. (2011) ' "Being there": Multidimensionality, reflexivity and the study of emotional lives, *The British Journal of Sociology*, 62, 462–481.

Brenton, M. (2013) 'Senior cohousing communities – an alternative approach for the UK?' in JRF ed. *Programme Paper: A Better Life* (York: Joseph Rowntree Foundation).

Brun, J. and Fagnani, J. (1994) 'Lifestyles and locational choices: Trade-offs and compromises: a case-study of middle-class couples living in the Ile-de-France region', *Urban Studies*, 31, 921–934.

Bruun, M. (2009) 'A private plot in the sun', Public and private space in Danish cooperative housing associations, paper presented at the ENHR Conference, Prague, 28 June–1 July 2009, Workshop 14 – Housing and Social Theory.

Bruun, M. (2011) 'Egalitarianism and community in Danish housing cooperatives: Proper forms of sharing and being together', *Social Analysis*, 55(2), 62–83.

Budgeon, S. and Roseneil, S. eds. (2004) 'Beyond the conventional family: Intimacy, care, and community in the 21st century', special issue of *Current Sociology*, 52(2).

Bunce, D. (2010) 'Relocatable homes: Medieval tenure in the 21st century?' *Urban Policy and Research*, 28, 277–292.

Burholt, V. (2011) 'Loneliness of older men and women in rural areas of the UK', in *Safeguarding the Convoy: A Call to Action from the Campaign to End Loneliness* (Oxfordshire: Age UK).

Burholt, V. and Wenger, G.C. (2004) 'Migration from South Asia to the UK and the maintenance of transnational intergenerational relationships', in Silverstein, M., Giarrusso, R. and Bengtson, V.L. eds. *Intergenerational Relations Across Time and Place Springer Annual Review of Gerontology and Geriatrics* (New York: Springer).

Burstow, P. (2005) *Dying Alone: Assessing Isolation, Loneliness and Poverty*, www.paulburstow.org.uk/resources/index/, accessed 24 August 2012.

Butler, J. (1999) 'Performativity's social magic', in Shusterman, R. ed. *Bourdieu: A Critical Reader* (Oxford: Blackwell).

Buzar, S. Ogden, P.E. and Hall, R. (2005) 'Households matter: The quiet demography of urban transformation', *Progress in Human Geography*, 29, 413–436.

Bynner, J. and Pan, H. (2002) 'Changes in pathways to employment and adult life?', in Bynner, J. Elias, P. McKnight, A., Pan, H. and Pierre, G. eds. *Young People's Changing Routes To Independence* (York: Joseph Rowntree Foundation, York Publishing Services).

Bynner, J., Ferri, E. and Shepherd, P. eds. (1997) *Twenty-something in the 1990s: Getting on, Getting by, Getting Nowhere* (Aldershot: Ashgate).

Cafferata, G.L. (1987) 'Marital status, living arrangements, and the use of health services by elderly persons', *Journal of Gerontology*, 42, 613–618.

Calhoun, C. (1998) 'Community without propinquity revisited: Communications technology and the transformation of the urban public sphere', *Sociological Inquiry*, 68, 373–397.

Calhoun, C. (2003) 'Belonging in the cosmopolitan imaginary', *Ethnicities*, 3, 531–553.

Cancian, F.M. (1986) 'The feminization of love', *Signs*, 11, 692–709.

Cancian, F.M. (1987) *Love in America: Gender and Self-development* (Cambridge: Cambridge University Press).

Caplow, T., Chadwick, B.A., Bahr, H.M., and Hill, R. (1982) *Middletown Families: Fifty Years of Change and Continuity* (Minneapolis: University of Minnesota Press).

Casper, L.M. and Bianchi, S.M. (2002) *Continuity and Change in the American Family* (Thousand Oaks, CA: Sage).

Castells, M. (1996) *The Rise of the Network Society* (Oxford: Blackwell).

Castro-Martín, T., Domínguez-Folgueras, M. and Martín-García, T. (2008) 'Not truly partnerless: Nonresidential partnerships and retreat from marriage in Spain', *Demographic Research*, 18, 436–468.

CGA Canada (2005) *Growing Up: The Social and Economic Implications of an Aging Population* (Certified General Accountants Association of Canada), www.cga-canada.org/enca/ResearchAndAdvocacy/AreasofInterest/AgingPopulation/Pages/ca_aging_report.aspx, accessed 3August 2012.

Champion, A. and Fisher, T. (2003) 'The social selectivity of migration flows affecting Britains larger conurbations: An analysis of the 1991 census regional migration tables', *Scottish Geographical Journal*, 119(3), 229–246.

Chan, K.S. and Chen, K.L. (2004) 'A comparison of offline and online friendship qualities at different stages of relationship development', *Journal of Social and Personal Relationships*, 21(3), 305–320.

Chandler, J. (1991) *Women without Husbands: An Exploration of the Margins of Marriage* (New York: St. Martin's Press).

Chandler, J., Williams, M., Maconachie, M., Collett, T. and Dodgeon, B. (2004) 'Living alone: Its place in household formation and change', *Sociological Research Online*, 9(3) www.socresonline.org.uk/9/3/chandler.html, accessed 5 October 2010.

Chang, K.-S. (2010) *South Korea under Compressed Modernity: Familial Political Economy in Transition* (London and New York: Routledge).

Chant, S. (1997) *Women-Headed Households: Diversity and Dynamics in the Developing World* (Basingstoke: Macmillan).

Charbonnau, J., Germian, A. and Molgat, M. (2009) *Habiter seul: un nouveau mode de vie?* (Québec: Presses de l'Université Laval).

Charles, N., Davies, C.A. and Harris, C. (2008) *Families in Transition: Social Change, Family Formation and Kin Relationships* (Policy Press: Bristol).

Chaudhuri, A. and Roy, K. (2009) 'Gender differences in living arrangements amongst older persons in India', *Journal of Asian and African Studies*, 44(3), 259–277.

Chen, M.A. (1998) *Widows in India: Social Neglect and Public Action* (New Delhi and Thousand Oaks, CA: Sage).

Chen, M.A. (2000) *Perpetual Mourning: Widowhood in Rural India* (USA: Oxford University Press).

Cherlin, A. (2009) *The Marriage-Go-Round: The State of Marriage and the Family in America Today* (New York: Alfred A. Knopf).

Chesnais, J.C. (1996) 'Fertility, family and social policy in contemporary Western Europe', *Population and Development Review*, 224, 729–739.

Chevalier, S. (2002) 'The cultural construction of domestic space in France and Great Britain', *Signs: Journal of Women in Culture & Society*, 27, 847.

Cieraad, I. ed. (1999) *At Home: An Anthropology of Domestic Space* (Syracuse, New York: Syracuse University Press).

Clapham, D., Mackie, P., Orford, S., Buckley, K. and Thomas, I. with Atherton, I. and McAnulty, A. (2012) *Housing Options and Solutions for Young People in 2020* (York: Joseph Rowntree Foundation).

Cole, J. and Thomas, L.M. eds. (2009) *Love in Africa* (Chicago: University of Chicago Press).

Coleman, J. (1988) 'Social capital in the creation of human capital', *American Journal of Sociology*, 94(1), 95–120.

Coontz, S. (1992) *The Way We Never Were: American Families and the Nostalgia Trap* (New York: Basic Books).

Coontz, S. (2005) *Marriage, a History: From Obedience to Intimacy or How Love Conquered Marriage* (New York: Viking/Penguin).

Cooper, C. (1976) 'The house as a symbol of the self', in Proshansky, H.M., Ittelson, W.H. and Rivlin, L.G. eds. *Environmental Psychology: People and their Physical Settings* (New York: Holt, Rinehart and Winston).

Cooper M.C. (1995) *House as a Mirror of Self: Exploring the Deeper Meaning of Home* (Berwick, ME: Nicolas-Hays).

Côté JE. (2000) *Arrested Adulthood: The Changing Nature of Maturity and Identity* (New York: New York University Press).

Côté JE. and Allahar AL. eds. (1996) *Generation On Hold. Coming of Age in the Late Twentieth Century* (New York and London: New York University Press).

Croll, E.J. (2006) 'The intergenerational contract in the changing Asian family', *Oxford Development Studies*, 34(4), 473–491.

Crompton, R. (2006) *Employment and the Family: The Reconfiguring of Work and Family Life in Contemporary Societies* (Cambridge: Cambridge University Press).

Crow, G. (2002) 'Community studies: Fifty years of theorization', *Sociological Research Online*, 7, 3 Special issue.

Crow, G. (2002b). 'Neither busybodies nor nobodies: Managing proximity and distance in neighbourly relations', *Sociology*, 36, 127–145.

Crow, G. (2008) 'Recent rural community studies', *International Journal of Social Research Methodology*, 11(2), 131–139.

Crow, G., Allan, G.A. and Summers, M. (2001) 'Changing perspectives on the insider/outsider distinction in community sociology', *Community, Work & Family*, 4, 29–48.

Crow, G. and Maclean, C. (2006) 'Community' in Payne, G. ed. *Social Divisions* (Basingstoke: Palgrave Macmillan).

Crow, H. (2010) *Factors Influencing Rural Migration Decisions in Scotland: An Analysis of the Evidence*. Rural and environment research and analysis directorate. Scottish Government. Web only publication. www.scotland.gov.uk/Publications/2010/09/09115845/0, accessed 1 October 2010.

Crystal, S. (1982) *America's Old Age Crisis: Public Policy and the two Worlds of Aging* (New York: Basic Books).

Cunningham-Burley, S. and Jamieson, L. eds. (2003) *Families and the State: Changing Relationships* (Basingstoke, NY: Palgrave Macmillan).

Daatland, S.O. and Herlofson, K. (2001) 'Service systems and family care – substitution or complementarity?' in Daatland, S.O. and Herlofson, K. eds. *Ageing, Inter-generational Relationships, Care Systems and Quality of Life. An Introduction to the OASIS Project* (Oslo:NOVA).

Davidson, K. (2004) 'Why can't a man be more like a woman?': Marital status and social networking of older men', *The Journal of Men's Studies*, 13(1), 25–43.

Dayaratne, R. and Kellett, P. (2008) 'Housing and home-making in low-income urban settlements: Sri Lanka and Colombia', *Journal of Housing and the Built Environment*, 23, 53–70.

De Jong Gierveld, J (1998) 'A review of loneliness: Concept and definition, determinants and consequences', *Review in Clinical Gerontology*, 8(1), 71–80

De Jong Gierveld, J., De Valk, H. and Blommesteijn, M. (2001) 'Living arrangements of older persons and family support in more developed countries', *Population Bulletin of the United Nations, Special Issue, Living Arrangements of Older Persons: Critical Issues and Policy Responses*, 42/43, 193–217.

De Paulo, B. (2006) *Singled Out: How Singles Are Stereotyped, Stigmatized, and Ignored, and Still Live Happily Ever After* (New York: St. Martin's Press).

De Paulo, B. (2011) *Singlism: What It Is, Why It Matters, and How to Stop It* (USA: Doubledoor Books).

De Vaus, D. and Richardson, S. (2009) 'Living alone in Australia: Trends in sole living and characteristics of those who live alone', *Occasional Paper 2009: Census Series Number 4* (Academy of the Social Sciences in Australia), www.assa.edu.au/publications/occasional_papers/2009_CS4.php, accessed 11 October 2012.

Dean, A., Kolody, B., Wood, P. and Matt, G.E. (1992) 'The influence of living alone on depression in elderly persons', *Journal of Aging and Health*, 4, 3–18.

Dermott, E. and Seymour, J. (2011) 'Developing displaying families': A possibility for the future of the sociology of personal life', in Dermott, E. and Seymour, J. eds. *Displaying Families* (Basingstoke: Palgrave Macmillan).

Di Leonardo, M. (1987) 'The female world of cards and holidays: Women, families and the work of kinship', *Signs*, 12, 440–453.

Di Santo, P. and Ceruzzi, F. (2010) *Migrant Care Workers in Italy: A Case Study, Interlinks, Health Systems and Long term care for Older People in Europe*, Funded by the European Commission under the Seventh Framework Programme Grant agreement no. 22303, www.euro.centre.org/data/1278594833_93987.pdf, accessed 15 August 2012.

Donovan, N. Pich, T. and Rubenstein T. (2002) *Geographic Mobility: A Discussion Paper. Performance and Information Unit* (London: Cabinet Office).

Dorling, D., Vickers, D., Thomas, B., Pritchard, J. and Ballas, D. (2008) *Changing UK: The Way We Live Now*. Report commissioned by the BBC. December 2008, www.sasi.group.shef.ac.uk/research/changingUK.html, accessed 11 October 2012.

Dreby, J. (2010) *Divided by Borders: Mexican Migrants and their Children* (Berkeley: University of California Press).

Duncan, S., Barlow, A. and James, G. (2005) 'Why don't they marry? Cohabitation, commitment and DIY marriage', *Child and Family Law Quarterly*, 17, 383–398.

Duncan, S. and Phillips, M. (2010) 'People who live apart together LATs – how different are they?', *The Sociological Review*, 58, 112–134.

Duncan, S. and Phillips, M. (2011) 'People who live apart together LATs: New family form or just a stage?', *International Review of Sociology: Revue Internationale de Sociologie*, 21,513–532.

Dupuis, A. and Thorns, DC. (1998) 'Home, home ownership and ontological security', *The Sociological Review*, 46(1), 24–47.

Durkheim, E. (1984) *The Division of Labour in Society* (Basingstoke: Macmillan).

Dykstra, P.A. and Hagestad, G.O. (2007) 'Roads less taken: Developing a nuanced view of older adults without children', *Journal of Family Issues*, 28(10), 1275–1310.

Dykstra, P.A. and Poortman, A.-R. (2010) 'Economic resources and remaining single: Trends over time', *European Sociological Review*, 26, 277–290.

Edwards, R., Franklin, J. and Holland, J. (2003) *Families and Social Capital: Exploring the Issues, Families & Social Capital ESRC Research Group Working Paper No. 1* (London: South Bank University).

Elder JR., G. (1998) 'The life course as developmental theory', *Child Development*, 69(1), 1–12.

Elliott, A. and Lemert, C. (2009) *The New Individualism: The Emotional Costs of Globalization* (London and New York: Routledge).

Elzinga, C. and Liefbroer, A. (2007) 'De-standardization of family-life trajectories of young adults: A cross-national comparison using sequence analysis', *European Journal of Population/Revue européenne de Démographie*, 23, 225–250.

Erikson, E. (1950) 'Growth and crises of the "healthy personality"', in Senn, Milton, J.E. ed. *Symposium on the Healthy Personality* (Oxford, England: Josiah Macy, Jr. Foundation).

Ermisch, J. (1999) 'Prices, parents, and young people's household formation', *Journal of Urban Economics*, 45, 47–71.

Ermisch, J. and Seidler T. (2008) 'Living apart together', in Ermisch, J. and Brynin, M. eds. *Changing Relationships* (London: Routledge).

Esping-Andersen, G. (1990) *The Three Worlds of Welfare Capitalism* (Cambridge: Polity).

Esping-Andersen, G. (1999) *Social Foundations of Postindustrial Economies* (Oxford: Oxford University Press).

European Commission (2011) *Active Ageing And Solidarity Between Generations – A Statistical Portrait Of The European Union 2012* (Luxembourg: Publications Office of the European Union).

Eurostat (2011) 'Marriage and divorce statistics', www.epp.eurostat.ec.europa. eu/statistics_explained/index.php/Marriage_and_divorce_statistics, accessed 12 August 2012.

Evans, M. (2003) *Love: An Unromantic Discussion* (Cambridge: Polity Press in association with Blackwell Publishers Ltd.).

Fagerström, C., Borg, C., Burholt, V. and Wneger, CG.(2007) 'Life satisfaction and associated factors among people aged 60 years and above in six European Countries', *Applied Research in Quality of Life*, 2(1), 33–50.

Feijten, P., Hooimeijer, P. and Mulder, C.H. (2008) 'Residential experience and residential environment choice over the life-course', *Urban Studies*, 45(1), 141–162.

Feinstein, L., Lupton, R., Hammond, C., Mujtaba, T., Salter, E. and Sorhaindo, A. (2008) *The Public Value Of Social Housing* (The Smith Institute), www.smith-institute.org.uk/file/ThePublicValueofSocialHousing.pdf, accessed 17 August 2012.

Finch, J. (2007) 'Displaying families', *Sociology*, 41, 65–81.

Finch, J. and Mason, J. (1993) *Negotiating Family Responsibilities* (Routledge: London).

Findlay, A.M., Stockdale, A. and Stewart, E. (2002) 'Professional and managerial migration from core to periphery: The case of English migration to Scottish Cities', *International Journal of Population Geography*, 8, 217–232.

Fine, B. (2001) *Social Capital Versus Social Theory: Political Economy and Social Science at the Turn of the Millenium* (Routledge: London).

Fischer, C. (1982) *To Dwell Among Friends* (Chicago: University of Chicago).

Ford, J., Quilgars, D., Burrows, R. and Pleace, N. (1997) *Young People and Housing, Rural Research Report Issue 31* (Salisbury: Rural Development Commission).

Franklin, J. (2007) *Social Capital: Between Harmony and Dissonance, Families & Social Capital ESRC Research Group Working Paper No. 22* (Families and Social Capital ESRC Research Group: London South Bank University).

Franklin, J. ed. (2004) *Politics, Trust and Networks: Social Capital in Critical Perspective, Families & Social Capital ESRC Research Group Working Paper No. 7* (Families and Social Capital ESRC Research Group: London South Bank University).

Franklin, J. ed. (2005) *Women and Social Capital, Families & Social Capital ESRC Research Group Working Paper No. 12* (Families and Social Capital ESRC Research Group: London South Bank University).

Fratiglioni, L., Wang, H.-X., Ericsson, K., Maytan, M. and Winblad, B. (2000) 'Influence of social network on occurrence of dementia: A community-based longitudinal study', *Lancet*, 355(9212), 1315.

Fukuda, S. (2009) 'Leaving the parental home in post-war Japan: Demographic changes, stem-family norms and the transition to adulthood', *Demographic Research*, 30, 731–816.

Fukunaga, R., Abe, Y., Nakagawa, Y., Koyama, A., Fujise, N., and Ikeda, M. (2012) 'Living alone is associated with depression among the elderly in a rural community in Japan', *Psychogeriatrics*, 12, 179–185.

Furedi, F. (2002) 'Singleton society', *Spiked Online*, www.spiked-online.com/Articles/00000002D3A7.htm, accessed 15 August 2012.

Furedi, F. (2004) *Where Have All the Intellectuals Gone?: Confronting 21st Century Philistinism* (Continuum International Publishing Group – Academi).

Furlong, A. and Cartmel, F. (2007) *Young People and Social Change. New Perspectives* (Maidenhead: Open University Press).

Furstenberg, F. (2010) 'On a new schedule: Transitions to adulthood and family change', *The Future of Children*, 20, 67–81.

Gardner, J. and Oswald, A. (2004) 'How is mortality affected by money, marriage, and stress?' *Journal of Health Economics*, 236, 1181–1207.

Garthwaite, K. (2012) 'Home alone? The implications of solo living for young people in their housing journeys into adulthood', *Youth and Policy*, 108, 73–87.

Gerson, K. (2010) *The Unfinished Revolution: Coming of Age in a New era of Gender, Work, and Family* (Oxford: Oxford University Press).

Gibson, C. and Argent, N. (2008) 'Getting on, getting up and getting out? Broadening perspectives on rural youth migration', *Geographical Research*, 46, 135–138.

Giddens, A. (1984) *The Constitution of Society: Outline of the Theory of Structuration* (Cambridge: Polity Press).

Giddens, A. (1990) *The Consequences of Modernity* (Cambridge: Polity Press).

Giddens, A. (1991) *Modernity and Self Identity* (Cambridge: Polity).

Giddens, A. (1992) *The Transformation of Intimacy: Sexuality, Love & Eroticism In Modern Societies* (Cambridge: Polity Press).

Gieryn, T. (2000) 'A space for place in sociology', *Annual Review of Sociology*, 26, 463–496.

Gilbert, M.R. (1998) "'Race', space and power: The survival strategies of working poor women', *Annals of the Association of American Geographers*, 884, 595–621.

Gillies, V., Ribbens McCarthy, J. and Holland, J. (2001) *Pulling Together, Pulling Apart: The Family Lives of Young People Aged 16–18* (London, UK: Family Policy Studies Centre/Joseph Rowntree Foundation).

Gillis, J. (2004) 'Gathering together', in Etzioni, A. and Bloom, J. eds. *We Are What We Celebrate: Understanding Holidays and Rituals* (New York: New York University Press).

Glanville, K., Maconachie, M., Sutton, C. and Chandler, J. (2005) *Solo Living in Devon: Project Report* (Plymouth: School of Sociology, Politics and Law, University of Plymouth).

Glaser, K. and Grundy, E. (1998) 'Migration and household change in the population aged 65 and over, 1971–1991', *International Journal of Population Geography*, 4, 323–339.

Glaser, K., Murphy, M., and Grundy, E. (1997) 'Limiting long term illness and household structure among people aged 45 and over, Great Britain 1991', *Ageing and Society*, 17, 3–20.

Goffman, E. (1959) *The Presentation of Self in Everyday Life* (New York: Doubleday).

Goldman, N., Korenman, S. and Weinstein, R. (1995) 'Marital status and health among the elderly', *Social Science and Medicine*, 4012, 1717–1730.

Goldscheider, F. (2000) *Why Study Young Adult Living Arrangements? A View of the Second Demographic Transition*, paper presented at Workshop 'Leaving Home – A European Focus', Max Planck Institute for Demographic research, Rostock, Germany, 06.09.2000–08.09.2000.

Goldscheider, F. and Goldscheider, C. (1999) *The Changing Transition to Adulthood: Leaving and Returning Home* (Thousand Oaks: Sage).

Goode, W. (1970 [1963]). *World Revolution and Family Patterns* (New York: Free Press).

Goode, W. (1974 [1959]). 'On the theoretical importance of love' in Coser, R.L. ed. *The Family: Its Structures and Functions* (Macmillan).

Gordon, T. (1994) *Single Women: On The Margins?* (Basingstoke: Macmillan).

Goulbourne, H., Reynolds, T., Solomos, J. and Zontini, E. (2010) *Transnational Families: Ethnicities, Identities and Social Capital* (London: Routledge).

Granovetter, M. (1973) 'The strength of weak ties', *American Journal of Sociology*, 786, 1360–1380.

Greenfield, E. and Russell, D. (2011) 'Identifying living arrangements that heighten risk for loneliness in later life: Evidence from the U.S. national social life, health, and aging project', *Journal of Applied Gerontology*, 30, 524–534.

Grundy, E. and Murphy, M. (2006) 'Marital status and family support for the oldest-old in Great Britain', in Robine, Jean-Marie and Crimmins, Eileen M. and Horiuchi, Shiro and Zeng, Yi, eds. *Human Longevity: Individual Life Duration and the Growth of the Oldest-old Population* (Dordrecht, The Netherlands: Springer).

Grundy, E. and Sloggett, A. (2003) 'Health inequalities in the older population: The role of personal capital, social resources and socio-economic circumstances', *Social Science and Medicine*, 565, 935–947.

Guilmoto, C.Z. (2011) 'Demography for anthropologists: Populations, castes and classes', in Clark-Decès, I. ed. *A Companion to the Anthropology of India* (Oxford: Wiley Blackwell).

Gullestad, M. (2001 [1984]) *Kitchen-Table Society: A Case Study of the Family Life and Friendships of Young Working-class Mothers in Urban Norway* (Oslo: Universitetsforlaget).

Gustavson, K. and Lee, C. (2004) 'Alone and content: Frail seniors living in their own homes compared to those who live with others', *Women and Aging*, 163(4), 3–18.

Hall, R. and Ogden, P. (2003) 'The rise of living alone in Inner London: Trends among the population of working age', *Environment and Planning*, 35(5), 871–888.

Hall, R., Ogden P.E. and Hill, C. (1997) 'The pattern and structure of one-person households in England and Wales and France', *International Journal of Population Geography*, 3 (2), 161–181.

Halpern, D. (2005) *Social Capital* (Cambridge: Polity Press).

Hansen, K. (2005) *Not So Nuclear Families: Class Gender and Networks of Care* (London: Rutgers University).

Hareven, T.K. (1991) 'The home and the family in historical perspective', *Social Research* 581, 253–285.

Hareven, T.K. (2000) *Families, History, and Social Change: Life-Course and Cross-Cultural Perspectives* (Boulder, CO: Westview Press).

Harloe, M. (1995) *The People's Home: Social Rented Housing in Europe and America* (Oxford: Blackwell).

Harriss, K. and Shaw, A. (2006) 'Family care and transnational kinship: British Pakistani Experience', in Ebtehaj, F., Lindley, B. and Richards, M. eds. *Kinship Matters* (Oxford: Hart).

Hartmann, H.I. (1979) 'The unhappy marriage of Marxism and feminism: Towards a more progressive union', *Capital & Class*, 3, 1–33.

Hashimoto, A. (1996) *The Gift of Generations: Japanese And American Perspectives On Aging And The Social Contract* (Cambridge: Cambridge University Press).

Hashimoto, A. (2004) 'Culture, power, and the discourse of filial piety in Japan: The disempowerment of youth and its social consequences', in Ikels, C. ed. *Filial Piety: Practice and Discourse in Contemporary East Asia* (Stanford: Stanford University Press).

Haskey J. (2005) 'Living arrangements in contemporary Britain: Having a partner who usually lives elsewhere, Living-apart-together', *Population Trends*,

122, 35–46, www.statistics.gov.uk/statbase/Product.asp?vlnk= 6303, accessed 2 September 2010.

Haskey, J. and Lewis, J. (2006) 'Living apart together in Britain: Context and meaning', *International Journal of Law in Context*, 2, 37–48.

Hays, J.C. (2002) 'Living arrangements and health status in later life: A review of recent literature', *Public Health Nursing*, 19(2), 136–151.

Hays, J.C. and George, L.K. (2002) 'The Life-Course trajectory racial differences', *Research on Aging*, 24(3), 283–330.

Hays, J.C. and George, L.K. (2002) 'The Life-Course trajectory toward living Alone, racial differences', *Research on Aging*, 24(3), 283–307.

Heath, S. (2008) *Housing Choices and Issues for Young People in the UK* (York: Joseph Rowntree Foundation), www.jrf.org.uk/sites/files/jrf/2325-young-people-housing.pdf, accessed 2 July 2012.

Heath, S. and Cleaver, E. (2003) *Young, Free and Single: Twenty-Somethings and Household Change* (Basingstoke: Palgrave Macmillan).

Hébert, R., Brayne, C. and Spiegelhalter, D. (1999) 'Factors associated with functional decline and improvement in a very elderly community-dwelling population', *American Journal of Epidemiology*, 1505, 501–510.

Heimtun, B. (2010) 'The holiday meal: Eating out alone and mobile emotional geographies', *Leisure Studies*, 29, 175–192.

Heimtun, B. (2012) 'The friend, the loner and the independent traveller: Norwegian midlife single women's social identities when on holiday', *Gender, Place & Culture*, 19, 83–101.

Henderson, S., Holland, J., McGrellis, S., Sharpe, S. and Thomson, R. (2007) *Inventing Adulthoods: A Biographical Approach to Youth Transitions* (London: Sage).

Hewitt, J.P. (2007) *Self and Society: A Symbolic Interactionist Social Psychology* (Boston: Allyn and Bacon).

Heywood, A. (2011) *The End of the Affair: Implications of Declining Home Ownership* (London: Smith Institute).

Hird, M.J. and Abshoff, K. (2000) 'Women without children: A contradiction in terms', *Journal of Comparative Family Studies*, 31, 3.

Hirsch, J.S., and Wardlow, H. (2006) *Modern Loves: The Anthropology of Romantic Courtship and Companionate Marriage* (Michigan: The University of Michigan Press).

Hiscock, R., Kearns, A., Macintyre, S. and Ellaway, A. (2001) 'Ontological security and psychosocial benefits from the home: Qualitative evidence on issues of tenure', *Housing, Theory and Society*, 18, 50–66.

Hochschild, A. (1978) *The Unexpected Community: Portrait Of An Old Age Subculture* (Berkeley: University of California Press).

Hochschild, A. (1990) *The Second Shift: Working Parents and the Revolution at Home* (London: Piatkus).

Hochschild, A. (2003) *The Commercialization of Intimate Life* (Berkeley: University of California Press).

Holdsworth, C. and Morgan, D. (2005) *Transition in Context Leaving Home Independence and Adulthood* (Maidenhead: Open University Press).

Holdsworth, C and Morgan, D. (2007) 'Revisiting the generalized other: An Exploration', *Sociology*, 41(3), 401–417.

Holmes, M. (2004) 'An equal distance? Individualisation, gender and intimacy in distance relationships', *The Sociological Review*, 52, 180–200.

Holmes, M. (2006) 'Love lives at a distance: Distance relationships over the lifecourse', *Sociological Research Online*, 11, 3, www.socresonline.org.uk/11/3/holmes.html, accessed 7 April 2010.

Holmes, M. (2010) 'The emotionalization of reflexivity', *Sociology*, 44, 139–154.

Hughes, G. and McCormick, B. (1981) 'Do council house policies reduce migration between regions?' *The Economic Journal*, 91(364), 919–937.

Hughes, G. and McCormick, B. (1985) 'Migration intentions in the U.K. which households want to migrate and which succeed?' *The Economic Journal*, 95, Supplement Conference Papers, 113–123.

Iacovou, M. (2004) 'Patterns of family living', in Berthoud, R. and Iacovou, M. eds *Social Europe, Living Standards and Welfare States* (Cheltenham: Edward Elgar Publishing Ltd).

Iacovou, M. (2010) 'Leaving home: Independence, togetherness and income', *Advances in Life Course Research*, 15, 4, 147–160.

Iacovou, M. and Skew, A. (2010) 'Household structure in the EU', in Atkinson, A. and Marlier, E. eds. *Income and Living Conditions in Europe* (Eurostat, Luxembourg: Publications Office of the European Union).

Ikels, C. (2004) *Filial Piety, Practice and Discourse in Contemporary East Asia* (Stanford: Stanford University Press).

Illouz, E. (2007) *Cold Intimacies: The Making of Emotional Capitalism* (Cambridge: Polity).

Irwin, S. (1995) *Rights of Passage. Social Change and the Transition from Youth to Adulthood* (London: UCL Press).

Jamieson, L. (1987) 'Theories of family development and the experience of being brought up'. *Sociology*, 21(4), 591–607.

Jamieson, L. (1998) *Intimacy: Personal Relationships in Modern Societies* (Cambridge: Polity Press).

Jamieson, L. (2000) 'Migration, place and class: Youth in a rural area', *Sociological Review*, 48, 203–223.

Jamieson, L. (2011) 'Intimacy as a concept: Explaining social change in the context of globalisation or another form of ethnocentricism?' *Sociological Research Online*, 16, 13.

Jamieson, L. (2013) 'Personal relationships, intimacy and the self in a mediated and global digital age', in Orton-Johnson, K. and Prior, N. eds. *Rethinking Sociology in a Digital Age* (Basingstoke: Palgrave Macmillan).

Jamieson, L., Anderson, M., McCrone, D., Bechhofer, F., Stewart, R. and Li, Y. (2002) 'Cohabitation and commitment: Partnership plans of young men and women', *Sociological Review*, 50, 354–375.

Jamieson, L., Backett Milburn, K., Simpson, R. and Wasoff, F. (2010) 'Fertility and social change: The neglected contribution of men's approaches to becoming partners and parents', *Sociological Review*, 58, 463–485.

Jamieson, L., Morgan, D., Crow G. and Allan, G. (2006) 'Friends, neighbours and distant partners: Extending or decentring family relationships?', *Sociological Research Online*, 11(3).

Jamieson, L., Stewart, R., Li, Y., Anderson, M., Bechhofer, F. and McCrone, D. (2003) 'Single, 20-something and seeking?', *Explorations in Sociology*, 63, 135–154.

Jamieson, L., Wasoff, F. and Simpson, R. (2009) 'Solo-Living demographic and family change: The need to know more about men', *Sociological Research Online*, 14, 2, Janelli, R.L. and Yim, D. (2004) 'The transformation of filial piety in contemporary South Korea', in Ikels, C. ed. *Filial Piety, Practice and Discourse in Contemporary East Asia* (Stanford: Stanford University Press).

Jankowiak, W.R. (2008) *Intimacies: Love and Sex Across Cultures* (New York: Columbia University Press).

Jarvis, H. (2011) 'Saving space, sharing time: Integrated infrastructures of daily life in cohousing', *Environment and Planning A*, 43, 560–577.

Jeffrey, C. (2010) *Time Pass: Youth, Class and the Politics of Waiting in India* (Stanford: Stanford University Press).

Jeffrey, C. (2011) 'Great expectations: Youth in contemporary India', in Clark-Decès, I. eds. *A Companion to The Anthropology of India* (Oxford: Blackwell).

Jeffery, P. (2013) 'India: Social consequences of demographic change', in Davin, D. and Harriss-White, B. (eds.), *China–India: Paths of Economic and Social Development* (Oxford: Oxford University Press).

Jenike, B.R. (2004) 'Alone in the family: Great-grandparenthood in Urban Japan' in Ikels, C. ed. *Filial Piety* (Stanford: Stanford University Press).

Jones, G. (1995) *Leaving Home* (Buckingham: Open University Press).

Jones, G. (1999) ' "The same people in the same places"? Socio-spatial identities and migration in youth', *Sociology*, 33, 1–22.

Jones, G. (2001) 'Fitting homes? Young people's housing and household strategies in rural Scotland', *Journal of Youth Studies*, 4(1), 41–62.

Kaufmann, J. (1994) 'Les ménages d'une personne en Europe', *Population*, 49, 935–958.

Kaufmann, V. (2002) *Re-thinking Mobility* (Ashgate: Aldershot).

Kellett, P. (2000) 'Voices from the barrio: Oral testimony and informal housing processes', *Third World Planning Review*, 22, 189–205.

Kellett, P. (2005) 'The construction of home in the informal city', *Critical Studies*, 27, 22–42.

Kennedy, T.L.M. and Tran, P. (2006) 'Connected lives: The project', in Purcell, P. ed. *Networked Neighbourhoods* (London: Springer).

Kesserling, S. and Vogl, G. (2008) 'Networks, scapes and flows – mobility pioneers between first and second modernity', in Canzler, W., Kaufmann, V. and Kesserling, S. eds., *Tracing Mobilities: Towards a Cosmopolitan Perspective* (Aldershot: Ashgate).

Kiernan, K. (1986) 'Leaving home: Living arrangements of young people in six west-European countries', *European Journal of Population/Revue européenne de Démographie*, 2, 177–184.

Killick, E. and Desai, A. (2010) 'Introduction: Valuing friendship', in Desai, A. and Killick, E. eds., *The Ways of Friendship: Anthropological Perspectives* (Oxford: Berghahn Books), 1–19.

Kirstensen, H. (2007) *Housing in Denmark* (Copenhagen: Centre for Housing and Welfare).

Klinenberg, E. (2001) 'Dying alone: The social production of Urban Isolation', *Ethnography*, 2(4), 501–531.

Klinenberg, E. (2002) *Heat Wave: A Social Autopsy of Disaster in Chicago* (Chicago: University of Chicago Press).

Klinenberg, E. (2012) *Going Solo: The Extraordinary Rise and Surprising Appeal of Living Alone* (New York: The Penguin Press).

Kohler, H.P., Billari, F.C. and Ortega, J.A. (2002) 'The emergence of lowest-Low fertility in Europe During the 1990s', *Population and Development Review*, 28, 641–680. doi: 10.1111/j.1728-4457.2002.00641.x.

Kono, M. (2000) 'The impact of modernisation and social policy on family care for older people in Japan', *Journal of Social Policy*, 29, 181–203.

Kuper, A. (1993) 'The English Christmas and the family: Time out and alternative realities', in Miller, D. ed. *Unwrapping Christmas* (Oxford: Clarendon Press).

Lamb, S. (2000) *White Saris and Sweet Mangoes: Aging, Gender and Body in North India* (Berkeley: University of California Press).

Langford, W. (1999) *Revolutions of the Heart: Gender, Power and the Delusions of Love* (London: Routledge).

Larsen, J., Urry, J. and Axhausen, K. (2005) *Social Networks and Future Mobilities*, report to the horizons programme of the department for transport (Lancaster and Zürich: Department of Sociology, University of Lancaster and IVT, ETH Zürich).

Larsen, J., Urry, J. and Axhausen, K. (2006) *Mobilities, Networks, Geographies* (Hampshire: Ashgate).

Larsen, J., Urry, J. and Axhausen, K. (2007) 'Networks and tourism: Mobile social life', *Annals of Tourism Research*, 34, 244–262.

Larsen, J., Urry, J. and Axhausen, K. (2008) 'Coordinating face-to-face meetings in mobile network societies', *Information, Communication & Society*, 11(5), 640–658.

Lasch, C. (1977) *Haven in a Heartless World: The Family Besieged* (New York: Basic Books).

Lasch, C. (1978) *The Culture of Narcissism: American Life in an Age of Diminishing Expectations* (New York: Norton).

Lasch, S. (1994) 'Reflexivity and its doubles: Structure, aesthetics, community', in Beck, U., Giddens, A. and Lasch, S. eds. *Reflexive Modernization: Politics, Tradition and Aesthetics in the Modern Social Order* (Cambridge: Polity).

Laslett, P. (1965) *The World We Have Lost* (London: Methuen).

Latour, B. (2005) *Reassembling the Social: An Introduction to Actor Network Theory* (Oxford: Clarendon).

Leonard, D. (1980) *Sex and Generation: A Study of Courtship and Weddings* (London and New York: Tavistock Publications).

Lesthaeghe, R. (2010) 'The unfolding story of the second demographic transition', *Population and Development Review*, 36, 211–251.

Lesthaeghe, R. and Moors, G. (2000) 'Recent trends in fertility and household formation in the industrialized world', *Review of Population and Social Policy*, 9(1), 121–170.

Lesthaeghe, R. and van de Kaa, D. (1986) 'Twee demografische transities?', in van de Kaa, D. and Lesthaeghe, R. *Bevolking – Groei en Krimp*, special issue of Mens en Maatschappij, (Deventer: Van Loghum Slaterus).

Levin, I. (2004) 'Living apart together: A new family form', *Current Sociology*, 52, 223–240.

Levin, I. and Trost, J. (1999) 'Living apart together', *Community, Work and Family*, 2, 270–294.

Lewis, J. (2001) *The End of Marriage* (London: Edward Elgar).

Lewis, J. (2006) 'Perceptions of risk in intimate relationships', *Journal of Social Policy*, 35(1), 39–57.

Leyshon, M. and DiGiovanna, S. (2005) 'Planning for the needs of young people: Affordable homes in rural communities', *Journal of Children, Youth and Environment*, 15(2), 254–277.

Liefbroer, A. and Goldscheider, F. (2007) 'Transitions to adulthood: How unique is Sweden in the European context?', in Bernhardt, E.M., Goldscheider, C., Goldscheider, F. and Bjerén, G. eds., *Immigration, Gender, and Family Transitions to Adulthood in Sweden* (Lanham, MD, University Press of America) 203–228.

Lim, S.S. (2008) 'Technology domestication in the Asian homestead: Comparing the experiences of middle class families in China and South Korea', *East Asian Science, Technology and Society*, 2, 189–209.

Lin, J. (1995) 'Changing kinship structure and its implications for old-age support in urban and rural China', *Population Studies*, 49, 127–145.

Lister, R. (1997) 'Citizenship: Towards a feminist synthesis', Special Issue on 'Citizenship: Pushing the Boundaries', *Feminist Review*, 57, 28–48.

Little, J. and Austin, P. (1996) 'Women and the rural idyll', *Journal of Rural Affairs*, 12(2), 101–111.

Liu, F. (2008) 'Negotiating the filial self: Young-adult only-children and intergenerational relationships in China', *Young*, 16, 409–430.

Livingstone, S. (2009) *Children and the Internet: Great Expectations Challenging Realities* (Cambridge: Polity).

Löfgren, O. (1993) 'The great Christmas Quarrel and other Swedish traditions', in Miller, D. eds. *Unwrapping Christmas* (Oxford: Clarendon Press).

Long, C.R. and Averill, J.R. (2003) 'Solitude: An exploration of benefits of being alone', *Journal for the Theory of Social Behaviour*, 33, 21–44. doi:10.1111/1468-5914.00204.

Lück, D. and Schneider, N.F. (2010) 'Introduction to the special issue on mobility and family: Increasing job mobility–Changing family lives', *Zeitschrift für Familienforschung-Journal of Family Research*, 22 (2).

Lyons-Lee, L. (1998) 'The 'graduate woman' phenomenon: Changing constructions of the family in Singapore', *Sojourn*, 13, 1–19.

MacDonald, R., Shildrick, T.A., Webster, C. and Simpson, D. (2005) 'Growing up in poor neighbourhoods: The significance of class and place in the extended transitions of "socially excluded" young adults', *Sociology*, 39(5), 873–891.

Maclean, C. (2003) ' "Making it their home": In-migration, time, social change and belonging in a rural community', in Allan, G. and Jones, G. eds. *Social Relations and the Life Course* (Basingstoke: Palgrave Macmillan).

Maclean, M. (2004) *Together and Apart: Children and Parents Experiencing Separation and Divorce* (London: Joseph Rowntree Foundation).

Maclean, M. and Eekelar J. (1997) *The Parental Obligation: A Study of Parenthood across Households* (Oxford: Hart Publishing).

MacVarish, J. (2006) 'What is "the problem" of singleness?', *Sociological Research Online*, 11(3).

Magazine, R. and Sanchez, M.A.R. (2007) 'Continuity and change in San Pedro Tlalcuapan, Mexico: Childhood, social reproduction and transnational migration', in Cole, J. and Durham, D. eds. *Generation and Globalization: Youth, Age and Family in the New World Economy* (Bloomington: Indiana University Press), 52–73.

Magaziner, J., Cadigan, D.A., Hebel, J.R. and Parry, R.E. (1988) 'Health and living arrangements among older women: Does living alone increase the risk of illness?', *Journals of Gerontology*, 435, 127–133.

Mallett, S. (2004) 'Understanding home: A critical review of the literature', *The Sociological Review*, 52(1), 62–89.

Manting, D. (1996) 'The changing meaning of cohabitation and marriage', *European Sociological Review*, 12(1), 53–65.

Mason, J. (2004) 'Managing Kinship over long distances: The significance of "the visit" ', *Social Policy and Society*, 3, 421–429.

May, V. (2011) 'Self, belonging and social change', *Sociology*, 45(3), 363–378.

Mayer, K.U. (1994) 'The postponed generation. Economic, political, social, and cultural determinants of changes in life course regimes', in Becker, H.A. and Hermkens, P.L.J. eds., *Solidarity of Generations. Demographic, Economic, and Social Change, and its Consequences* (Amsterdam: Thesis Publishers).

McAllister, F. and Clarke, L. (1998) *Choosing Childlessness* (London: Family Policy Studies Centre).

McDonald, P. (2000a) 'The "Toolbox" of public policies to impact on fertility – a global view', paper presented at seminar on 'Low Fertility, Families and Public Policies', organised by European observatory on family matters, Sevilla, 15–16 September 2000.

McDonald, P. (2000b) 'Gender equity in theories of fertility transition', *Population and Development Review*, 26(3), 427–439.

McNay, L. (2000) *Gender and Agency: Reconfiguring the Subject in Feminist Theory*, (Cambridge: Polity Press).

Mead, G.H. (1934) *Mind, Self and Society* (Chicago: University Chicago Press).

Mensch, B., Singh, S. and Casterline, J. (2005) 'Trends in the timing of first marriage among men and women in the developing world', *Population Council Working Papers*, 202, 1–57.

Mercer (2011) 'Employee holiday entitlements around the World', www.mercer.com/press-releases/holiday-entitlements-around-the-world#, accessed 10 July 2012.

Mesch, G.S. and Talmud, I. (2010) *Wired Youth: The Social World of Adolescence in the Information Age* (London: Routledge).

Michael, Y.L., Berkman, L.F., Colditz, G.A. and Kawachi, I. (2001) 'Living arrangements, social integration, and change in functional health status', *American Journal of Epidemiology*, 1532, 123–131.

Michielin, F. and Mulder, C.H. (2008) 'Family events and the residential mobility of couples', *Environment and Planning A*, 40(11), 2770–2790.

Mifflin, E. and Wilton, R. (2005) 'No place like home: Rooming houses in contemporary urban context', *Environment and Planning A*, 37, 403–421.

Miller, D. (1993a) 'A theory of Christmas', in Miller, D. ed. *Unwrapping Christmas* (Oxford: Clarendon Press).

Miller, D. (1993b). 'Christmas against materialism in Trinidad', in Miller, D. ed. *Unwrapping Christmas* (Oxford: Clarendon Press).

Miller, D. (2001) 'Possessions', in Miller, D. ed. *Home Possessions* (Oxford: Berg).

Miller, D. (2010) *Stuff* (Cambridge: Polity Press).

Miller, D. (2011) *Tales from Facebook* (Cambridge: Polity Press).

Miller, D. and Slater, D. (2000) *The Internet: An Ethnographic Approach* (Oxford: Berg).

Mitchell, B.A. (2006) 'Changing courses: The pendulum of family transitions in comparative perspective', *Journal of Comparative Family Studies*, 37(3), 325–343.

Mody, P. (2008) *The Intimate State: Love-Marriage and the Law in Delhi* (New Delhi: Routledge India).

Moeran, B. and Skov, L. (1993) 'Cinderella Christmas: Kitsch, consumerism and youth in Japan', in Miller, D. ed. *Unwrapping Christmas* (Oxford: Clarendon Press) 105–133.

Molgat, M. and Vézina, M. (2008) 'Transitionless biographies? Youth and representations of solo living', *Young*, 16 (4), 349–371.

Morgan, D.H.J. (2009) *Acquaintances: The Space Between Intimates and Strangers* (Open University Press: McGraw Hill).

Morley, D. (1986) *Family Television: Cultural Power and Domestic Leisure* (London: Comedia).

Morley, D. (2000) *Home Territories: Media, Mobility and Identity* (Abingdon: Routledge).

Mui, A.C. and Burnette, D. (1994) 'A comparative profile of frail elderly persons living alone and those living with Others', *Journal of Gerontological Social Work*, 21(3–4), 5–26.

Mulder, C.H. (2007) 'The family context and residential choice: A challenge for new research', *Population. Space and Place*, 13(4), 265–278.

Mulder, C.H. and Cooke, T.J. eds. (2009) 'Family ties and residential locations', *Special Issue. Population Space and Place*, 15(4), 299–304.

Murata, C., Kondo, T., Hori, Y., Miyao, D., Tamakoshi, K., Yatsuya, H., Sakakibara, H. and Toyoshima, H. (2005) 'Effects of social relationships on mortality among the elderly in a Japanese rural area: An 88-month follow-up study', *Journal of Epidemiology*, 153, 78–84.

Murphy, M., Glaser, K. and Grundy, E. (1997) 'Marital status and long-term illness in Great Britain', *Journal of Marriage and the Family*, 591, 156–164.

Murphy, M., Grundy, E. and Kalogirou, S. (2007) 'The increase in marital status differences in mortality up to the oldest age in seven European countries, 1990–99', *Population Studies*, 613, 287–298.

Mutongi, K. (2007) *Worries of the Heart: Widows, Family and Community in Kenya* (Chicago: University of Chicago Press).

Nemoto, K. (2008) 'Postponed marriage: Exploring women's views of matrimony and work in Japan', *Gender and Society*, 22, 219–237.

Netuveli, G., Wiggins, R.D., Hildon, Z., Montgomery, S.M. and Blane, D. (2006) 'Quality of life at older ages: Evidence from the English longitudinal study of ageing wave 1', *Journal of Epidemiology Community Health*, 60, 357–363.

Newton, J. (2008) 'Emotional attachment to home and security for permanent residents in caravan parks in Melbourne', *Journal of Sociology*, 44, 219–232.

Nico, M. (2010) 'Individualized housing careers in early adulthood: Conditions and constraints in a familistic society', *Sociological Research Online*, 15(1), 6

OECD (2005) *Ageing Populations: High Time for Action* OECD Publishing. www.oecd.org/employment/emp/34600619.pdf, accessed 15 August 2012.

OECD (2011a) *The Future of Families to 2030: A Synthesis Report OECD 2011*, International Futures programme, www.oecd.org/dataoecd/19/31/49093502.pdf. accessed 15 August 2012.

OECD (2011b) *Doing Better for Families, Paris*. www.oecd.org/els/familiesandchildren/doingbetterforfamilies.htm, accessed 15 August 2012.

Ogden, P.E. and Hall, R. (2000) 'Households, reurbanisation and the rise of living alone in the principal French cities, 1975–1990', *Urban Studies*, 37(2), 367–390.

Oinonen, E. (2008) *Families in Converging Europe: A Comparison of Forms, Structures and Ideals* (Palgrave Macmillan: Basingstoke).

ONS (2011) 'Households and families', *Social Trends 41* (Office for National Statistics).

Orrange, R. (2003) 'The emerging mutable self: Gender dynamics and creative adaptations in defining work, family, and the future', *Social Forces*, 82, 1–34.

Oxley, H. (2009) *Policies for Healthy Ageing: An Overview*, OECD healthy working papers, No. 42 (OECD Publishing).

Padilla, Mark B., Jennifer, S., Hirsch, Miguel, Munoz-Laboy, Robert, E., Sember. and Richard, G. Parker. eds. (2007) *Love and Globalization: Transformations of Intimacy in the Contemporary World* (Nashville: Vanderbilt University Press).

Pahl, R. and Spencer, L. (2003) *Personal Communities: Not Simply Families of 'Fate' or 'Choice'*, Working Papers ISER 2003–2004.

Pahl, R. and Spencer, L. (2004) 'Personal communities: Not simply families of "fate" or "Choice"', *Current Sociology*, 52(2), 199–221, doi: 10.1177/0011392104041808.

Parreñas, R.S. (2005) *Children of Global Migration: Transnational Families and Gendered Woe* (Stanford: Stanford University Press).

Parsons, T. and Bales, R. (1956) *Family, Socialisation and Interaction Process* (London: Routledge and Kegan Paul).

Pateman, C. (1988) *The Sexual Contract* (Cambridge: Polity Press).

Perissinotto, C.M., Stijacic Cenzer, I.and Covinsky, K.E. (2012) 'Loneliness in older persons: A predictor of functional decline and death', *Arch Intern Med*. Published online 18 June 2012. doi:10.1001/archinternmed.2012.1993

Pfau-Effinger, B. (1998) 'Gender cultures and the gender arrangement – A theoretical framework for cross-national gender research', *Innovation*, 11, 147–166.

Pfau-Effinger, B. (2000) 'Conclusion: Gender cultures, gender arrangements and social change in the European context', in Duncan, S. and Pfau-Effinger, B. eds. *Gender, Economy and Culture in the European Union* (London: Routledge). 262–276.

Pizzetti, P., Manfredini, M. and Lucchetti, E. (2005) 'Variations in late-age mortality by household structure and marital status in Parma, Italy', *Ageing and Society*, 25, 305–318.

Popenoe, D. (1993) 'American family decline, 1960–1990: A review and appraisal', *Journal of Marriage and the Family*, 55(3), 527–542.

Portacolone, E. (2011) 'The myth of independence for older Americans living alone in the Bay Area of San Francisco: A critical reflection', *Ageing and Society*, 31, 803–828.

Prinz, C. (1995) *Cohabiting, Married or Single: Portraying, Analyzing and Modeling new Living Arrangements in the Changing Societies of Europe* (Avebury: Aldershot).

Putnam, R. (1995) 'Bowling alone: America's declining social capital', *Journal of Democracy*, 6(1) Jan 1995, 65–78.

Putnam, R. (2000) *Bowling Alone: The Collapse and Revival of American Community* (New York: Simon and Schuster).

Putnam, R., Feldstein, L. and Cohen, D. (2003) *Better Together: Restoring the American Community* (New York: Simon and Schuster).

Rabe, B. and Taylor, M. (2010) 'Residential mobility. quality of neighbourhood and life course events', *Journal of the Royal Statistical Society: Series A Statistics in Society*, 173(3), 531–555.

Raine, L. and Wellman, B. (2012) *Networked: The New Social Operating System.* (Cambridge, MA: The MIT Press).

Rajan, S.I. ed. (2008) *Social Policies for the Elderly Experiences from South Asia* (New Delhi: Routledge).

Rebhun, L.A. (1999) *The Heart Is Unknown Country: Love in the Changing Economy of Northeast Brazil* (Stanford: Stanford University Press).

Reeve, K. (2011) *The Hidden Truth about Homelessness: Experiences of Single Homelessness in England* (London: CRISIS, Centre for Regional Economic and Social Research).

Reher, D.S. (1998) 'Family ties in Western Europe: Persistent contrasts', *Population and Development Review*, 242, 203–234.

Reimondos, A., Evans, A. and Gray, E. (2011) 'Living-apart-together LAT relationships in Australia', *Family Matters*, 87.

Reynolds, J. and Wetherell, M. (2003) 'The discursive climate of singleness: The consequences for women's negotiation of a single identity', *Feminism and Psychology*, 13, 489–510.

Reynolds, J., Wetherell, M. and Taylor, S. (2007) 'Choice and chance: Negotiating agency in the narrative of singleness', *The Sociological Review*, 55, 331–351.

Reynolds, T. (2005) *Caribbean Mothers: Identity and Experience in the UK* (London: Tufnell Press).

Ribbens McCarthy, J., Edwards, R. and Gillies, V. (2003) *Making Families: Moral Tales of Parenting and Step-Parenting* (London, UK: Sociology Press).

Riesman, D., Denny, R. and Glaser, N. (1961) *The Lonely Crowd; A Study Of The Changing American Character* (New Haven, CT, US: Yale University Press).

Riley, D. (2002) 'The right to be lonely', *Differences*, 13, 1–13.

Ronald, R. and Hirayama, Y. (2009) 'Home alone: The individualization of young, urban Japanese singles', *Environment and Planning A*, 41, 2836–2854.

Rose, G. (2003) 'Family photographs and domestic spacings: A case study', *Transactions of the Institute of British Geographers*, 28, 5–18.

Rose, N. (1996) *Inventing Our Selves: Psychology, Power and Personhood* (Cambridge: Cambridge University Press).

Roseneil, S. (2006) 'On not living with a partner: Unpicking coupledom and cohabitation', *Sociological Research Online*, 11, 3.Roseneil, S. (2010) 'Intimate citizenship: A pragmatic, yet radical, proposal for a politics of personal Life', *European Journal of Women's Studies*, 17(1), 77–82.

Roseneil, S. and Budgeon, S. (2004) 'Cultures of intimacy and care beyond "the family": personal life and social change in the early 21st Century', *Current Sociology*, 52, 135–159.

Rosenfeld, M.J. (2007) *The Age of Independence: Interracial Unions, Same Sex Unions, and the Changing American Family* (Cambridge, MA: Harvard University Press).

Salmela-Aro, K., Taanila, A., Ek, E. and Chen, M. (2012) 'Role configurations in young adulthood, antecedents, and later wellbeing among Finns born in 1966', *Longitudinal and Life Course Studies*, 3(2), 228–242.

Sanderson, W.C. and Scherbov, S. (2010) 'Remeasuring aging', *Science*, 10, 329 (5997), 1287–1288.

Santore, D. (2008) 'Romantic relationships, individualism and the possibility of togetherness: Seeing Durkheim in theories of contemporary intimacy', *Sociology*, 42(6), 1200–1217.

Sargisson, L. (2010) 'Cohousing: a utopian property alternative?', www.psa.ac.uk/journals/pdf/5/2010/1225 1085.pdf. Accessed 20 January 2013.

Sargisson, L. (2012) 'Second-wave cohousing: A modern utopia?' *Utopian Studies*, 23 (1), 28–56.

Sassler, S. and Miller, A.J. (2011) 'Waiting to be asked: Gender, power, and relationship progression among cohabiting couples', *Journal of Family Issues* 32, 482–506.

Savage, M., Bagnall, G. and Longhurst, B. (2005) *Globalization and Belonging* (London: Sage).

Schnaiberg, A. and Goldenberg, S. (1989) 'From empty nest to crowded nest: The dynamics of incompletely launched young adults', *Social Problems*, 36, 251–269.

Schofer, E. and Meyer, J.W. (2005) 'The worldwide expansion of higher education in the Twentieth Century', *American Sociological Review*, 70, 898–920.

Schor, J. (2010) *Plenitude: The New Economics of True Wealth* (Penguin Press: New York).

Schneider, N. and Limmer, R. (2008) 'Job mobility and living arrangements', in Canzler, W., Kaufmann, V. and Kesserling, S. eds. *Tracing Mobilities: Towards a Cosmopolitan Perspective* (Aldershot: Ashgate).

Schulenberg, J. and Schoon I. (2012) 'The transition to adulthood across time and space: Overview of special section', *Longitudinal and Life Course Studies*, 3(2), 228–242.

Scottish Household Survey (2006) 'Scotland's people: Scottish household survey questionnaire January to December 2006', Scottish Executive National Statistics.

Searle-Chatterjee, M. (1993) 'Christmas cards and the construction of social relations in Britain today', in Miller, D. ed. *Unwrapping Christmas* (Oxford: Clarendon Press).

Sennett, R. (1998) *The Corrosion of Character: Personal Consequences of Work in the New Capitalism* (New York: Norton).

Settersten, R.A. (2007) 'Passages to adulthood: Linking demographic change and human development', *European Journal of Population/Revue européenne de Démographie*, 23(3–4), 251–272, doi: 10.1007/s10680-007-9132-8.

Seyfang, G. and Smith, A. (2007) 'Grassroots innovations for sustainable development: Towards a new research and policy agenda', *Environmental Politics*, 16(4), 584–603.

Sharp, E.A. and Ganong, L. (2007) 'Living in the Gray: Women's experiences of missing the marital transition', *Journal of Marriage and the Family*, 69, 831–844.

Sharp, E.A. and Ganong, L. (2011) " 'I'm a Loser, I'm Not Married, Let's Just All Look at Me": Ever-Single women's perceptions of their social environment', *Journal of Family Issues*, 32, 956–980.

Shorter, E. (1975) *The Making of the Modern Family* (Basic Books).

Shove, E. (2003) *Comfort, Cleanliness and Convenience: The Social Organization of Normality*. (Berg: Oxford).

Shove, E., Pantzar, M. and Watson, M. (2012) *The Dynamics of Social Practice: Everyday Life and How It Changes* (Sage: London).

Shove, E. and Warde, A. (2002) 'Inconspicuous consumption: The sociology of consumption, lifestyles, and the environment', in Dunlap, R.E., Buttel, F., Dickens, P. and Gijswijt, A. eds. *Sociological Theory and the Environment: Classical Foundations, Contemporary Insights* (Rowman & Littlefield), 230–251.

Silva, E. (2007) 'Security, self and the home' in Carter, S., Jordan, T. and Watson, S. eds. *Security: Sociology and Social Worlds* (Manchester: Manchester University Press).

Silva, E. (2010) *Technology, Culture, Family: Influences on Home Life* (Basingstoke: Palgrave Macmillan).

Silva, E. and Smart, C. eds. (1999) *The New Family?* (London: Sage).

Silverstein, M. and Bengston, V. (1994) 'Does intergenerational social support influence the psychological well-being of older parents? The contingencies of declining health and widowhood', *Social Science & Medicine*, 387, 943–957.

Simmel, G. (1950 [1858–1918]). *The Sociology of Georg Simmel (Translated by Kurt Wolff)*. Glencoe, IL: Free Press.

Simpson, R. (2006) 'The intimate relationships of contemporary spinsters', *Sociological Research Online*, 11(3).

Simpson, R. (2009) *Contemporary Spinsterhood: Gender, Partnership Status and Social Change* (Saarbrücken: VDM Verlag).

Sinardet, D. and Mortelmans, D. (2009) 'The feminine side to Santa Claus. Women's work of kinship in contemporary gift-giving relations', *Social Science Journal*, 46, 124–142.

Sixsmith, A.J. (1986) 'Independence and home in later Life', in Phillipson, C., Bernard, M. and Strange, P. eds. *Dependency and Interdependency in Old age: Theoretical Perspectives and Policy Alternatives* (London: Croom Helm).

Skolnick (1991) *Embattled Paradise: The American Family in an Age of Uncertainty* (New York: Basic Books).

Slater, D. (1997) *Consumer Culture and Modernity* (Cambridge: Polity Press).

Smart, C. (2007) *Personal Life* (Cambridge: Polity).

Smart, C., Davies, K., Heaphy, B. and Mason, J. (2012) 'Difficult friendships and ontological insecurity', *The Sociological Review*, 60, 91–109.

Smart, C., Neale, B. and Wade, A. (2001) *The Changing Experience of Childhood: Families and Divorce* (Cambridge: Polity).

Smart, C. and Shipman, B. (2004) 'Visions in monochrome: Marriage and the individualization thesis', *Sociology*, 55(4), 491–509.

Smith, A., Wasoff, F. and Jamieson, L. (2005) 'CRFR Briefing 20: Solo living across the adult lifecourse', Edinburgh, www.crfr.ac.uk/briefingslist.htm#rb20. Accessed 20 August 2012.

Smith, D. (1987) *The Everyday World As Problematic: A Feminist Sociology* (Milton Keynes: Open University Press).

Sobotka, T. (2004) *Postponement of Childbearing and Low Fertility in Europe*, PhD thesis, University of Groningen (Amsterdam: Dutch University Press).

Song, J. (2006) 'Family breakdown and invisible homeless women: Neo-liberal governance during the Asian Debt Crisis in South Korea, 1997–2001', *Positions: East Asia Cultures Critique* 14, 37–65.

Song, J. (2010) ' "A room of one's own": The meaning of spatial autonomy for unmarried women in neoliberal South Korea', *Gender, Place and Culture*, 17, 131–149.

South, S.J. and Crowder, K.D. (1997) 'Residential mobility between cities and suburbs: Race, suburbanization, and back-to-the-city moves', *Demography*, 34(4), 525–538.

Southerton, D. (2009) *Communities of Consumption: Place, Geographical Mobility and Identification* (Saarbrücken, Germany: VDM Publishing).

Southerton, D. (2011) 'Consumer culture and personal life', in May, V. ed. *Sociology of Personal Life* (Basingstoke: Palgrave Macmillan).

Speare, A. Jr, Avery, R., and Lawton, L. (1991) 'Disability, residential mobility, and changes in living arrangements', *Journals of Gerontology: Social Sciences*, 46, S133–S141.

Spencer, L. and Pahl, R. (2006) *Rethinking Friendship: Hidden Solidarities Today*, (Princeton: Princeton University Press).

Stacey, J. (2011) *Unhitched: Love Marriage and Family Values from West Hollywood to Western China* (New York: New York University Press).

Stockdale, A. (2002) 'Out migration from rural Scotland: the importance of family and social networks', *Sociologia Ruralis*, 42(1), 41–64.

Stockdale, A. (2004) 'Rural out-migration: Community consequences and individual migrant experiences', *Sociologia Ruralis*, 44(2), 167–194.

Stone, J., Berrington, A. and Falkingham, J. (2011) 'The changing determinants of UK young adults' living arrangements', *Demographic Research*, 25, 629–666.

Stone, L. (1979) *The Family, Sex and Marriage in England 1500–1800* (Harmondsworth: Penguin).

Strathern, M. (1988) *The Gender and the Gift: Problems with Women and Problems with Society in Melanesia* (Berkeley: University California Press).

Strohm, C., Selzer, J.A., Cochran, S.D. and Mays, V. (2010) ' "Living apart together" relationships in the United States', *Demographic Research*, 21, 177–214.

Swartz, T.T. (2009) 'Intergenerational family relations in adulthood: Patterns, variations, and implications in the contemporary United States', *Annual Review of Sociology*, 35, 191–212.

Swidler, A. (2003) *Talk of Love: How Culture Matters* (Chicago: University of Chicago Press).

Taylor, Y.(2012) *Fitting Into Place?: Class and Gender Geographies and Temporalities*, (Aldershot: Ashgate).

Therborn, G. (2004) *Between Sex and Power: Family in the World 1900–2000* (London: Routledge).

Therborn, G. (2011) *The World: A Beginner's Guide* (Cambridge: Polity Press).

Thomson, R. and Holland, J. (2002) 'Imagining adulthood: Resources, plans and contradictions', *Gender and Education*, 14, 378–350.

Thornton, A. (2005) *Reading History Sideways: The Fallacy and Enduring Impact of the Developmental Paradigm on Family Life* (Chicago: Chicago University Press).

Thornton, A., Axinn, W.G. and Xie, Y. (2007) *Marriage and Cohabitation* (University of Chicago Press: Chicago).

Tomassini, C., Glaser, K., Wolf, D., van Groenou, M. and Grundy, E. (2004) 'Living arrangements among older people: an overview of trends in Europe and the USA', *Population Trends*, 115, 24–34.

Trawick, M. (2003) 'The person beyond the family', in Das, V. ed. *The Oxford India Guide Companion to Sociology and Social Anthropology* (Oxford: Oxford University Press), 1158–1178.

Trimberger, K. (2006) *The New Single Woman* (Boston: Beacon Press).

Trost, J. (1998) 'LAT relationships now and in the future', in Matthijs, K. ed. *The Family: Contemporary Perspectives and Challenges* (Louvain, Belgium: Leuven University Press).

Tyler May, E. (1988) *Homeward Bound: American Families in the Cold War Era* (New York: Basic Books).

Tyler, T.R. (2002) 'Is the internet changing social life? It seems the more things change, the more they stay the same', *Journal of Social Issues*, 58, 195–205.

Uberoi, P. (2006) *Freedom and Destiny: Gender, Family and Popular Culture in India* (New Delhi: Oxford University Press).

Ulbrich, P.M. and Warheit, G.J. (1989) 'Social support, stress and psychological distress among older black and white adults', *Journal of Aging and Health*, 1, 286–305.

Unger, J. (1993) 'Urban families in the eighties', in Davis, D. and Harrell, S. eds. *Chinese Families in the Post-Mao Era* (Berkeley: University of California Press).

Urry, J. (2002) 'Mobility and Proximity', *Sociology*, 36, 255–274.

Urry, J. (2007) *Mobilities* (Cambridge: Polity).

US Census Bureau 'Current Population Survey – Definitions and Explanations' www.census.gov/population/www/cps/cpsdef.html. Accessed 12 September 2012.

Vachhani, S.J. and Pullen, A. (2011) 'Home is where the heart is? Organizing women's work and domesticity at Christmas', *Organization*, 18, 807–821.

Verderber, S. (2008) 'Emergency housing in the aftermath of Hurricane Katrina: An assessment of the FEMA travel trailer program', *Journal of Housing and the Built Environment*, 23, 367–381.

Vézina, M. (2011) 'Quality of personal networks: Does living alone make a difference?' Component of Statistics Canada Catalogue no. 11-008-X, *Canadian Social Trends*.

Victor, C. (2011) *Loneliness in Old Age: The UK Perspective, in Safeguarding the Convoy: A Call to Action from the Campaign to End Loneliness* (Oxfordshire: Age UK).

Victor, C., Scambler, S. and Bond, J. (2009) *The Social World of Older People: Understanding Loneliness and Social Isolation in Later Life* (Maidenhead: Open University Press/McGraw Hill Education).

Viry, G. (2012) 'Residential mobility and the spatial dispersion of personal networks: Effects on social support', *Social Networks*, 34, 59–72.

Viry, G., Kaufmann, V. and Widmer, E.D. (2009) 'Social integration faced with commuting: more widespread and less dense support networks', in Ohnmacht, T., Maksim, H. and Bergman, M. eds. *Mobilities and Inequality* (Aldershot: Ashgate), 121–143.

Vullnetari, J. and King, R. (2008) 'Does your granny eat grass?' On mass migration, care drain and the fate of older people in rural Albania', *Global Networks*, 8, 139–171.

Wajcman, J. and Martin, B. (2002) 'Narratives of identity in modern management: The corrosion of gender difference', *Sociology*, 36, 985–1002.

Walker, A. (2005) 'A European perspective on quality of life in old age', *European Journal of Ageing*, 2(1), 2–12.

Wall, R. (1989) 'Leaving home and living alone: An historical perspective', *Population Studies: A Journal of Demography*, 43(3), 369–389.

Walter-Ginzburg, A., Blumstein, T., Chetrit, A. and Modan, B. (2002) 'Social factors and mortality in the old-old in Israel: The CALAS study', *Journals of Gerontology Series B-Psychological Sciences and Social Sciences*, 575, S308–S318.

Wang, H. and Wellman, B. (2010) 'Social connectivity in America: Changes in adult friendship network size from 2002 to 2007', *American Behavioural Scientist*, 53(8), 1148–1169.

Warde, A. (2005) 'Consumption and theories of practice', *Journal of Consumer Culture*, 5(2), 131–153.

Warde, A. and Martens, L. (2000) *Eating Out: Social Differentiation, Consumption and Pleasure* (Cambridge: Cambridge University Press).

Wardhaugh, J. (1999) 'The unaccomodated woman: Home, homelessness and identity', *Sociological Review*, 47(1), 91–109.

Wasoff, F., Jamieson, L. and Smith, A. (2005) 'Solo-living, individual and family boundaries across the adult lifecourse', in McKie, L. and Cunningham-Burley, S. eds. *Families and Society: Boundaries and Relationships* (Bristol: Policy Press).

Webb, J. (2004) 'Organisations, self identity and the new economy', *Sociology*, 40, 719–717.

Weber, M. (1968) *Economy and Society* (New York: Bedminster).

Weber, M. (1976) *The Protestant Ethic and the Spirit of Capitalism* (London: Allen and Unwin 1930 edition, translated by Talcott Parsons, original essays 1904/5).

Weeks, D.J. (1994) 'A review of loneliness concepts with particular reference to old age', *International Journal of Geriatric Psychiatry*, 9(5), 345–355.

Weeks, J., Donovan, C. and Heaphy, B. (1996) *Families of Choice: Patterns of Non-Heterosexual Relationships – A Literature Review*, Social Science Research Papers 2 (London: South Bank University).

Weeks, J., Heaphy, B. and Donovan, C. (2001) *Same Sex Intimacies: Families of Choice and Other Life Experiments* (London: Routledge).

Wellman, B. (2001) 'Physical place and cyberplace: The rise of personalized networking', *International Journal of Urban and Regional Research*, 25, 227–252.

Wellman, B., Hogan, B., Berg, K., Boase, J., Carrasco, J.A., Côté, R., Kayahara, J., Kennedy, T.L.M. and Tran, P. (2006) 'Connected lives: The project' in Purcell, P. ed. *Networked Neighbourhoods* (London: Springer).

Wenger, C.G. (1984) *The Supportive Network: Coping with Old Age* (London: George Allen and Unwin).

Wenger, C.G. (1992) *Ageing in Liverpool: Demographic Profile of Elderly People Living in the Community*, Working Paper Centre for Social Policy Research and Development, University of Wales, Bangor.

Wenger, C.G. (1993) 'The formation of social networks: Self-help, mutual aid and old people in contemporary Britain', *Journal of Ageing Studies*, 7(1), 25–40.

Wenger, C.G. (1997) 'Review of findings on support networks of older Europeans', *Journal of Cross-Cultural Gerontology*, 12, 1–21.

Wenger, C.G. and Burholt, V. (2004) 'Changes in levels of social isolation and loneliness among older people in a rural area: a twenty-year longitudinal study', *Canadian Journal on Aging*, 232, 115–127.

Wenger, C.G., Dykstra, P.A., Melkas, T. and Knipscheer, K. (2007) 'Social embeddedness and late-Life parenthood community activity, close ties, and support networks', *Journal of Family Issues*, 28(11), 1419–1456.

Wenger, C.G. and Liu, J.M. (2000) 'Family support in Beijing China and Liverpool UK: Differences and similarities', *Hallym International Journal of Aging Korea*, 2, 85–91.

Wessendorf, S. (2010) 'Local attachments and transnational everyday lives: Second-generation Italians in Switzerland', *Global Networks*, 10(3) 365–382.

West, P. (1984) 'The family, the welfare state and community care: Political rhetoric and public attitudes', *Journal of Social Policy*, 13(4), 417–446.

Weston, K. (1997) [1991] *Families We Choose: Lesbians, Gays, Kinship*, 2nd edition, (New York: Columbia University Press).

Weston, K. (1998) *Long Slow Burn: Sexuality and Social Science* (New York: Routledge).

White, N.R. (2003) 'Changing conceptions: Young people's views of partnering and parenting', *Journal of Sociology*, 39, 149–164.

Whitehead, A. (1976) 'Sexual antagonism in Herefordshire', in Barker, D. and Allen, S. eds. *Dependence and Exploitation in Work and Marriage* (London: Tavistock).

Widmer, E. (2004) 'Couples and their networks', in Scott, J., Treas, J. and Richards, M. eds. *The Blackwell Companion to the Sociology of the Family* (Oxford: Blackwell).

Wiener, J.M. and Tilly, J. (2002) 'Population ageing in the United States of America: implications for public programmes', *International Journal of Epidemiology*, 31(4), 776–781, doi: 10.1093/ije/31.4.776.

Williams, J. (2005) 'Homes for the future – accommodating one-person households the sustainable *way*', in *(Proceedings) Second International Conference On Sustainable Planning & Development*, Bologna, September 2005.

Williams, J. (2007) 'Innovative solutions for averting a potential resource crisis – the case of one-person households in England and Wales', *Environment Development and Sustainability*, 9, 325–354.

Williams, M., Maconachie, M., Ware, L., Chandler, J. and Dodgeon, B. (2008) 'Using longitudinal data to examine living alone in England and Wales 1971 to 2001', in Edwards, R. ed. *Researching Families and Communities: Social and Generational Change* (Abingdon: Routledge), 164–180.

Willmott, P. (1987) *Friendship Networks And Social Support* (London: Policy Studies Institute).

Wolinsky, F.D., Callahan, C.M., Fitzgerald, J.F. and Johnson, R.J. (1992) 'The risk of nursing home placement and subsequent death in nursing home among older adults', *Journals of Gerontology: Social Sciences*, 47, S173–S182.

Xin, M. and Chuliang, L. (2008) 'What determines living arrangements of the elderly in Urban China?' in Gustafsson, B., Shi, L. and Sicular, T. eds. *Inequality and Public Policy in China* (Cambridge: Cambridge University Press).

Yamada, M. (2005) *Meisou suru kazoku: Sengo kazoku moderu no keisei to kaitai [Runaway family: Declining of postwar family model in Japan]* (Tokyo: Yuhikaku).

Yan, Y. (2003) *Private Life Under Socialism: Love, Intimacy and Family Change in Chinese Village 1949–1999* (Stanford: Stanford University Press).

Yan, Y. (2009) *The Individualization of Chinese Society* (Oxford: Berg).

Yan, Y. (2010) 'Introduction: Conflicting images of the individual and contested process of individualization', in Hansen, M.H. and Svarverud, R. eds. *iChina: the Rise of the Individual in Modern Chinese Society* (Copenhagen: NIAS).

Yang, K. and Victor, C. (2011) 'Age and loneliness in 25 European nations', *Ageing & Society* 31, 1368–1388.

Yi, Z., Coale, A., Choe, M.K., Zhiwu, L., and Li, L. (1994) 'Leaving the parental home: Census-based estimates for China, Japan, South Korea, United States, France, and Sweden', *Population Studies*, 48, 65–90.

Young, H. and Grundy, E. (2009) 'Living arrangements, health and well-being', in Stillwell, J., Coast, E. and Kneale, D. eds. *Understanding Population Trends and Processes: Fertility, Living Arrangements, Care and Mobility* (Dordrecht: Springer) 1, 127–150.

Young, M. and Willmott, P. (1957) *Family and Kinship in East London* (Harmondsworth: Penguin).

Zaretsky, E. (1976) *Capitalism, the Family and Personal Life* (Pluto Press).

Zhang, H. (2004) ' "Living Alone" and the rural elderly: Strategy and agency in Post-Moa Rural China', in Ikels, C. ed. *Filial Piety: Practice and Discourse in Contemporary East Asia* (Stanford: Stanford University Press), 63–87.

Zontini, E. and Reynolds, T. (2007) 'Ethnicity, families and social capital: Caring relationships across Italian and Caribbean transnational families', *International Review of Sociology*, 17, 257–277.

Index

Printed and bound in the United States of America